UNTOLD
POWER

UNTOLD POWER

The Fascinating Rise and Complex Legacy
of First Lady Edith Wilson

REBECCA BOGGS ROBERTS

VIKING

VIKING
An imprint of Penguin Random House LLC
penguinrandomhouse.com

Image credits appear on pages 287 and 288.

LIBRARY OF CONGRESS CATALOGING-IN-PUBLICATION DATA
Names: Roberts, Rebecca Boggs, author.
Title: Untold power : the fascinating rise and complex legacy of First Lady
Edith Wilson / Rebecca Boggs Roberts.
Description: [New York, New York] : Viking, [2023] | Includes
bibliographical references and index.
Identifiers: LCCN 2022040220 (print) | LCCN 2022040221 (ebook) |
ISBN 9780593489994 (hardcover) | ISBN 9780593490006 (ebook)
Subjects: LCSH: Wilson, Edith Bolling Galt, 1872–1961. | Presidents'
spouses—United States—Biography. | Wilson, Woodrow, 1856–1924. |
United States—Politics and government—1913–1921.
Classification: LCC E767.3.W55 R63 2023 (print) |
LCC E767.3.W55 (ebook) | DDC 973.91/3092 [B]—dc23/eng/20220920
LC record available at https://lccn.loc.gov/2022040220
LC ebook record available at https://lccn.loc.gov/2022040221

Printed in the United States of America
1st Printing

Designed by Alexis Farabaugh

Behind the scenes at the White House, where peering eyes cannot see . . . there is a picture of heroic determination on the part of a worried woman to save her husband's life and fight to the bitter end the political calumny that is being avalanched upon the man who gave several years to public service and now lies a victim to nervous exhaustion.

Between the President and the outside world stands Mrs. Woodrow Wilson, as devoted and faithful a companion as ever nursed a sick man.

DAVID LAWRENCE, "PRESIDENT WILSON'S WIFE
IS HEROINE OF WHITE HOUSE DRAMA,"
NEW YORK EVENING POST, DECEMBER 5, 1919

Or, more sinister still, must we look for the woman in the case? Has the female of the species already succeeded in putting a working Presidentess in the White House?

"PRESIDENT REASSERTS AUTHORITY," BRISTOL
(TN) HERALD COURIER, FEBRUARY 20, 1920
(BLIND ITEM FROM THE BALTIMORE SUN)

CONTENTS

INTRODUCTION

She hated the title "First Lady," preferring to be known by the name on her calling cards: Mrs. Woodrow Wilson. But for some months at the end of 1919 and beginning of 1920, Edith Bolling Galt Wilson held the most political power of any First Lady in history.[1] Even today, by the simple fact of her marriage, the First Lady is one of the most famous and publicly scrutinized women in America. That was dramatically more true a hundred years ago, when many fewer women had the opportunity to achieve national prominence in their own rights. Yet the role of First Lady comes with no job description, no constitutional duties or legal guidelines.[2] She is, therefore, a blank slate for the projections of a critical public. As scholar Molly Meijer Wertheimer puts it, "all First Ladies become symbols of American womanhood and as such they are expected to conform to the public's image of the 'ideal woman' of their times."[3]

But the times, of course, they keep a'changin'. So not only can a First Lady rarely rely on the precedents of her predecessors, but sometimes the public's expectations change in real time while she fills the role. Edith became First Lady when she married President Woodrow Wilson at the end of 1915, after the death of his first wife, Ellen. Unlike wives who rise up through the political ranks with their husbands, she didn't have the luxury of an on-ramp to national attention. She had to develop a public persona overnight. She chose the role of devoted second wife, living only for the health and success of her brilliant husband. She also wanted to be known as a gracious social presence, in contrast to the earnestly awkward first Mrs. Wilson. Edith was praised for her choice as soon as the engagement was announced. "Mrs. Galt is regarded as a woman of rare beauty and charm," the Washington *Evening Star* wrote approvingly. "Those who have known her best predicted today that she would be, as the first lady of the land, a popular hostess as well as a comfort and support to the President in his daily work."[4] If she was hoping to reflect the 1915 feminine ideal, she chose her image perfectly.

But the years Edith served as First Lady, 1915–1921, saw profound changes in women's social roles. World War I required women to take on traditional male jobs and do them well. Suffrage activists pushed for recognition of women's rights, not only securing the vote but also challenging the notion that public life was the exclusive domain of men. And while Edith was never a suffragist, she did take on more public roles than any First Lady before her. She was the first to stand behind the president when he took the oath of office. She was the first to accompany her husband on business calls with cabinet secretaries. She was the first to travel abroad while her husband was in office. She was welcomed and celebrated by royalty in England and Italy in a way no leader's wife had been before. She was admired globally for her public visibility, which was all still very much in the service of her husband, never for her own agenda. When she accompanied her husband to Europe in 1918, one English reporter gushed, "No queen could have had a more queenly manner, no great lady could be more gracious, no woman more utterly winning than President Wilson's wife."[5] Edith kept that clipping in her scrapbook.

So when her husband collapsed from a stroke in October 1919, no one should have been surprised when Edith inserted herself between his sickroom and the public. She would protect him from anything that might make his condition worse, which included most of the duties of the presidency. From the day of their marriage she had cast herself as his devoted helpmate, there to make his life easier both in private and in public, and she would continue that role until her husband recovered. For a little while, that was enough. A sympathetic public worried over their fallen leader and supported his wife as gatekeeper. But what no one knew, what they could not know because Edith controlled the truth so closely, was just how sick Woodrow was, how many decisions he could not make, and how long his illness lasted. For weeks, he was almost totally incapacitated. For months after that, he was weak, easily confused, with slurred speech, limited vision, and a useless left arm. He tired early and was sometimes unable to control his emotions.[6] He slept a lot. Meanwhile, it was Edith who met with cabinet secretaries, Edith who drafted public statements, Edith who made decisions about who could visit her husband, what issues to tackle, and which to ignore. As history has revealed just how thoroughly and how long Edith maintained control over the executive branch, Americans have professed themselves amazed that this unambitious woman, this wife who wanted nothing more than to serve her adored husband, had the confidence, brains, and cunning to pull off a conspiracy of this magnitude.

But anyone who pays the slightest bit of attention to Edith before her 1915 marriage shouldn't be surprised at all. Edith's obituary in

1961 described her as "a most retiring woman to that date, she entered public life in that peculiar white-hot glare that surrounds the White House in a near-election year."[7] This is typical of the accounts that completely fail to even attempt to understand Edith, painting her as a not-very-bright country mouse who magically became the nation's most powerful woman overnight. Many adjectives can accurately describe Edith, but retiring is not one of them. She was fierce, clever, gracious, funny, loyal, and brave. Also petty, snobbish, jealous, and bigoted. She had a somewhat fickle regard for the truth. These are not character traits she developed in the "white-hot glare" of public attention. Her whole history reveals a woman of uncommon shrewdness, ingenuity, and a little ruthlessness. Were she a man, her story would be celebrated as an up-by-your-bootstraps American dream.

An Appalachian girl from dilapidated southern gentry without much formal education, Edith managed to move to Washington on her own as a teenager and thrive in the flashy society of the nation's capital in the Gilded Age. Beautiful and popular, she tripped lightly through romantic attachments before they became too serious. When she eventually married, she did so for stability and security, not love. She became the first licensed woman driver in DC and blithely ignored traffic rules as she tooled around town in her electric car. After her first husband died, she took over his jewelry business and made it profitable. She enjoyed years as an independent woman of means, beholden to no one, traveling the world and pleasing only herself. She prided herself on being the bedrock of her family, supporting her mother and sister and employing her three youngest brothers. When she caught the eye of the recently widowed president, she made it clear his desperate romantic pursuit would be much more successful if he augmented his mushy love notes with discussions of foreign policy.

While the president was smitten from their first date, Edith dragged her feet on marriage, hesitant to give up her independence and fretful the public would think she coveted the office, not the man. Maintaining the monthslong facade that Woodrow was mentally perfect and fully capable of executing the duties of his office was, for Edith, entirely in keeping with her history.

Of course, one of the reasons Edith's public persona as Mrs. Woodrow Wilson seems to clash with her actual decisions while Woodrow was sick is that Edith herself wanted it that way. She worked very hard to cultivate her own image as a devoted wife, maybe a little naive, who was dedicated to protecting and serving her heroic husband. Her own memoir, helpfully titled *My Memoir*, hides so much more than it reveals, glossing over inconvenient truths, shading others, and occasionally lying to her readers outright. Edith began the memoir on a train in 1927. She was so annoyed with other published accounts of her husband's presidency (and it does seem as though everyone involved in that administration wrote a memoir) that she began her own story to set her version of the record straight. She claimed she had no expectation of publication; after all, no First Lady had ever published a memoir before. At first, she was "writing the truth for my own satisfaction."[8] But she continued to work on the book for ten years, publishing it in 1938. In the foreword she stated, "I have revealed the truth about personal matters which has been often distorted by the misinformed. And if I take the public into my confidence about these matters, it is because the high office which my husband held robs them of a private character and makes me feel that they belong to history."[9] Like many women in power before and since, she was highly invested in reputation management, in pleasing and winning the approval of as many people as she could. She claimed she was doing so on behalf of her husband, but of course she was curating her own image at the same time. She had to walk a thin line to do so—downplaying her own influence and ambition while boasting just a bit about the prominence she brought to the complicated job of First Lady. And she did elevate that role, pioneering the realm of public diplomacy that so many First Ladies have taken on since then. That chapter of her life is well documented by other sources. But because no one was recording the life of Edith Wilson before 1915, her memoir is often the only source for her years before the White House. Knowing her tendency to embroider the truth, I have, where possible, tried to verify her version of events, or at least the dates and ages of the players. When primary sources are unavailable, I have tried to add context to the times and places of Edith's life through other related histories. For the many years Edith lived after her husband's death, her life was documented more widely. I am especially grateful to have been able to talk to a few people who knew her, like her great-nephew Cary Fuller and Woodrow's great-grandson Thomas Sayre. And it is my unique privilege to have access to the unpublished chapters of Edith's memoir, which take place after Woodrow's death. I am enormously indebted to Farron Smith at the Edith Bolling Wilson Birthplace Museum for trusting me with this rare and delightful material.

Hidden under these layers of tangential sources and carefully curated accounts is the real story of Edith Bolling Galt Wilson. So far, she's existed in the historical record only as a blank screen for projection: Lady Macbeth to some observers, a cheap floozy to others, the ideal of true devoted womanhood to an archaic few. The handful of biographies that do exist either see her entirely through the lens of her famous husband or reduce her to a stock character. She has played whatever role observers assigned her: a shape-shifter for the ages, even now, fifty years after her death. She is not a hero; she is also not a villain. Very few people in American history are either, and I believe that our collective insistence on picking one category or the other for all of our most influential people has left us (at best) confused about how and through whom our history is made. It will no longer do to project convenient narratives onto the lives of others or hide in fear behind the screens of those projections. In addition to the social damage this hall-of-fame version of history has caused, it is inaccurate—not to mention boring. Saints are dull. It's time for a fuller picture of this remarkable woman, in all her strengths and weaknesses. So here is Edith Wilson's story in a spirit of empathy, curiosity, fascination, care—and accountability.

UNTOLD
POWER

PROLOGUE

By December of 1919, First Lady Edith Wilson had finally settled into a routine. October had been a white-knuckled horror show as President Woodrow Wilson's health lurched from crisis to crisis. He would seem to be recovering strength, only to be thrown back by a fever or infection. When each day dawned, Edith wondered if it would be her husband's last. November brought its own terrors. The president's life no longer hung in the balance, but he was far from healthy. Meanwhile, debate raged over the Treaty of Versailles and the inclusion of Woodrow's beloved League of Nations. Even close friends were telling her the president was killing his own project by insisting the Senate ratify the treaty with no changes or amendments.[1] Her husband continued to swear amendments were impossible, even immoral, and if she urged him to compromise she was betraying his principles.[2] By a healthy margin of 38–53, the Senate voted the treaty down on November 19, but its supporters vowed to fight another day.

Now it was December. Chilly but sunny, Washington had yet to see a real snowfall. The president remained seriously ill. Virtually no one was allowed to see him. Edith met all inquiries with the same polite but firm brush-off: The president was mentally as sharp as ever; he was merely suffering from nervous exhaustion. He was not accepting meetings, but she would be happy to relay any important messages and return any necessary replies. This seemed to satisfy the bulk of would-be visitors. Most of them were content to conduct their business in writing, usually addressed directly to her.

Conspiring with the president's doctor, Cary Grayson, and secretary, Joe Tumulty, Edith had begun to think she just might be able to manage this state of affairs for as long as she must. But then the cracks in the scheme began to appear, starting with blowback from the secretary of state, Robert Lansing, never Woodrow's biggest fan in the cabinet, who found the silence from the White House infuriating.

Long before the stroke, Lansing had realized his position was impossible. Lansing disagreed with the president over the urgency of going to war, how the war was conducted, and the tactics and specifics of the peace process. He did not believe his counsel in these matters had been given the respect he was due.[3] In fact, he and his boss disagreed so often, the president had seriously considered firing him in September.[4] Before he could act on that impulse, Woodrow had collapsed in his train car.

Lansing did not trust the Wilson White House to tell the truth about the president's health. He suspected the situation was much more dire than the public was being led to believe. Stuck in a job he hated with a boss who wouldn't or couldn't act, Lansing was not alone in his frustration. Several Republican members of the Senate were also deeply suspicious. The most vocal and colorful member of this faction was Albert B. Fall of New Mexico. With his walrus mustache and ten-gallon hat, Fall was one of the first two senators elected from New Mexico when it joined the union in 1912. He was not chosen for his record of moral rectitude. A trial lawyer, he regularly represented murderers and gunmen in court and was so deep in the pocket of the oil industry that friends and enemies alike called him "Petroleum" Fall.[5] In 1922, as secretary of the interior in the Harding administration, Fall would go on to earn the distinction of being the first cabinet secretary ever sentenced to jail, convicted of taking bribes in the infamous Teapot Dome scandal.[6]

Fall had lately taken to yelling to everyone who would listen that Woodrow was not capable of serving as president. He had even shouted on the Senate floor, "We have a petticoat government! Wilson is not acting! Mrs. Wilson is President!"[7] For the most part, people ignored him. But the one thing Fall hated more than the Wilson administration was the Carranza government in Mexico, which had thwarted petroleum interests for years. As a senator from a border state, Fall enjoyed blaming the Mexican government for everything from labor unrest to the high price of oil. Then, in December of 1919, a U.S. consular agent named William Jenkins was kidnapped in the city of Puebla. And Fall was handed the perfect opportunity to kill two birds with one stone.

Secretary Lansing, no longer deferring to the president on matters of foreign policy, sent a strongly worded letter to Mexico demanding Jenkins's release. It stopped just short of threatening war.[8] The Senate Foreign Relations Committee met to consider next steps. Lansing appeared before the committee and described his aggressive letter. The senators, knowing the peace-seeking president could not have approved such belligerent tactics, asked Lansing if he had consulted with his chief executive. With visible anger, Lansing replied that no, he had not consulted with the president at all since September. As far as Lansing knew, not a single member of the cabinet had met with the president about anything in months.

That was all the justification Senator Fall needed.[9] He introduced a resolution appointing a delegation of the Senate committee to visit the president to hear his views on the Mexican situation. He graciously volunteered to go himself. The Democrats on the committee chose Gilbert Hitchcock of Nebraska, a very reluctant recruit to this enterprise. Hitchcock, like literally everyone else, knew this was not actually a visit about the Jenkins kidnapping. It was a recon mission.

And so the stage was set for a showdown.

FALL CORNERED WILSON'S secretary, Joe Tumulty, in the Capitol and demanded an immediate meeting with the president, playing up the urgency of helping an American in foreign custody. Tumulty, who knew Fall's vehemence had very little to do with Mexico, couldn't possibly refuse and still maintain the fiction that Woodrow was running the government. He feared the standard White House brush-off would give Fall an excuse to start impeachment proceedings.

He decided to go all in, agreeing to a meeting that very day, December 5, at two thirty in the afternoon.[10] Fall, counting on the usual stonewalling, was surprised by Tumulty's helpfulness and grew suspicious. He even suggested the meeting could wait a couple of days. But this had now become a high-stakes game of chicken, and Tumulty would not be the first to flinch. He insisted a timely meeting was just what everyone wanted. Fall agreed and helpfully alerted the entire Washington press corps.

Tumulty ran back to the White House and warned Edith and Cary Grayson that a Senate delegation was on the way. Everyone involved later described the day in theatrical terms; they knew they were putting on a show.

Tumulty called in Robert Woolley, head of publicity for the Democratic Party, to help stage a "dress rehearsal."[11] Together Tumulty, Woolley, Grayson, and Edith surveyed the props and cast they had available. Woodrow, who by necessity would star in this little production, had good days and bad days. His entire left side was still paralyzed. He tired easily, and sometimes his speech slurred. In his weakness and exhaustion, he could find it hard to concentrate on a conversation, and Edith would have to gently prod him to respond. But he also had windows of clarity and wit. Maybe today would be one of those days?

The team decided Edith would stay in the room during the senators' meeting. Between her and the sympathetic Hitchcock, perhaps they could keep the mood light and the conversation flowing. The patient-slash-leading man knew exactly what was going on. He dubbed Fall's visit a "smelling committee" and comprehended just how high the stakes were. But all he could do was let his team get on with the preparations and rest up for his moment in the spotlight.

First they had to figure out where to set the stage. The president spent most of his day in bed. Edith had once tried to prop him up in a wheelchair, but he had listed to the side alarmingly. White House usher Ike Hoover had finally come up with the genius idea to rent a rolling beach chair from a vendor in Atlantic City, which was somewhat more stable.[12] But the whole apparatus was a little clownish and not very presidential.

The production team decided that the president would have to receive the senators lying down in bed, with only his head elevated.[13] Edith covered his useless left side with a blanket, tucked up under his chin. Tumulty placed a copy of the Senate report on Mexico on a table within easy reach of his good right hand. Grayson placed chairs for the senators that would limit their view of the president's left side and made sure the chairs were well lit while the bed remained in shadow. As Ike Hoover described it, "it was quite impossible for one coming from a well-lighted part of the house to see anything to his satisfaction."[14]

Stage manager Edith surveyed her star, realizing her costuming options were limited. He had worn a formal silk dressing gown to briefly greet the king of the Belgians, but it bunched up uncomfortably in bed, and Woodrow much preferred a beloved old brown sweater. It was a little moth-eaten, but the interests of ease and comfort outweighed formality here, so the sweater went on. With no visitors, Edith had not insisted on the president being shaved regularly, and now a white wispy beard on his gaunt gray face did nothing to boost the illusion of vitality.[15] The president submitted to a shave. It was all they could do. As two thirty approached, everyone took their places, crossed their fingers, and hoped for the best.

Fall and Hitchcock arrived at the White House right on time, trailed by more than one hundred newspapermen. It was the first time Edith had allowed press at the White House since the stroke, which of course triggered pandemonium as well as some skepticism. As *The New York Times* dryly put it, "there was apparently an effort to have it appear that those around the President wanted the fullest publicity."[16] They all knew the real reason for this meeting and stood by ready to publicize every detail Senator Fall provided on the president's condition. While the reporters waited downstairs, the senators were escorted up to the president's bedroom. As rehearsed, Grayson met them at the door. Fall asked if the meeting had a time limit. Grayson, keeping up the pretense that this visit was wholly welcome, answered, "No, not within reason, Senator."[17]

Then he opened the door.

Edith tried not to let her loathing for Fall show. She gripped a pencil in one hand and a notebook in the other so she could avoid shaking his hand.[18] Then she watched helplessly as Fall entered the room and approached the president's bed.

Woodrow astonished everyone by greeting Fall with a firm handshake and waving him casually to the chair that was staged for him. Hitchcock followed timidly behind. As Edith recounted in her memoir, Fall, not sure what to make of this scene, ventured a tepid "I have been praying for you, sir."

The president, without missing a beat, replied, "Which way, Senator?"

As Fall laughed, Edith breathed a sigh of relief and began taking notes. "If agreeable, I wish Mrs. Wilson to remain," said the president, as if her presence were expected.

"You seem very much engaged," Fall commented to Edith.

"I thought it was wise to record this interview so there would be no misunderstandings or misstatements made," Edith shot back.[19]

Fall asked if the president had even seen the Foreign Relations Committee report on Mexico. Just as rehearsed, Woodrow grabbed the report off his bedside table with his good right hand. "I have a copy right here," he crowed, waving it triumphantly.

And so the meeting proceeded. Woodrow was charming. Fall was thwarted. Edith fumed. Hitchcock smiled and nodded with utter terror in his eyes. Grayson hovered in the doorway, cautiously optimistic. The meeting was going so well that when he was called away to the telephone, he felt confident leaving the drama to play out.

Fall, disappointed that he hadn't caught the president drooling or incoherent, turned his focus to the ostensible reason for the meeting. He attempted to play up the Jenkins kidnapping and urge the president to take stronger action against Mexico. But then, in a piece of stagecraft even this play's planners could not have foreseen, Grayson returned from his phone to call to announce that Jenkins had just been released. Grayson felt, he said later, "like an actor making a sensational entrance."[20] Fall had no choice but to wrap the meeting up. Woodrow spoke of getting on his feet again soon and wished his visitors well.

Almost giddy with relief, Grayson escorted Fall and Hitchcock downstairs to face the waiting reporters. They didn't even pretend to ask about Mexico but peppered both senators with questions about the president's condition.

Hitchcock led off, describing the president's mental alertness, his healthy color, and even his old brown sweater in glowing terms. Senator Fall was forced to agree, saying Woodrow "seemed to me to be in excellent trim, both mentally and physically."[21] The resulting news coverage was everything Edith and her confidants could have wished for. *The New York Times* was typical, stating, "The two Senators who interviewed the President with the ill-concealed purpose on the part of members of the Foreign Relations Committee to ascertain the truth or falsity of the many rumors that he was in no physical or mental condition to attend to important public business, came away from the White House convinced that his mind was vigorous and active."[22] The president acted his part so well, the senators even gave him more credit than he was due. As Edith gushed in her memoir, Fall "assured the reporters that the president was mentally fit and that he had the use of his left side and his right which was of course an overstatement for Mr. Wilson's left side was nearly useless."[23]

Although Woodrow's critics continued to demand less secrecy from the White House, the immediate rumors of his condition had been publicly, triumphantly quashed. For the moment, everyone believed the president was running the country.

Edith just had to make sure everyone kept believing it until it was true or until the 1920 election, whichever came first.

Chapter One

A VIRGINIA CHILDHOOD

1872–1891

Aunt Lizzie took one look at her infant niece and declared, "Oh, sister, she is the ugliest child you ever had." Since baby Edith was the seventh child born to William and Sallie Bolling, there was a decent data pool for this assessment. Of course Edith's mother objected, although perhaps not as strongly as she might have. "She is no such thing," Sallie retorted, but then allowed, "but even if she is she is so sweet and good you forget it."[1] As it turned out, none of these characterizations was quite accurate. Edith was certainly not ugly, and no one ever accused her adult self of being sweet. As for good, well, that is for history to judge.

Regardless of her merits, Edith did not have the childhood she thought she deserved. Her aristocratic forebears colonized Virginia in the early seventeenth century. They weren't the Pilgrims or political revolutionaries of history books but royalists. Armed with land grants, they left England to exploit the resources of the new world and increase their own wealth. One of these ancestral cavaliers was Robert Bolling, who married a woman named Jane Rolfe, granddaughter of colonist John Rolfe and Pocahontas, forever enabling future Bollings to trace their family tree back to that rarest of seedlings: literal American royalty. Through Jane Rolfe, Edith, as she proudly proclaimed throughout her life, was a ninth-generation descendant of Pocahontas. Edith's branch of these self-proclaimed "Red Bollings" (as distinguished from the "White Bollings" Robert produced with his second wife) settled along the James River near Lynchburg. Edith's grandfather, Archibald Bolling, owned a tobacco plantation where he enslaved over a hundred people.[2] Edith was reared on romanticized tales of these antebellum days, in "spacious times" when there were "slaves and abundance."[3] Even the terrible war years were recounted with a certain idealized air. The plantation house Rose Cottage served as a Confederate hospital, with the women of the family acting as nurses. Archibald's daughter Mary Jefferson, known to Edith as Aunt Jeff, tended a wounded German soldier named Rudolf Teusler. Though Rudolf spoke little English, he fell desperately in love with Jeff, and when he recovered, they ran off to Germany together. After a childhood spent surrounded by such stories, Edith became imbued with the belief that her family was a cut above. It was a world she felt she belonged to. The casual racism and snobbery of unquestioned superiority remained character traits throughout her long life. She always believed she was to the manor born.

But by the time of Edith's birth on October 15, 1872, the manor was long gone. Union triumph in the Civil War and subsequent emancipation upended her family's wealth and social status. As Edith lamented on the very first page of her memoir, "the old order passed, and they found themselves, like thousands of others, with everything swept away, and unable to live on a plantation with no one to work it and no money."[4] By the end of the war, Edith's parents held mastery only over a warren of cramped rooms above three storefronts on a commercial block of Main Street in Wytheville, Virginia. Wytheville is a modest Blue Ridge Mountain town in the state's narrow southwest corner—closer geographically and culturally to Appalachian West Virginia, North Carolina, and Tennessee than to the plantations of the James River. The Bolling home looks like it has a third story, but the top level is a false gable—complete with false windows—only the depth of the brick facade. Edith imagined that her grandfather had taken ownership of this building in payment of a debt, but the truth is much more mundane: William, who had been practicing law in Wytheville with his uncle William Terry, simply bought the property at auction with his mother in 1860.[5] Originally purchased to provide the newlywed William with rental income, the Wytheville house, too, served as a Confederate hospital, which for a time rendered it "untenantable."[6] But that was where the family moved in 1866 and, after it was "scrubbed and patched up,"[7] made their home.

Fortunately, William Bolling had a profession beyond tobacco planter. He practiced law with substantial success and in 1870 became a circuit court judge, a man of some stature in Wytheville. He and Edith shared the same curly dark hair, low brow, and long, straight nose. He had a flair for reading aloud and entertained his family with Dickens and Shakespeare and Milton and "even some of the racy seventeenth-century playwrights."[8] Every Sunday, he took his oratory talents to the masses, becoming the most popular lay reader at St. John's Episcopal Church. By contrast, his wife, Sallie, was timid and deferential, and "no one ever heard her say an unkind thing."[9] Doe-eyed and placid, Sallie was untiring in her domestic duties. Edith believed her "radiantly happy," and the marriage was serene. But even a man of William's stature and success could afford little in postwar Virginia, with a raft of children of his own and an unending succession of long-term visitors. Despite their efforts, the Main Street house was "shabby and inadequate."[10] And crowded. The Bollings had eleven children: Rolfe, Gertrude, Annie Lee, Will, Bertha, Charles, Edith, Randolph, Wilmer, Julian, and Geraldine (Charles and Geraldine died as babies). Also resident were William's fierce invalid mother, his prim mother-in-law, his sister Aunt Jeff, now widowed and back from Germany with her son, Rudolf Jr., Sallie's judgmental sister Lizzie, and assorted other dependents. Cousins and friends and passing acquaintances would visit and stay for months. Judge Bolling's resources were stretched to the limit. He found himself a long way from the wealth of his childhood, when he had once been given an enslaved boy as a birthday present.[11]

Their loss of material plenty led the Bollings to emphasize their wealth of pedigree. They proudly claimed membership among the First Families of Virginia, those who traced their ancestry to the Jamestown settlers of the early 1600s and took credit for "civilizing" America. The First Families of Virginia claim was a sacred trust. In his 1893 novel *Pudd'nhead Wilson*, Mark Twain explained this snobbery even as he mocked it: "In their eyes it was a nobility. It had its unwritten laws, and they were as clearly defined and as strict as any that could be found among the printed statutes of the land. The F.F.V. was born a gentleman; his highest duty in life was to watch over that great inheritance and keep it unsmirched."[12] No degradation of home or bank account could tarnish the shine of sterling bloodlines.

Additionally, the Bollings' direct descent from Pocahontas, a status symbol that Virginians continue to hold precious over four hundred years after her death, gave them a further claim to an even more elite lineage. This heritage was so important, in fact, that the Virginia legislature would eventually tie itself in knots trying to carve the "Pocahontas exception" out of racial purity and antimiscegenation laws well into the twentieth century.[13]

The Bollings remained unreconstructed Confederates. Even in her 1938 memoir Edith identified herself as a "Rebel."[14] Edith's family was hardly unusual in its failure to accept the reality of a postwar South. As one scholar of Reconstruction put it, "Confederate defeat not only destroyed the dream of an independent nation for the slaveholding South; it also shook the very foundations of the antebellum household. Adapting to new constellations of household organization, reshaped by wartime deaths and emancipation, was an emotional and material challenge for white Virginians."[15] Shocked by their losses, the Bollings steadfastly maintained that the war had been fought to preserve a gracious and beautiful way of life and that their enslaved laborers, ignorant and hopeless, were devoted to the family's well-being.[16] The chief storyteller of these Lost Cause myths was Edith's grandmother Anne Wigginton Bolling. Equal parts terrifying and inspirational, Grandmother Bolling was thrown from a horse as a young woman, and the resulting spinal injury left her stooped and immobile. Throughout Edith's childhood, her grandmother was almost entirely housebound, only able to leave if she was physically carried to a carriage. She held court from her bedroom at the center of the Bolling house, a bespectacled tyrant dwarfed by severe black dresses over hoopskirts, adorned only with a mourning brooch of human hair, ruling from a rocking-chair throne. The tanned skin of a dead dog, a treasured possession, was draped across the back of that rocking chair until the day she died.

Using criteria known only to herself, Grandmother Bolling chose favorites among her nine surviving grandchildren. "She simply did, or did not, like you," Edith wrote in her memoir, "and there was the end of it, and no compromise."[17] If you were deemed unworthy, like Edith's next-older sister, Bertha, the best you could hope for was to be ignored. More likely you were constantly belittled. It was a formative fact of Edith's youth that she was her grandmother's favorite. Grandmother Bolling's favor was a mixed blessing. She did not countenance relaxation or idleness. Young Edith was required to sleep in her grandmother's four-poster bed, constantly available for her nightly needs. "I used to make a game of counting the times she would call on me to wait on her, and sometimes it was thirty-nine or forty in a night."[18] Edith had to wash and iron her grandmother's white lace caps, which were elaborate and required fussy attention. But these chores were nothing compared with the canaries. The back of the Bolling home had a broad wooden porch with a view of the mountains. And it was here that the canaries ruled—dozens of them, lavished with the love and affection Grandmother Bolling denied most of her human descendants. With her exacting grandmother watching her every move, Edith cleaned their many cages, fed them, watched their nests and hatchlings. Never shy in her opinions, Edith unequivocally hated the canaries. She claimed the only time she ever enjoyed their care was when one died and she and her brother Will were allowed to preside over elaborate bird funerals, complete with spool-box coffins and marble-chip tombstones.[19]

But Edith also credits her grandmother with the bulk of her limited education. "For myself I can truly say she taught me nearly everything I know. From her I learned to read and write. She even tried to teach me French, which she had learned to read by herself. The Bible she knew from cover to cover, and we read it together morning and night. She taught me to knit, to sew, to embroider, hemstitch and crochet, and to cut and fit dresses."[20] Despite her grandmother's demanding coldness, Edith always believed she owed much to "the tiny lady who sat enthroned on a dog-skin."[21]

Edith's maternal grandmother, Lucy White Logwood, might have provided a softer counterpoint to severe Grandmother Bolling. Warm-hearted and given to singing in the evening, Grandmother Logwood could always be counted on for sweet treats like coconut balls or pralines. But she was not all comfort and sugar—she insisted that no proper female should allow her ankles to show or any part of her person to come in contact with the back of a chair. Even her evening ballads inevitably featured tragic ends for girls who strayed from social norms.[22] Regardless, her influence was not long felt. While Edith was still young, Aunt Lizzie confounded predictions of lifelong spinsterhood by marrying a Confederate veteran twice her age. They moved to Albemarle County in the central part of Virginia, and Grandmother Logwood went with them. But her daughter Sallie continued her example of proper female behavior, in accordance with the cult of True Womanhood that so dominated women's literature of the nineteenth century.[23] The pillars of True Womanhood were piety, purity, submissiveness, and domesticity, all traits Sallie embodied to her core. At times each of these ideals clashed with Grandmother Bolling's example (and Edith's own inclination) of frankness, strong opinions, and self-confidence. Throughout her life, Edith constantly juggled the contradictions among these conflicting early lessons.

Edith was, by her own account, a precocious child. Born seventh among the eleven Bolling children (sixth of the surviving nine), she had to distinguish herself somehow. Judge Bolling undertook the religious education of his children himself. For efficiency's sake, he taught them in cohorts of three. Thus Edith was classified as the youngest member of the second sibling class. When her brother Will turned fourteen and was ready to be presented to the bishop for his confirmation, Edith insisted she knew all the same material he did and, despite being only nine, was equally prepared to be confirmed. A doubtful bishop quizzed her but found her confidence was well founded. Thoroughly charmed, the bishop instructed, "Tell your father, little girl, you are the best prepared candidate I have examined, and I *want* you in the class tomorrow."[24]

Edith adored her father and seems to have been something of a pet with him. In 1886, when she was thirteen, he suggested that she, of all his children, should accompany him to his board meeting at the University of Virginia in Charlottesville. Edith had never been out of Wytheville. She was delighted with every aspect of the trip: riding on a train, staying in a hotel, seeing Thomas Jefferson's home at Monticello. When his meetings were over, Edith's father put her alone on a train to Gordonsville to visit her Aunt Jeff. This was Edith's first taste of travel, and she was excited to be trusted to do it all by herself. The busyness enthralled her, and she remembered it vividly many years later. As she described in her memoir in 1939, the station was "full of people changing from the Richmond to the Washington train, and fortifying themselves with legs of fried chicken from the big trays that were carried on the heads of tall black negro women. Dressed in calico dresses and big white aprons, the chicken vendors smiled as only darkies can smile."[25]

Like her formidable grandmother, Edith's confidence in her own abilities and opinions was not always a power she used for good. One memorable night, Edith and her sister were forced to entertain the tedious sons of the local Episcopal minister. Dutifully, they brought the boys to their library, an attractive upstairs room with a small balcony.

But Edith's patience for these dullards ran out quickly. "We thought they would never go home. Finally I said, 'I'll bet you can't jump from that balcony to the ground!' They took the dare and climbed over the rail and carefully let themselves down until they were hanging from the floor by their hands. I ran out and stomped on their fingers."[26] (While young Edith was at times obnoxious, she was not homicidal. It is reassuring to report that the bottom of the library window, which still stands, is only about ten feet off the ground.)

Edith's father and grandmother provided the entirety of her education until she turned fifteen in 1887, when she was sent to board at Martha Washington College for Young Ladies. "The Martha," as students called it, was about sixty miles west of Wytheville in Abingdon, just shy of the Tennessee border. The curriculum included math, physics, chemistry, and Latin but placed special emphasis on music, literature, art, and elocution. The Bollings chose it specifically for the music teacher, as Edith had expressed an interest in improving her piano skills. And with her oldest brother, Rolfe, working in a local bank and living nearby, it was an appropriate and proper institution for a gently bred young flower of the FFV.

Edith hated it. After her informal home schooling, she hated the rigidity of schedules and rules and routines. She hated that the music room was kept so cold her fingers would stiffen too much to play. She hated the terrible, meager food and the girls who called her "the gray spider" because she was so tall and skinny. But mainly she hated the headmaster, a "narrow, cruel, and bigoted" man "whom Dickens could have chosen for the head of Dotheboys Hall."[27] She fled back home in June of 1888 and refused to return. The institution seems to have forgiven the *Nicholas Nickleby* comparison: today "the Martha" is a luxury inn and spa where you can enjoy your tea in the Edith Wilson Parlor.

Back in Wytheville, Edith found a quieter household than the one she had left. Rolfe had moved to Abingdon, and Gertrude had married Alexander Hunter Galt and moved all the way to Washington, DC. Will was studying to be a doctor. Aunt Jeff and Rudolf moved to Richmond. But there were still plenty of people about—Edith's parents and Grandmother Bolling, along with some boarders to bring in extra income. Annie Lee, twenty-three, and Bertha, nineteen, were both living at home. The youngest boys, Randolph, Wilmer, and Julian, were not yet teenagers. On Edith's very first night back, a gentleman came to call on one of her older sisters. He was "a New Yorker and had money. He kept fine horses and entertained in a much more elaborate style than our modest townspeople were accustomed to." He took one look at fifteen-year-old Edith and, according to her, "fell in love with me as soon as I entered the room."[28] The charming Yankee was thirty-eight years old. Edith claimed the romantic feelings were entirely one-sided, and she regarded him merely as a kind older man. But her parents remained unconvinced. Despite their tight budget and the utter failure of Edith's first attempt at boarding school, it was decided she should go away as soon as possible.

So the fall she turned seventeen, Edith was packed off to the state capital to attend the Richmond Female Seminary, widely known as Powell's School. Richmond was still emerging from the ashes of the Civil War—in some places quite literally. In 1865, retreating Confederate soldiers started fires that burned about a quarter of the city's buildings. But by 1889, fueled by the economic engines of railroads and tobacco, rebuilt Richmond was busy enough to seem to provincial Edith "a seething mass of humanity and distractions."[29] There was even a brand-new electric streetcar system, the nation's first. At Powell's

School, about thirty boarders shared a handsome brick building on East Grace Street, while day students from Richmond's most prominent families came and went. The school promised "the best advantages in Music, Art, and Languages" and, crucially for the strapped Bollings, "terms very moderate for the advantages given."[30] As much as she had hated Martha Washington, Edith adored her second attempt at school. No Dickensian condemnations for Mr. Powell—he was "father, counselor, and comrade to each of us." The girls formed "one big family" and enjoyed the adolescent pleasures of breaking the occasional rule or cutting the occasional class. Edith and her roommate Lucy Day, along with the two girls next door, would remain lifelong friends.[31] But Edith's happy year was cut short in May of 1890, when Mr. Powell almost died in an accident with that shiny new streetcar. The girls were told to pack up and go home.

Edith consoled herself that if Powell recovered, she could return to Richmond for another year. But it was not to be. By the time fall rolled around, it was time to send her younger brothers to school, and the family could not afford more education for a mere daughter. Edith, not quite eighteen, was left without anything to keep her busy in the short term or a plan for her future in the long term. Many girls her age would have been thinking of marriage and surveying the neighborhood for eligible beaux. But Edith always claimed she didn't want to marry. She had thrived in the bustle of Richmond, with its crowds and trains and shops. She loved mingling with sophisticated city girls in their fashionable clothes. Despite the dictates of True Womanhood, she was beginning to suspect she could never be satisfied with a quiet domestic life in Wytheville.

Edith's growing malaise was nipped in the bud by her oldest sister,

Gertrude, who had moved to the nation's capital with her husband when Edith was thirteen. Now she issued an invitation: come stay in Washington for four entire months.

Today, Washington and Wytheville are separated by only three hundred miles of easy highway. In 1890, they might as well have been different planets.

Chapter Two

WOMAN OF WASHINGTON

1891–1908

The capital city unfolded before Edith like a menu of options for the woman she wished to become. Washington in the 1890s was a great place to reinvent yourself if you were young and beautiful. The city was even more attractive if you were rich, which Edith was decidedly not. In the last decade of the nineteenth century, the capital boomed with new residents and sparkled with new money. Some of this growth was by design. The rapid population increase and military occupation of the Civil War years left Washington so chaotic and battered there was serious talk of moving the nation's capital west to a more central city like Saint Louis. The oft-quoted imperative "Go West, young man," attributed to Horace Greeley in 1865, is actually a direct insult to postwar DC. The full (disputed)* quotation:

---

* It is possible Greeley never said this at all, or said a different form of it, or was quoting someone else. Thomas Fuller, "'Go West, Young Man!'—an Elusive Slogan," *Indiana Magazine of History* 100, no. 3 (September 2004).

"Washington is not a place to live in. The rents are high, the food is bad, the dust is disgusting and the morals are deplorable. Go West, young man, go West and grow up with the country." Random islands of federal buildings and row houses connected by unpaved, muddy avenues had (mostly) sufficed for the prewar Washington population of 75,000 but proved almost unlivable for the 177,000 souls who packed the district by 1880.[1] In response, the leaders of the city's new territorial government, led by Alexander "Boss" Shepherd, undertook massive public works projects to make their hometown more appealing. The streets were graded and paved. Miles and miles of sewers, gas mains, and water mains were installed.[2] A horse-drawn streetcar system was established. The city's trees had been a major war casualty, cut down to feed the constant need for firewood and for soldiers to have clear sight lines for their weapons.[3] Under Shepherd's direction, sixty thousand new trees were planted. All of this modernization, rationalization, and beautification served the mission of keeping the seat of government in Washington by transforming it from a provincial village to a glittering city that could compete with the capitals of Europe.

It was a mission that largely succeeded. One hundred thousand additional new residents arrived before the turn of the century.[4] Talk of moving the capital quieted to the occasional territorial grumble. The expensive, modern city infrastructure led directly to a real estate boom, with new neighborhoods like the Palisades and Chevy Chase springing up where once there had been only farmland. And a second, less intentional motivation for moving to Washington emerged: the gates of high society there were easier to crash than the exclusive circles of Boston, Philadelphia, or New York.[5] Those with undistinguished pedigrees who found themselves in possession of shiny new Gilded Age fortunes of questionable origins could achieve social prominence in

Washington, join (or found) the "right" clubs, and marry their children into blue bloodlines.[6] Writers of the time, including Mark Twain,[7] who coined the term "the Gilded Age," and Edith Wharton,[8] its most astute critic, created characters who escaped claustrophobic New York society for relative freedom in DC. Washington was simply too young a city for the social arbiters to insist upon colonial antecedents—the roots of even the oldest local families were relatively shallow. And the transitory nature of elected government meant "important" citizens were constantly coming and going before anyone who cared could discover who their people were.[9] There was, of course, a small, insular group of permanent DC families known as the "cave dwellers."[10] But they stuck to themselves in the elegant townhouses around Lafayette Square next to the White House, while the fabulously wealthy parvenus built palaces up Massachusetts Avenue beyond Dupont Circle, pushing the axis of prosperity north and west. By the mid-1880s, one newspaper claimed it was as fashionable to have a winter home in Washington as it was to have a summer place in Newport.[11] Each grander than the last, many of these monuments of excess still exist, now repurposed into institutions like the Cosmos Club, the Anderson House Museum, and the embassy of Indonesia.[12]

This was the Washington Edith Bolling discovered in the winter of 1890, when she moved in with her sister Gertrude and brother-in-law Alexander Hunter Galt and their baby, Alexander Bolling Galt (with a surfeit of Alexanders, both father and son went by their middle names). The Galts lived on G Street Northwest, between Nineteenth and Twentieth Streets, in Foggy Bottom—not quite as desirable as Dupont Circle but eminently respectable. Edith had just turned eighteen and was finished with school forever. She eagerly anticipated her transformation from child of Appalachia to woman of Washington. She knew in her heart she was never meant to be a country mouse, or indeed a mouse of any variety. Now standing a statuesque five-foot-nine, Edith had thick dark hair and brows that contrasted with her ivory skin. Her many admirers couldn't seem to agree if her eyes were gray,[13] violet,[14] or light blue[15] but invariably used descriptors like *dancing* or *twinkling*. Her voice, pitched low, carried a southern lilt her friends called a "Shenandoah Twist."[16] She loved beautiful clothes and dressed, within the confines of her budget, to enhance her ample curves. With very little money and limited social connections, the legendary galas at Massachusetts Avenue mansions were not yet open to her. But many of the revitalized city's new attractions were within easy reach of a young white woman with more pedigree than wealth. After years of delay and infighting, the Washington Monument was finally finished in 1884 and opened to the public in 1888. And although its reign as the world's tallest structure was brief, eclipsed by the Eiffel Tower in 1889, the Washington Monument was a hugely popular destination, attracting over fifty thousand visitors a month. In September 1890, the U.S. Congress took a departure from its habitual refusal to support the capital city and agreed to fund the creation of a "pleasuring ground" in Rock Creek Valley.[17] The Smithsonian Institution kept busy expanding its collection of live animals from around the U.S., including three different kinds of bears. The menagerie grew so fast that little care was taken to separate predator and prey, to the eternal grief of a Rocky Mountain goat and a California antelope.

And then there was the music. If not exactly an accomplished musician, Edith was certainly a competent one. And she was a very appreciative fan. It was the music in Washington that confirmed Edith's suspicion she would never be satisfied within the confines of Wytheville. She and Gertrude went to the opera and the theater as often as they could, which was several times a week. Her letters to her sister Bertha back home in Virginia are full of theater parties ("one of the sweetest little German plays I ever saw") and fashion ("Gertrude wore her lavender waist with crimson roses and I wore my blue dress with La France roses").[18]

Just a few days before her visit to DC was scheduled to end, Edith was handed a once-in-a-lifetime chance to see Adelina Patti in concert. She had despaired of ever hearing the legendary soprano, knowing she couldn't afford the five-dollar ticket. But at the last minute a friend of Hunter's called up with the offer of an extra seat, right in the front row. Edith could have it, but only if she could get downtown to Albaugh's Opera House before eight. Not stopping to change into appropriate evening dress, Edith flew out of her sister's house and raced for the street corner. She paced the G Street sidewalk, the dusk gathering and the minutes ticking by, as she waited impatiently for a herdic. How to describe the city herdics? No memoirist[19] of nineteenth-century Washington failed to mention these remarkable conveyances.[20] They were a vaguely hearse-like variety of horse-drawn bus, long and narrow with a door in the back and seats along the sides. In theory, they ran regular routes, but they were notoriously unpredictable and painfully slow.

In her memoir, Edith described this night in colorful detail: How the herdic seemed to stop every block, and no passenger had exact change, causing an excruciating delay while the driver searched his pockets for coins. How her companions were embarrassed by her green plaid day dress. How transported she was by Patti's performance (she did make it on time, after running the last two blocks) as she sat "drinking in the liquid, exquisite notes."[21]

As an afterthought, she mentioned that when she floated back to G Street "in a sort of dream" after this wonderful evening, she discovered Norman Galt sitting down to a chafing dish full of oysters with Gertrude and her husband. He had come to call on her. Again.

Norman Galt was Hunter's cousin and by all accounts a perfectly nice and very respectable man. With his father, uncle, and brother, Norman ran Galt & Bro. jewelers on Pennsylvania Avenue. Galt's had been a Washington fixture as long as anyone could remember— Norman's grandfather James Galt opened its doors in 1802, when Thomas Jefferson occupied the White House (he bought a silver service from Galt's)[22] and the city of Washington was little more than a construction site. With baby cups and engagement rings and ceremonial plaques, the elite of Washington marked their life passages with silver and jewelry from Galt's. Mary Todd Lincoln, roundly mocked in the press for her profligate spending, bought brooches and bouquet holders and coffee spoons from Galt's. There was still a considerable balance due on Mrs. Lincoln's account when the president was assassinated. Norman's father forgave most of the debt.[23]

As befitted the honorable owner of a long-standing high-end business, Norman served on the local Chamber of Commerce and Board of Trade. He volunteered on the boards of the Arlington Fire Insurance Company and the Children's Hospital. He was active in the vestry of St. Thomas' Parish Episcopal church.[24] He was, in other words, the very definition of an upstanding citizen. He was also something of a fusspot. Tall and dark with gray eyes and a neat mustache, Norman was always immaculately dressed. He took two baths a day and changed his shirt at least twice. He never wore the same suit for two days running.[25] And he was, in his quiet, fastidious way, absolutely smitten with Edith. The feeling was decidedly not mutual. When he began dropping by his cousin's house with small tokens of his affection, Edith professed herself baffled. "It did not occur to me that

Norman Galt's frequent visits were in any way due to his interest in me. He was about nine years my senior, but he seemed much older, and I never gave him a thought. He sent me flowers and candy; but I was used to that—as all Southern girls were—and felt it only a natural attention."[26] Edith returned to Wytheville as scheduled in the spring of 1891, and Norman floated the idea of joining Gertrude and Hunter when they came south to visit the following summer. Edith agreed, still claiming to believe he just needed a break from his lonely city life and willfully ignoring any evidence of courtship.

After a season in the capital, the sleepy foothills of Wytheville must have felt more provincial than ever. There was nothing for Edith in her hometown. Grandmother Bolling was still terrorizing descendants and coddling canaries on Main Street, retaining her "usual vigor of mind and character" well into her eighties.[27] The oldest siblings had married and moved away. But the house was still crowded with boarders and relatives and hangers-on. Edith didn't even last a year before she moved back to Washington. The confidence and independence instilled by Grandmother Bolling easily beat out the lessons of submissiveness and domesticity modeled by Edith's mother, Sallie. It would not be the last time that happened.

Without a lot of other options, Edith finally decided to notice Norman. "Not until I had been there two months did I realize Norman was in love with me. We were the best of friends, and I liked him immensely, but I did not want to marry anyone." This is not a case of the quiet, steady boy next door being transformed by love into a dashing Prince Charming. But a dashing Prince Charming would probably not have gotten very far with Edith anyway. Despite her youth and inexperience, practical Edith was one to be overcome not by epic romance but by something much more prosaic. "His patience and persistence overcame me, and after four years of close and delightful friendship we were married."[28] The wedding took place at St. John's Church in Wytheville, just down Main Street from the Bollings' home. It was April 30, 1896, Norman's thirty-second birthday. Edith was twenty-three.

Until they could afford a house of their own, Edith and Norman lived with Norman's father in his big brownstone on a fashionable block of H Street NW, between Fourteenth and Fifteenth. The senior Mr. Galt had built houses for his older son and daughter upon their marriages but told the new couple he could not afford to do the same for them. As soon as they could, Edith and Norman moved to a tiny house they laughingly (but proudly) called "the Palace." Their first guests were Edith's parents, visiting from Wytheville for Thanksgiving. "My father and mother arrived in time to take the first meal with us, and see all the simple but sweet furnishings—with the *new* still on them."[29] In those first few years together, the Galt marriage seems, if not exactly a love story for the ages, a solid partnership of mutual respect. "All my family were devoted to Norman," Edith wrote. And if she conspicuously omitted her own devotion, she did admit, "No one could have been better or lovelier than he to each and every one of them. He was sound in his judgments, and unfailing in his eagerness to help the younger boys and do everything he could for anyone I loved."[30]

But after only a few short years of contentment, the losses started to pile up. In 1898 Reginald Fendall, the husband of Norman's sister Annie, and "a delightful man," dropped dead of a stroke in a room at the Waldorf Astoria in New York. Twenty-four hours later, as Mr. Galt Sr. was arranging to have the body sent back to Washington, *he* dropped dead of heart failure. Grandmother Bolling died just two weeks later, followed shortly by Aunt Jeff. Then Norman's brother Charles became a hopeless invalid and entirely dependent on Norman and Edith. Not long after that, in the summer of 1899, Edith's beloved father, William Bolling, died at age sixty-two. It was this last loss that wounded Edith most deeply. Her father was her role model and trusted confidant, "not only a father but a comrade—who shared our joys and sorrows, who understood our complexities."[31] He was also the cornerstone holding up the entire Bolling family infrastructure: Edith's sister Bertha and her two youngest brothers, Wilmer and Julian, who were still only teenagers. Edith's mother, Sallie, who had deferred to her husband in all things since her marriage at seventeen. All those hapless relatives who overstayed their welcome in Wytheville. They had all depended on the wisdom, hospitality, and resources of William Bolling. And with his sudden death it all threatened to come crashing down. A heartbroken Sallie decided she couldn't possibly keep the Wytheville house on her own. And so the family scattered: Sallie and Bertha at first to Annie Lee's home in Tennessee. Randolph and Wilmer to Bridgeport, Connecticut. Fifteen-year-old Julian to Washington to live with Norman and Edith and attend private school. Eventually Sallie and Julian joined the Connecticut contingent as well, and the Virginian Bollings tried to replant themselves in Yankee soil. "They took a small house on Fairfield Avenue," Edith wrote, "where all the old things from Virginia were transplanted and where for five years they made a center around which we all gathered whenever we could."[32]

Finally, in the fall of 1903, there was some good news. Edith gave birth to a son in September. Effusive letters of congratulations poured in from the family in Bridgeport. Edith's sister Bertha gushed on September 23, "I am wild to see him and you both, and to know who he is like, and what you will name him!"[33] In classic younger-brother fashion, Wilmer promised, "Name him for me & I will leave him a fortune!"[34] From the shocked tone of most of these letters, it seems Edith and Norman had not told the family they were expecting. "Of all the astonishing things that have happened, this knocks me more completely off my feet!"[35] wrote stunned sister-in-law Annie, Rolfe's wife. "I am really taken so much by the delightful surprise," Edith's mother wrote in the second of two letters from September 23, "that I am, even yet, three hours after the happy news reached me, bewildered and wondering if this is the day of miracles."[36] But perhaps the lack of advance warning stemmed from the grim fact that the birth was dangerously premature—for within a week, the notes of congratulations turned to condolences. The baby (who seems never to have been named, despite Wilmer's generous proposal) lived only three days. By September 27, Bertha's initial gushing turned to equally heartfelt sympathy. "My heart is so full of the sorrow that has followed our joy!"[37] Rolfe's more measured note, tacked onto the end of his wife Annie's longer letter, followed a day later. "I have just time to express my deep sorrow & regret at the sad news," he wrote. "Our hearts go out to you in tenderest love & sympathy."[38] Edith was hospitalized. But she felt the need to write to her mother and assure her all was well. Sallie Bolling, who had given birth to eleven children, responded with a kind rebuke, cloaked in the anatomical euphemisms of the day. "I rejoice that you are convalescing rapidly and feel equal to writing; I rather fear you ought not to have made this effort and while it was the greatest relief to see again your dear, familiar hand, you must not attempt to write again until you gain strength for it is all important now that you be still until all the muscles have assumed their former position and function."[39] Two weeks later, Edith was home from the hospital when her mother wrote again. The letter was nominally meant to wish Edith a happy thirty-first birthday but included plenty of motherly fussing. "Suppose you are now moving around your room & sitting room.

Which will be such a relief after the long time in bed. Be careful though until after the 22nd [one month after the birth], then you should be strong and well."[40] Although Edith was indeed eventually strong and well, she was unable to have more children.

In her 1939 memoir, Edith detailed the terrible losses she and Norman endured in 1898 and 1899. But she made absolutely no mention of the birth or death of her son. Maybe it was simply too painful, which would certainly be understandable, even decades later. It is tempting to attach broader significance to the omission, however. Edith's memoir, like all memoirs, presented a carefully curated image of herself and her history. On page after page, she made it clear that she wanted to be seen as a practical, useful person of good judgment who was dedicated to her second husband. Perhaps she felt any mention of the brief life of her only child undermined that image by making her seem too tragic, too vulnerable, too much of a woman. Or maybe, in a book written to glorify Woodrow Wilson and Edith's devotion to him and his work, a baby was simply too obvious a reminder that before Woodrow, Edith and Norman had a real, consummated marriage. After all, Edith's memoir scarcely mentions Norman himself, and never with anything like love. Biographer Phyllis Lee Levin had her own theory: "Any hint of affection or love was denied him [Norman] in Edith's *Memoir*, as though she wished to preserve, at least mentally, her virginal state, or feared that such affirmation might invalidate the passion of her second marriage."[41]

But the inescapable fact remained that Edith and Norman were married for almost twelve years. If Edith remained dispassionate about her husband, he was unfailingly good to her and her whole extended family. When Edith's mother and brothers inevitably gave up Connecticut as too cold and too Yankee, they all moved down to

Washington, where Norman hired the three young Bolling men at Galt's. And Edith, although she adored her father and felt his loss keenly, seemed to thrive on taking his place as the cornerstone of her family. It was a role she would play for the rest of her life. Edith's mother made it clear that "she would have to depend on us now that Father was gone, and we must not expect her to decide things, for it made her nervous and unhappy. And it was to us all the greatest privilege to shield her and her gentle spirit from anything that chilled or wounded it."[42]

With a profitable business and her family close at hand, Edith enjoyed the next few years. Norman made plans to buy out his relatives, becoming the sole proprietor of Galt's. They moved out of "the Palace" and into a house at 1308 Twentieth Street NW between N and O, near Dupont Circle. The building was demolished in 1960 to make way for an apartment block. But photos show a narrow, elegant, three-story brick townhouse with a small balcony and decorative slate roof. It was not enormous, but it was sophisticated and fashionable. They went every Sunday to St. Thomas' Parish Episcopal church, just on the other side of Dupont Circle. Edith and Norman Galt were now eminently respectable—if the highest of society sniffed at those "in trade," they still occupied a position of considerable status and responsibility in nonfederal Washington.

Their prosperity brought some material pleasures. In 1904, Edith became the first woman documented to receive a driver's license[43] in Washington, which allowed her to "operate an automobile of the electric type in the District of Columbia." Although cars were still a novelty in the early years of the twentieth century, electric "runabouts" (picture a golf cart designed to look like a small Victorian carriage, steered by a kind of tiller from the bench seat) became popular with urban women of means like Edith. For years, the fashionable way for modern women to travel independently around town had been the bicycle. Edith Benham Helm, the daughter of proper Washingtonians who would go on to serve as the First Lady's social secretary, was an avid cyclist who regularly biked around DC. She described the "extraordinary costume" called a "divided skirt," which had "long flowing petticoats on either leg, which was supposed to be very modest and give the illusion of skirts while riding the bicycle."[44] Edith never learned to ride a bike (although she would attempt to learn years later in the basement of the White House, with hilarious results) and would probably have dismissed the divided skirt as a crime against fashion. Another society hostess claimed the divided skirt was "so hideous and uncomfortable I feel as if I were in a bag."[45] So her little electric car opened up an independence of movement Edith had never known: faster than a horse, more flexible than a trolley, and more ladylike than a bicycle. Electric car manufacturers were not unaware of the appeal to women who found gas cars too noisy and smelly. They began to market electric cars to women particularly, even including built-in vanity cases and cut-glass bud vases on the dashboards (Edith preferred an orchid in hers). If Edith claimed to be "the first woman in Washington to own and drive an electric car,"[46] she was not alone for long. *Motor* magazine reported in 1904: "The [electric runabout] appears to be the most popular form of automobile for women, at any rate in the National Capital. . . . Indeed, judging from the number of motors that one sees driven by women on a fine afternoon, one would imagine that nearly every belle in Washington owned a machine."[47] Edith became a familiar sight to the locals as she buzzed around town in her Columbia Victoria at its top speed of thirteen miles per hour. The traffic cop at the corner of Fifteenth and Pennsylvania knew her by sight and "always held up traffic for me, allowing me to cross, and giving me a salute."[48] Society hostess Dolly Gann remembered, "I used to see her often when she occupied a house in the same block where we lived, in O Street. She was accustomed to drive about the city in an electric runabout, a luxury which I myself possessed."[49]

As Edith was learning to enjoy her thirties as a married woman of status and means, so too was the city of Washington coming into its own. Teddy Roosevelt and his rowdy family occupied the White House, bringing a new public liveliness that had been missing from previous administrations.[50] First, they redid the White House interior. Ellen Maury Slayden, who was married to a Democratic congressman, approved. Slayden wrote a very gossipy memoir of her time in Washington and was not afraid to express her opinion. "If Roosevelt had never done anything else, the metamorphosis of the White House from a gilded barn to a comfortable residence that he has accomplished would entitle him to his country's gratitude."[51] After redoing the residence, the Roosevelts set about remaking Washington society. Any president and his family always held social status due to the eminence of the office. But never before had they dictated trends in high society. As that deeply entrenched society insider Henry Adams put it, "No one in society seemed to have the ear of anybody in Government. No one in Government knew any reason for consulting any one in society."[52] That all changed with Roosevelt's oldest daughter, Alice. With her beauty, outspokenness, and willingness to court scandal, Alice Roosevelt was a celebrity fashion icon by the time of her teenage debut in 1902 and *the* society hostess after her marriage to Congressman Nicholas Longworth in 1906. Alice stayed in Washington after her marriage as her husband rose to power in the House, and she almost single-handedly created a new connection between federal politics and the Washington "smart set." Political social life, at least for the wives, was tedious, predictable, and strictly proscribed. Ellen Maury Slayden called it "a damnable iteration of each social season; every winter the same thing, nothing changed but the names and the clothes—and not always the latter."[53] But Alice scorned previously unavoidable political expectations, such as the endless formal calls political wives made upon each other on rotating days of "at homes." As one biographer noted, "One function of calling was to climb the social ladder. She was already at the top. Regardless of the job Nick held, Alice Roosevelt Longworth would always be a Roosevelt and the president's daughter (even when Theodore Roosevelt was no longer president; even when he was dead). She needed no acceptance from the cave dwellers (long-term residents in the capital city), for although she had not been born in Washington, she had lived there much of her life, and showed every sign of staying."[54] She was also, as it happened, the driver of an electric runabout, and although she did not adopt the practice as early as Edith did, Alice did much to advance driving's social acceptance. "The First Daughter . . . added a legitimacy to the heretofore risqué combination of women and automobiles, and opened the avenues for women drivers."[55]

The infrastructure and architecture of the city was changing too, and fast. Inspired by the "White City" of the 1893 World's Columbian Exposition in Chicago, the federal McMillan Commission in 1902 debuted an ambitious project. It wholly reimagined the monumental core[56] of federal Washington, resurrecting Pierre L'Enfant's eighteenth-century plan for what would become the National Mall.[57] By 1907, the McMillan Plan had been largely adopted, and its biggest recommendations implemented in dramatic fashion. The unsightly railroad tracks that ran in front of the Capitol were removed, and train traffic was rerouted north and east to the grand new Beaux Arts Union Station.

That year, 1907, was also the year President Roosevelt spoke at the laying of the cornerstone of a new National Cathedral at the summit of Mount St. Alban.[58] The cathedral was designed in the Gothic Revival style, but almost all of the other new buildings rising up around Washington shared an obvious White City genetic connection. Many familiar, iconic white marble Washington landmarks were established in the early years of the twentieth century, including the Smithsonian National Museum of Natural History, the Department of Agriculture, the Cannon House Office Building, and the Carnegie Library (now an Apple Store). All around Edith, Washington was growing up and out of its awkward stage. The "overgrown village"[59] a teenage Edith had wondered at just fifteen years earlier was rapidly transforming into the gleaming world capital its founders had envisioned. A few years later, in 1912, Montgomery Schuyler would write in *Scribner's Magazine*, "He who visits Washington now after ten years finds so great a transformation that he is fain to take his bearings anew from the ancient landmarks and is relieved to find the Capitol and the Monument still predominant."[60] Between the glamour of society and the grandness of the architecture, Washingtonians now felt they could boast of their hometown anywhere in the world.

Edith and Norman tested that theory with trips to Europe in 1905 and 1907. They settled into international travel with ease. In July 1905, Edith sent a postcard to her mother, writing casually of the beauty of the Welsh roses. In a 1907 letter to Gertrude and Hunter from Lucerne, she claimed she and Norman were "leading a quietly delightful life."[61] There is no amazement at the foreignness of the sights and sounds, no bafflement around food or language, no fish-out-of-water insecurities from a rookie traveler. Edith could always find the confidence to adapt to any new circumstances. They stayed at luxury hotels, saw all the recommended sights, and took in some opera. Edith fell quite in love with travel, and especially with Paris, where the girl from Wytheville delighted in ordering her gowns from the legendary House of Worth.

As the first decade of the century ticked by, the Galts and Bollings found a steady happiness after the death of their patriarch. Edith's brothers Randolph, Wilmer, and Julian all lived in Washington and worked for Galt's, and their income helped support their mother and sister Bertha, who shared an apartment in town.[62] Edith and Norman each had some minor health issues, the most serious being appendicitis for Edith in 1906. Edith was terrified of the hospital, so Norman arranged for her to have her appendix removed at home on Twentieth Street. Years later, Edith described the scene to a biographer: "The library was fitted out as an operating room with clean sheets covering the floor and furniture, and an operating table brought in. The anesthetist required no more paraphernalia than a gauze cone and a bottle of ether; and the instruments were boiled in dishpans."[63] Happily Edith survived this makeshift OR.

Norman was not so lucky when he fell ill on Christmas Eve, 1907. After a short illness, which has variously been described as a liver infection, the grippe, or Russian influenza, Norman died at home on January 28, 1908. He was forty-three years old. *The Washington Times* declared his death had "shocked business friends"; they knew he had been sick, but "that he would succumb to the disease was entirely unexpected."[64] The *Washington Post* obituary claimed, "Mr. Galt's personality won for him a large circle of friends and his pride in the civic beauty of Washington made him one of the foremost citizens of the District."[65] The funeral was held at St. Thomas' Parish Episcopal church. His pallbearers represented his various allegiances: the church vestry, the Arlington Fire Insurance Company, the board of the Children's Hospital, the Chamber of Commerce, the Board of Trade, and the Commercial National Bank. He was buried at Oak Hill Cemetery in Georgetown, alongside his infant son.

The loss of Norman takes up about a third of a sentence in Edith's memoir. Here is the entirety of her description of the death of the man she was married to for almost twelve years: "Three years passed and then, in January, 1908, after a brief illness my husband died, and I was left with an active business either to maintain or liquidate, upon which all my income was dependent."[66] There is not much else to go on—few letters from this time period survive, which is probably a function of the fact that Edith's closest family members lived nearby. So what to make of this airy dismissal of Norman? Was Edith, who took care of everybody and cared deeply about her family, really so unmoved by his death? And if she wasn't, why did she want to present herself that way? Perhaps it was simply expedience—a desire to rush through the relatively anonymous first forty years of her life to devote more memoir space to the juicy White House saga. This seems unlikely. Edith did very little without thoughtful consideration of how it would look, and she must have realized her brevity would come across as cold. Maybe, as Levin speculated, she believed her apathy toward Norman would contrast becomingly with her passion for Woodrow. It is also entirely possible that after a lifetime of historians treating her as if she had sprung Athena-like, fully formed, into the world the day she met the president, and ceased to exist the day he died, some part of her believed her own lived experience outside of that window was simply unimportant. Which is demonstrably untrue. The years Edith spent growing up in Washington as Washington grew up around her—years in which Norman was present every day—were formative. She learned she could

thrive away from her provincial hometown and without the wisdom
and resources of her father. She discovered she was considered fashionable and sophisticated, even in an increasingly cosmopolitan city.
And she became the dependable, sensible woman her family relied on—
rather than the stubborn, unpredictable girl who depended on them.
And that transformation, more than anything else, might explain her
minimization of Norman. In a deeply patriarchal world, her husband's
death allowed her to become the independent, worldly, woman-about-
town that she always imagined, but perhaps never before wholeheartedly believed, she could be.

Chapter Three

MERRY WIDOW

1908–1914

I n 1910, Edith stood on the deck of the grand Red Star Line steamship SS *Finland* and watched American shores recede. Her sister Bertha joined her at the rail, eagerly anticipating her first European adventure. But if Bertha was a little giddy, Edith was simply relieved. Sometimes she felt like she hadn't taken a deep breath since Norman's death two years earlier. His loss had been the cause of many sleepless nights. She missed him, of course—she had grown rather fond of her steady, dependable husband in twelve years of marriage. But it wasn't loneliness that kept Edith up at night; it was the pressing question of what to do about Galt's. Edith inherited the family jewelry business in Norman's will. In 1908, this was still unusual. By the turn of the century, the rights of women to inherit property and to enter into contracts had been codified in every state, even, finally, Edith's home state of Virginia. But women's property laws were not enacted for feminist reasons; it's not as if late-nineteenth-century men suddenly recognized women as capable, equal partners. Instead, these laws were generally an attempt to keep a family from drowning in debt when the patriarch died by protecting widows' property from creditors. They were interpreted very narrowly in the courts, and consequently women's ability to own and operate businesses was severely limited well into the twentieth century.[1] If Norman had had an obvious male heir, he might have made a case to control Edith's interest in the business. But with no children, a dead father, and an invalid brother, Norman was able to leave Galt's to Edith entirely.

Unfortunately for Edith, he also left the business's debts. Although it was a profitable company, Norman had not yet paid off his investment in buying out the other partners. Perhaps, Edith thought, the easiest thing to do would just be to sell the business, recoup what she could, and be done with it. Or maybe she could take on a new partner? But she felt keenly that Norman had entrusted her with a business his family had run successfully for over a century. And Edith's family was deeply involved too: three of her brothers worked for Galt's, and they each contributed to the support of Bertha and their mother. If Galt's closed, the ripple effects would be personal and disastrous. Hence the sleepless nights.

Edith received, inevitably, "much advice from friends and relatives, no two of whom ever gave the same counsel."[2] And although Edith protested she "had no experience in business affairs, and hardly knew an asset from a liability,"[3] she did, as always, trust herself to rise to the occasion. And again her trust was well placed. Ultimately she figured out a way to keep the business, support her family, and pay off Norman's debts. Instead of borrowing money, she took no salary for herself and relied on the lessons of her frugal childhood to make it through the crisis. "We were offered all the credit we wanted, both from banks and from business houses from whom we bought goods. But credit meant paying interest on money borrowed, so we did not take it . . . and thus kept our friends and our independence and asked no favors."[4] She trusted the day-to-day running of the store to the longtime manager, Henry Bergheimer. But she remained actively involved in the business, meeting regularly with Bergheimer and her lawyer, closely tracking Galt's profits and losses.

And now, in 1910, Edith had earned that rare role for the time: an independent woman of comfortable means. She had no debts, no children, no need for chaperones. And she was only thirty-eight; she still had half a lifetime ahead to enjoy her status. She habitually wore black—not in mourning for Norman but because it flattered her rosy cheeks and dark hair. She was looking forward to this vacation. She wanted to show Bertha the places she had already visited in Europe, plus explore a few new ones. And, of course, augment her wardrobe. The heavily corseted S shape of Edwardian fashion was giving way to lighter, less restrictive styles and huge ornamental hats. Both of these innovations appealed to Edith. As the ship steamed east, she turned her back on the U.S. and looked ahead toward a new adventure.

And it was an adventure. Edith had been to Europe before, but Bertha had stronger language skills, so they turned out to be excellent travel companions. They admired Flemish architecture in Antwerp, enjoyed the Butter Market in Middelburg, and tried to decide if the Oberammergau Passion Play was sacrilegious. We know from Edith's letters that they were joined by two gentlemen for at least some of this trip, a fact Edith pointedly omitted from her memoir. Warren Van Slyke and his friend Herbert Biggs are nowhere mentioned in Edith's account. Van Slyke was in love with Edith,[5] although she seemed indifferent to his ardor. And Biggs corresponded with Bertha, "assuring you that last summer's voyage over will be often in my mind."[6] The four also attended at least one event together in New York in the summer of 1911.[7] But if this trip was a sort of extended double date, that's not how Edith wanted it to be remembered. She just wanted a break from the pressures and loneliness of home.

The Washington Edith left behind was progressing too. The boisterous Roosevelt children and their equally boisterous father left the White House in 1909. Their retirement was reluctant; Theodore Roosevelt regretted his pledge not to run for a third term. His handpicked successor was William Howard Taft, who easily beat three-time Democratic loser William Jennings Bryan. The Taft children were older than the Roosevelt clan—by the time their father was inaugurated, Robert was at Yale and Helen was about to leave for Bryn Mawr. But Charlie Taft was just twelve and did his best to follow in the mischievous Roosevelts' footsteps, tying dinner guests' shoelaces together and shooting spitballs at a portrait of Andrew Jackson.[8] Like the elder Roosevelts, the Tafts loved to entertain, and they attempted many outdoor parties in the style they had hosted while living in the Philippines. Alas, the Washington weather rarely cooperated with these events, and the lush tropical feel of Manila gardens was hard to replicate at the White House. First Lady Helen Taft did manage to leave one important botanical legacy in the capital, however: the iconic cherry blossoms that line the Tidal Basin were her idea.

In the summer of 1909, Washingtonians flocked across the Potomac to Fort Myer, where the Wright brothers were attempting daily flights. Some were there to see and be seen, others to marvel at the wonder of the new two-passenger Wright flyer. Cabinet secretaries came to assess the surveillance and weaponry potential of this new invention.[9]

In March 1911, Washingtonians watched in horror as their wooden baseball park burned, then watched in amazement as the new steel-and-concrete Griffith Stadium was built so fast it was finished (or finished enough) to host the Senators' opening day that September. New apartment buildings seemed to spring up overnight but still couldn't keep up with demand—many were fully rented before they were fully built. The population of Washington continued to grow, adding over fifty thousand new residents between 1900 and 1910. A full third of the city residents were Black—the largest percentage of Black residents of any city in the country.

After Norman's death, Edith chose to live alone for the first time in her life, despite offers from each of her siblings to move into the townhouse on Twentieth Street and keep her company. She enjoyed having to please only herself when she was home. It was the only chapter in her life when she could truly claim the independence she had longed for. She buzzed around town in her electric car, always beautifully dressed with a fabulous hat, going to the theater and to check in at Galt's. She never took on the role of society hostess, claiming she preferred small family parties to glittering salons. But in her own way, she was a figure of respect and status in Washington social life.

Yet she was often lonely. She didn't have a particularly wide circle of friends outside of her family. One exception was a man named James Gordon, a Scottish mining engineer who had married a woman from Virginia. When his wife died, James and his only child, Alice Gertrude, known as Altrude, rattled around together in a big house on Sixteenth Street. Edith occasionally had dinner with James, and she watched Altrude grow into a dashing debutante who enjoyed dancing, tennis, and driving way too fast. That changed in the spring of 1911, when James was diagnosed with cancer. Altrude, just nineteen, was crushed. Before he died, James asked Edith if she would look out for his daughter. In retrospect, this is an interesting choice. The Gordons were wealthy and well connected. Presumably James could have asked any number of friends to take an interest in Altrude. Perhaps he thought Edith's practical smarts would temper his daughter's frivolity. Perhaps he thought Edith needed a friend. Whatever the reason, Edith took her responsibility seriously.

The first thing she did was propose the remedy that had proven so helpful to her the previous year: a trip. Altrude was, according to Edith, "lovely to look at, very intelligent and, like me, lonely."[10] For her part, Altrude "had known Mrs. Galt only casually as a young person knows a friend of her parents. I remembered her best one Sunday in church, a very tall woman with violet-blue eyes, dark hair, and lovely, clear skin."[11] Altrude agreed to the trip, then immediately regretted it. Edith had second thoughts too, calling herself "all kinds of a fool for saddling herself with an unknown teenager."[12] They simply didn't know each other very well, and there was a twenty-year age difference between them. Many closer friendships have wrecked on the rocky terrain of international travel. But they were both game for the challenge— besides, they were too polite to back out. So just two months after James Gordon's death, they found themselves steaming across the Atlantic on the SS *Lapland*. "We decided to take each other on faith and go to Europe together. We stayed five months."[13] Happily, they enjoyed each other's company. They toured Antwerp, Milan, and Lake Como. In Brussels, fed up with big, crowded hotels, they took a chance on a two-star Baedeker guesthouse. The place was lovely but creepy. All the doors were locked. Every morning, the concierge was waiting outside their room and escorted them directly out the front door, not allowing them to explore the hotel. At dinner, they were the only patrons in the dining room. Edith and Altrude spun up a Gothic fantasy of gruesome skeletons of previous guests hidden behind all the locked doors. They were tempted to leave, although the hotel was convenient and comfortable. After three weeks and no other guests, the mystery was solved. Their ever-present concierge admitted the proprietor was away and the hotel was actually closed, but he and the chef, the only staff on site, had wanted to make them as comfortable as they could.[14]

By October 1911 the pair were in Paris. They were expecting to stay only a week, as Edith had to get back home to take care of some business with Galt's. "Neither of us was eager to get back to Washington and to an empty home. So when a cable came saying our business matters had been delayed until January, we decided we would stay until December, and return just in time for Christmas."[15] The extended visit allowed for more shopping, a pastime the two women enjoyed together throughout their long friendship. "Like all the rest of American femininity, Altrude and I invested almost our last penny in dresses and hats."[16]

Edith must have really dreaded that empty house, since she stayed in Washington only six months. By the summer of 1912 she was back in Europe, this time with her sister Bertha, but no beaux. "That was a Presidential election year, but so little was my interest in political affairs that I could hardly have told who the candidates were."[17] Back in Washington, of course, the talk was of little else. Taft was not a particularly popular president, and Roosevelt was frustrated that his more conservative successor had strayed from the original progressive agenda. He decided to challenge his former protégé for the Republican nomination. It was ugly, with hotly contested public primaries and intense private horse trading throughout the spring of 1912. But at the Republican convention in Chicago, the Taft forces prevailed. The incumbent president would be the Republican nominee in 1912. "We seem to be seeing the last of Roosevelt," Democratic congressional wife Ellen Maury Slayden wrote in her diary on June 23, "but he goes out tumultuously shouting prize-ring vulgarity in support of his utterly selfish ambition."[18] Just one day later she had cause to revise her prediction. "We had barely finished the story of how the steam roller had crushed T.R. beyond recognition when news came that he was leading a new party organized immediately after Taft and Sherman were nominated. Not 'bolters' at all, but just a few righteous men meant to save Sodom, I presume, and elect any old Democrat that we want to put up."[19] Roosevelt's decision to run under the banner of his newly formed Progressive Party (known somewhat affectionately as the Bull Moose Party) was widely predicted to split the Republican vote and elect a Democrat, any Democrat, for the first time in twenty years.

But who would that Democrat be? A sizable cast competed for the nomination. The inevitable William Jennings Bryan was in the mix, despite having lost the presidency for the Democrats in 1896, 1900, and 1908. Ultimately he decided not to run, but as the leader of the party's liberals, his endorsement was actively sought by the remaining hopefuls. These included Speaker of the House Champ Clark of Missouri, majority leader Oscar Underwood of Alabama, and Ohio governor Judson Harmon, who had served as Grover Cleveland's attorney general. But behind this pack of career politicians, a dark horse edged up to the front. He was fifty-five-year-old Woodrow Wilson, a man who had spent his career as a college professor and president of Princeton University. By the time the 1912 election heated up, Wilson had held his first political office, governor of New Jersey, for a little over a year.

In that short time, Wilson won the affection of party progressives. He refused to support a corrupt machine-backed candidate for Senate, championed legislation that required primaries for all elected offices, and passed a workers' compensation bill. He cultivated his reputation as an independent intellectual, unsullied by the dirtier side of politics. And with the divisions of the Civil War and Reconstruction still vivid in many voters' memories, Wilson seemed like a geographical unicorn—governor of a northern state with an East Coast elite–friendly association with Princeton, but born in Virginia, raised in Georgia and South Carolina, and southern by heritage and manner. By the time the Democratic National Convention began in Baltimore in June of 1912, Wilson and Clark had won most of the primaries. But it was still anybody's nomination to win. Roosevelt announced his split from the Republicans just the day before the Democrats met, making it clear overnight that whichever nominee emerged from Baltimore was very likely to become the nation's twenty-eighth president. The convention was "one of the most exciting and bitterly contested in the history of the Democratic Party."[20] Roosevelt's daughter Alice Longworth crowed, "It was comforting to see that there was no more sweet harmony in the Democratic ranks than in those of the erstwhile Republican Party."[21] The delegates sweated through ballot after ballot, with no clear winner emerging, even after days of loud speechmaking and quiet backroom deals. Bryan hesitated to make a big endorsement speech, but on every ballot he joined the Nebraska delegation in voting for Clark. The tide seemed to turn in Clark's favor. Then the powerful party operatives of New York's infamous Tammany Hall joined the Clark camp. This gave Clark the majority of the delegates' votes, but not the two thirds required for nomination.

Wilson was not in Baltimore to watch these subplots play out. He was with his family at the governor's summer mansion in Sea Girt, New Jersey. But the telephone and telegraph lines between Baltimore and the Jersey Shore buzzed constantly with updates from friendly reporters and Wilson's campaign workers.[22] When Tammany went for Clark, Wilson's campaign manager, William McCombs, thought the battle was lost. He called Sea Girt and urged the governor to withdraw his name. After all, the vote of the Tammany bosses had always proved decisive in the past.[23] Wilson agreed, hung up the phone, and started planning a vacation to England's Lake District.[24]

But before McCombs could release Wilson's delegates, a call came in from Wilson's deputy campaign manager, William McAdoo. McAdoo insisted McCombs was lost in the past, still fighting the last election. Tammany's sway was no longer absolute. Wilson should keep fighting. Ellen Wilson agreed. She told her husband it was irrational to throw in the towel at this point; after all, what did he have to lose? Wilson often took his wife's advice, and in this instance he didn't need a lot of convincing. He told McAdoo to keep his delegates in line.

McAdoo quickly proved he had a much better read on the convention atmosphere than McCombs did. William Jennings Bryan announced he was withdrawing Nebraska's support from Clark and told anyone who would listen he would never support a candidate endorsed by the corrupt fat cats of Tammany Hall. The Clark supporters tried to rally, but from then on, his support declined on every ballot. Meanwhile, McCombs made a deal to secure the Indiana delegates by adding Governor Thomas Marshall to the ticket as Wilson's vice president. In the drama of the convention, however, no one thought to mention this deal to Wilson.[25] The two men had never met.[26] When the Indiana delegation switched to Wilson, the Illinois delegation followed. Finally, on the forty-sixth ballot, Wilson won the nomination of the Democratic Party.

And so the general-election stage was set with a drama American voters don't see very often: a cast of three. And there were some dramatic moments. In October, an unhinged former saloonkeeper shot Roosevelt in the chest at a campaign event. The bullet passed through his coat pocket, where his steel eyeglass case and the bulky copy of his lengthy speech kept the bullet from inflicting too grave a wound. Roosevelt went on to deliver the speech as scheduled, and the bullet remained lodged in his chest till the day he died in 1919. Then rumors began to circulate that Wilson was having an affair with a woman named Mary Peck. They had met in Bermuda in 1908, and he was immediately taken with this irreverent bohemian who balanced his more pompous tendencies. They had written dozens of suggestive letters back and forth in the years since. She had just finalized her divorce in the summer of 1912—was Wilson behind it? Some of Roosevelt's advisers wanted him to play up the scandal, maybe pay Mary Peck for the letters. Ultimately Roosevelt refused. "It wouldn't work," he said. "You can't cast a man as Romeo who looks and acts so much like the apothecary clerk."[27] But aside from these mini dramas, the plot was a foregone conclusion. Ellen Maury Slayden spoke for many Americans when she wrote, "Roosevelt beats the air and shouts, 'Liar, crook,' etc.; Wilson continues a series of philosophical discourses, and Taft signs bills and plays golf. It looks as if nothing but an accident can prevent Wilson's election, not because the country wants him especially, but because of Roosevelt's madness in splitting the GOP."[28]

As predicted, the general election was a landslide. Wilson carried forty states, Roosevelt six, and Taft just two. Socialist Eugene Debs won 6 percent of the popular vote but carried no states. Edith, still abroad, barely registered the news. "I was in Paris on Election Day, and when the local papers announced the victory of Wilson and Marshall I was glad because the Democrats had won, but beyond the fact that they were Democrats, Messrs. Wilson and Marshall were little more than names to me."[29] Of course, Edith couldn't have voted in 1912 even if she had been home on Election Day. But she regularly claimed that she wasn't at all politically involved before she became First Lady. She knew some readers of her memoir would find that unusual—many Americans assume all adults within the city limits of DC live and die for politics alone. But Edith, a local business owner, was firmly part of the permanent city population that had little to do with the federal government. Before 1913 Edith never attended a single official government affair.[30]

The Wilson family moved to Washington in March of 1913. It was not their natural habitat. First Lady Ellen Wilson was shy and self-conscious. She was extremely well-read and enjoyed being Woodrow's confidant and political adviser. But the public role did not come easily to her. As her biographer Kristie Miller wrote, "Ellen Axson Wilson was quiet, intellectual, dutiful, and frugal. Such qualities are admirable, but not always admired in a first lady."[31] Others were not so gentle. Ellen Maury Slayden dismissed her as "short, round-faced, round-pompadoured, red-cheeked and not becomingly dressed."[32] Ellen much preferred to stay behind the scenes and hand the public social roles over to her three daughters: Margaret, twenty-six, Jessie, twenty-five, and twenty-three-year-old Eleanor, known as Nell. The Misses Wilson, while more eager than their mother to participate in Washington society, were not any more prepared. For help, they brought in Belle Hagner, who had served as social secretary to Edith Roosevelt. Belle was the daughter of proper Washingtonians and parlayed her society insider status into a genteel profession. This was not uncommon—several local young ladies with more breeding than wealth found that serving as a social guide to capital newcomers was an acceptable and reliable way to earn a living. Nell was a little concerned Belle's previous position might make her unfriendly to Democrats but soon discovered she "knew all there was to know about the intricacies of Washington social life"[33] as "she introduced us to the mysteries of Washington etiquette, and solved all the problems of precedence."[34] The social custom that prohibits the president and First Lady from accepting private invitations does not extend to the whole first family, but Belle advised the girls not to attend the same events as each other. On any given night, the first daughters could be found around the city, dancing at military barracks, enjoying diplomatic dinners, and attending Marine Corps Band concerts.

ELLEN ALSO INVITED Helen Bones, a cousin of Woodrow's, to live at the White House and serve as personal secretary. The first task for Helen and Belle would normally be to plan and execute the inaugural ball, one of the biggest events on the federal social calendar. But the president decided not to have one. "He thought it was not in keeping with simple democratic ideals, and in spite of loud outcries and protests from Washington society and tradespeople, he stuck to his decision." His daughters were disappointed. Nell, who had ordered a gorgeous ball gown and was looking forward to showing it off, wrote, "I knew he was right, but wished desperately that he wouldn't be so Jeffersonian."[35] This very first night set the tone for Washington in the first Wilson administration, a reset after the glamorous parties of the Roosevelt and Taft years. "The social life in official circles followed its usual course," wrote diplomatic political hostess Dolly Gann, "possibly in a somewhat modified tempo, owing to the Wilson family's lack of interest in formal entertaining."[36] Opinionated Ellen Maury Slayden had a less measured reaction. Despite being a Democrat, she took an instant dislike to the Wilsons. She knew Woodrow when they were

both at the University of Virginia, where "he was admired for his intellect then but never beloved. . . . We girls thought him too stuck on
himself."[37] Her snark extended to the president's daughters. "The lady
Wilsons are all in place and all smiles—the family really has more than
a fair share of teeth."[38] When she learned of the new administration's
social strictures, she threatened, "The Jeffersonian simplicity and intel-
lectuality will drive me to drink."[39] The president excused his lack of
social visibility by claiming to value small-*d* democratic simplicity, and
there was some truth to that. But he also found the public side of his
office frivolous, even counterproductive. He defined three roles for the
presidency: govern the country, lead the party, and be accessible to the
American people. Before he even took office he decided that "no one
man could do all three things at the same time, successfully. And to
him it was quite obvious which of the three roles was least important."
He told his family and advisers that "all unnecessary social life must be
curtailed, speaking trips and hours of hand-shaking eliminated. He
not only must attend properly to the duties of the office, but must have
time to think."[40]

But presidential inaugurations always include unavoidable pomp
and circumstance. At the time, Inauguration Day was March 4 (it was
changed to January 20 with the passage of the Twentieth Amendment
to the Constitution in 1933), and the Wilson family took the train
down from Princeton on March 3. After his landslide victory, the incoming president could reasonably expect a huge, cheering crowd to
greet his family at Union Station. But a group of suffragists, organized
by Alice Paul, planned a massive march down Pennsylvania Avenue
that day, in support of a constitutional amendment enfranchising
women. Theodore Roosevelt's Progressive Party had supported a federal amendment in the election, but Wilson's Democrats said it was an

issue best left to the states. The event, the first civil rights march to use the nation's capital as a backdrop, drew thousands of spectators. When only a modest crowd met the Wilsons' train, the president-elect reportedly asked, "Where are all the people?" The police answered, "Watching the suffrage parade."[41]

But the family got their crowds the next day, when, as tradition dictates, the outgoing and incoming presidents rode together from the White House to the Capitol for the inauguration ceremony. The day started cloudy but turned sunny and pleasant by midmorning. Vice President Marshall and President Wilson were duly sworn in by Chief Justice Edward White. Then, standing on the steps of the Capitol's east front, the new president addressed the crowd. His speech was solemn. "This is not a day of triumph," he declared. "It is a day of dedication. . . . I summon all honest men, all patriotic, all forward-looking men, to my side.* God helping me, I will not fail them, if they will but counsel and sustain me."[42]

The swearing-in is traditionally followed by an inaugural parade. Streets are blocked off all around the federal core of Washington, and visitors flock to town, filling up hotels and restaurants and sidewalks. It is not unusual for jaded local Washingtonians to skip the crowds and traffic headaches and stay home. That was certainly Edith Galt's plan when she found herself at home that March. She had seen McKinley's and Roosevelt's inaugurations, back when she was new to DC, but now it was old news. She was somewhat amazed to discover her sister-in-law Annie planned to come to town to join the throngs of visitors. Annie was a big supporter of the new president and had even campaigned for

---

* This quotation ultimately became one of four engraved in the Wilson Bay at Washington National Cathedral, Woodrow Wilson's final resting place.

him, despite her inability to cast a vote. For her part, Annie was equally amazed at Edith's lack of enthusiasm. "This is a Democrat, and a great man,"[43] she insisted. Besides, Edith had the perfect spot for watching the parade: the balcony at Galt's, right on Pennsylvania Avenue. Edith told Annie she was welcome to the balcony but happily stayed quietly at home. A few days later, Annie secured an appointment, with a guest, to visit the White House and shake the president's hand. Again Edith refused to participate. But she did drive Annie to the White House in her electric runabout, then drove a few circuits around the block until it was time to pick her up again. Annie returned home to Baltimore, baffled by Edith's "inexplicable attitude."[44]

Instead of a ball, after the inauguration ceremony and the parade, the Wilsons hosted a simple White House tea party for family and friends. The event was much more a dignified ritual than a raucous celebration, so it was something of a surprise when Woodrow's sister Annie Wilson Howe took a spill down a marble stair and cut her forehead. In rushed Dr. Cary Travers Grayson, a young naval medical officer who had served as White House physician to President Taft. Taft had recommended Cary Grayson to his successor the day before, saying, "Here is an excellent fellow that I hope you will get to know. I regret to say that he is a Democrat and a Virginian, but that's a matter that can't be helped."[45] Now, with Cary's careful, prompt, and discreet care of Annie Howe, Woodrow was convinced of the doctor's worth. He asked Cary to stay on and continue to serve as White House physician. It was the beginning of a lifelong friendship.

As it happened, Cary was also a friend of Edith's. They had known each other for years, possibly since the birth and death of her son in 1903. But they became closer that year when Cary began courting Altrude Gordon. It was a match Edith wholeheartedly supported. Cary was popular in town, "a catch for hostesses, always impressive in his naval uniform, a martinet about physical fitness, and a superb dancer."[46] In the spring of 1913, Cary was thirty-four and Altrude was twenty-one, not that she told him that fact. "You are a man with a marvelous memory for dates," Altrude wrote in January. "Have you an equally good one for ages? I hope not. For I fear that in an unguarded moment I confided mine to you! I am in a state of mental anguish, for I cannot remember whether or not I did such a rash thing."[47] Their friendship progressed through the spring of 1913, but Cary was very busy and Altrude had other suitors. By August, Edith and Altrude were once again crossing the Atlantic for a European adventure. They were accompanied by Altrude's grouchy cousin Pat, who was one of those contrary tourists who travel only to confirm their hatred of other nations. His complaining started on the voyage over: the ship was too slow, the cayenne pepper Altrude used to settle her stomach made him sneeze, the cattle on board gave him hay fever.[48] Edith and Altrude tried their hardest to ignore him. Edith's "on deck" letter to her sister Bertha (the two wrote long, newsy letters to each other when they weren't together, addressing each other as "Bert" and "Tete") didn't even mention Cousin Pat. Instead, she described in hilarious detail their "imposing stewardess," who "is so English Altrude can't understand a word she says." They had beautiful weather for most of the crossing, so "Altrude and I go way out on the bow and take our rugs and read aloud."[49] Edith read *The Inside of the Cup*, a bestselling novel of social criticism by Winston Churchill (the American writer, no relation to the English statesman). Little did Edith know she would have occasion to meet this author just a few years later.

Once in England, Cousin Pat insisted on hitting all the major tourist attractions. Edith had no interest in slogging through the Tower of

London just to hear Pat grouse about it, so while he toured, she found a shady spot on the Tower grounds to sit and write some letters. As soon as she sat down, a suspicious guard approached and told her that while she could keep her pen and paper, her bag had to be sealed and checked at the gate. Edith was baffled. The guard explained that militant suffragettes, led by Emmeline Pankhurst, had been staging violent protests and vandalizing British landmarks. "We don't trust women these days,"[50] he told Edith. She was embarrassed and self-conscious. The incident did not endear her to the suffrage cause, which she never supported.

Disgusted with England, Cousin Pat insisted on seeing Paris next. He was not a fan. After only a few days, he gave up and booked the next passage home. Liberated from his unpleasant company, Edith and Altrude escaped to the Pyrenees, where they had many adventures involving, according to Edith's memoir, donkeys and omelets. They also explored Biarritz, Madrid, Seville, and Gibraltar and spent a memorable two days in Tangier. They were growing more adventurous in their travels, and ever closer as friends.

Meanwhile, the Wilson administration was settling into the capital. Woodrow Wilson was a man who kept his own counsel, preferring just a few close advisers and his wife, Ellen, to a panel of experts. Some of the men who had guided him through the campaign were rewarded with plum appointments: William McAdoo became secretary of the treasury, and New Jersey political operative Joseph Tumulty became the president's secretary, who functions as his chief of staff. Other appointments were more overtly political, like William Jennings Bryan as secretary of state. If Woodrow was concerned that Bryan would steal the spotlight for himself, he didn't show it. For one thing, he hoped his administration could concentrate almost wholly on his domestic agenda. And if Bryan did start offering unsolicited advice, the president did not have to take it. His closest political adviser had no official role to speak of. Edward Mandell House, known to all as Colonel House (it was a courtesy title; he never served in the military) was a political insider who was one of the first to recognize the national potential of the governor of New Jersey. He was offered a job in the administration but turned it down, preferring to stay behind the scenes.

In April 1913, Woodrow took the unusual step of addressing a joint session of Congress in person, the first president to do so since John Adams. As Nell put it, "for a hundred and thirteen years the President's message had been droned off with expressionless speed, by a congressional clerk, while the gentlemen to whom they were addressed chatted and yawned."[51] Not for this administration: the president went down to the Capitol and addressed a packed gallery. He introduced his domestic agenda, which he called the New Freedom, and outlined three key priorities: tariff reform, banking reform (which would be accomplished through the creation of the Federal Reserve System), and business reform (encouraged by the establishment of the Federal Trade Commission). This was the way the president had always preferred to work: have a good think, make a plan, lay it out clearly, and stick to it. But the office does not generally lend itself to that model. As Wilson biographer John Milton Cooper put it, "as president, he came closest to working that way during the first year and a half, when he concentrated on the New Freedom legislative program. Seldom again would he enjoy the luxury of focusing so much on tasks of his own choosing."[52]

As it happened, Edith was one of the many eager spectators in the Capitol gallery that night. Her mother and her sister Bertha wanted to go see the president speak, and Edith offered to take them. They had only two tickets, so Edith planned to wait outside during the speech.

But the crowd was so large and enthusiastic that when the doors opened, Edith found it was impossible to step aside. "We were swept in, and on, and on, to the very front where in the gallery on the right side I found myself next to the big clock on the front row, immediately above the Speaker's rostrum. In a few minutes I was looking down on the tall, slender figure of Woodrow Wilson, President of the United States."[53] Edith did not record her impressions of the speech. But a few years later, when she was a regular visitor at the White House, Woodrow showed her a picture of that night. Edith "pointed out myself tucked away in a corner above his head."[54]

The Wilson family were also finding their way in DC. In November 1913, middle daughter Jessie married Francis Sayre in a White House ceremony. It was a grand affair, despite the bride's instincts to keep the wedding quiet and private. Jessie was like her mother, serious and conscientious, devoted to social reform and Christianity. Using his own eccentric criteria, her father divided the family up into the "proper" members (Ellen and Jessie), the "vulgar" members (himself and Nell), and Margaret, who switched between the two camps. After a European honeymoon, the Sayres moved to Massachusetts, where Francis was a professor at Williams College.

Just weeks later, Nell dropped the bomb that she was also engaged. Ellen and Woodrow were less than delighted by this news. Nell had been secretly engaged to a man named Ben King for months. But now she told her parents she had broken off with King and meant to marry none other than William McAdoo, the secretary of the treasury. More than twice Nell's age, "Mac" was a widower with seven children, two of whom were older than Nell.[55] After much hand-wringing, "the elder Wilsons could not resist the couple's being, as Ellen put it, 'simply mad over each other,' and they gave their consent."[56]

Nell and Mac's wedding in May of 1914 was a much smaller affair than Jessie and Francis's had been. Ellen, who for months had explained away her fatigue and weakness as a side effect of being First Lady, was by then clearly in truly poor health. To spare her mother the exhaustion of another giant White House wedding, Nell insisted on "as small and quiet a wedding as possible."[57] Cary Grayson was the best man. After the honeymoon, the bride and groom moved out of the White House but stayed in Washington.

Even as Ellen was failing, Woodrow was thriving. Under the guidance of Cary, the president was eating healthy food and getting regular exercise. He had long suffered from digestive issues he described as "a turmoil in Central America" and "disturbances in the equatorial regions."[58] He treated these symptoms with a variety of quack medicines. Cary was convinced a few preventative measures would make a tremendous difference. He conspired with the White House kitchen to prepare simple, healthy food for breakfast. The president's valet would report back on what was eaten and what was left on the tray, until the doctor was able to build a reliable rotation of popular dishes.[59] Exercise came in the form of almost daily golf. Woodrow's devotion to the game was not matched by his talent. Years later, Secret Service agent Edmund Starling recalled his briefing the first day he was assigned to guard the president. Joseph Murphy, head of the White House detail, explained the schedule. "He doesn't like to do it, but he leaves here every morning for the links at eight thirty." "Does he play well?" Starling asked. The reply was unequivocal. "He's terrible.[60] So is Grayson." But even terrible golf had its benefits. As John Cooper describes that time, "just about everything seemed to be going right for Woodrow Wilson as the summer of 1914 began. Several people remarked on how good he looked then and how the presidency seemed to agree with him. He had been healthy most of the time since his inauguration. His skin was tan from his golf games with Dr. Grayson, and he found time for reading."[61]

But Washington summers are notoriously awful: hot and swampy with endless mosquitoes and daily thunderstorms. Most of the family was desperate to get out of town to a cooler clime. The summer before, sight unseen, Ellen and Woodrow had rented a house in Cornish, New Hampshire. Cornish was something of an artists' colony, and the house they rented, "Harlakenden," belonged to Winston Churchill, whose novel *The Inside of the Cup* was still topping the bestseller lists. Ellen and her daughters spent much of the summer of 1913 there, and the president, who was negotiating with Congress over the New Freedom agenda, would visit when he could. The trip was so successful, the family planned to repeat it in the summer of 1914.

This decision affected Edith's travel, too. Altrude and Cary's romance was getting serious, although Altrude "professed herself unwilling to make a decision controlling her future."[62] So instead of going to Europe as usual, Edith cooked up a plan for her and Altrude to take a walking and canoeing trip through Maine. For a woman who enjoyed London hotels and Paris fashion, this might seem like an odd choice for vacation. But the woods of Maine had a huge advantage over the capitals of Europe: proximity to New Hampshire, where Cary was expecting to spend at least some of the summer. "Possibly he could slip away now and then, join us in Maine and assist Altrude in her thinking, amid surroundings more conducive to reflection than the formal and busy life of Washington."[63] Edith and Altrude began their trip in Kineo, near Moosehead Lake, where they hoped Cary could join them. But he was detained in Washington. The women lingered in Kineo for a while, hoping each week that Cary could get away. Altrude sent teasing letters. "Won't you join us? I feel that it would do you more good than anything in the world. . . . I promise that we would leave no deep laid schemes and that Mrs. Galt is no managing mama!!"[64] But after three weeks and no Cary, they proceeded to the next part of their trip, a fishing and camping trek through the Rangeley Lake region, where they would be entirely unreachable.

Cary was stuck in Washington for both political and personal reasons. The assassination of Archduke Franz Ferdinand of Austria in Sarajevo in June 1914 sparked a crisis between Austria-Hungary and Serbia. Throughout the summer, their allies weighed in, escalating the conflict. By late July, war in Europe was inevitable. The president wasn't going anywhere. And as Woodrow's doctor and adviser, Cary would stay with him.

But Cary's medical skills were needed for a more personal reason: Ellen Wilson was fading fast. In the first week of August, as Germany declared war on Russia and France, German troops invaded Belgium, and Great Britain declared war on Germany, Ellen was clearly dying. Woodrow told his daughters to keep the awful news from Europe from their mother. The White House communications office more or less hid the seriousness of Ellen's illness from the press. But on August 5 they issued a statement: the First Lady was critical. The diagnosis was "Bright's Disease, with complications,"[65] an archaic term that referred to various serious kidney ailments. As she drifted in and out of consciousness, she whispered to Cary, "Doctor, if I go away, promise me that you will take good care of my husband."[66] She died on August 6, 1914. She was fifty-four.

Woodrow was utterly bereft. He had relied on Ellen for so much: her sound judgment and good advice, her unfailing instinct to take care of him and make him feel loved. Jessie and Nell were married and gone. Margaret, who was attempting a singing career, was away more often than she was home. The only woman left in the White House was Cousin Helen Bones. Woodrow was lost. As White House usher Ike Hoover described it, "President Wilson appeared retiring, uncommunicative, and rather ill at ease in company; but with his own family—who were all of the gentle sex—he was at his best. They pampered and petted him and looked up to him as their lord and master. He could do no wrong in their eyes."[67] He was facing a massive international crisis with no foreign policy experience whatsoever. He told his daughter, "I was not intended to lead the country in a war. Mine should have been a constructive, not a destructive administration."[68] He blamed himself for Ellen's death, convinced the pressures of his position had sent her to an early grave. He had lost his support system, the people who loved him best. "A sadder picture no one could imagine," Cary wrote to Edith. "A great man with his heart torn out."[69] At times he wasn't sure he would survive the loss. "I never dreamed such loneliness and desolation of heart possible," he wrote to Mary Peck.[70] He was not alone: Joe Tumulty was there, and Colonel House, and Ellen's brother Stockton Axson. Cary came every day. But no matter how sympathetic they were, they were men. Woodrow had always been very clear: to feel whole, to do his best work, to live up to his potential, he needed a woman by his side.

Chapter Four

ROMANCED BY
THE PRESIDENT

1915

I f Edith were to be completely honest with herself, she had to admit
that Cary Grayson was getting annoying. She loved him, she really
did, and she was happy to abet his on-again, off-again romance
with Altrude. Edith had barely survived a terrible case of ptomaine
poisoning in Maine, and in the fall of 1914 she returned to Washington recovered but weak. Cary came to check on her every day. His soli-
citousness was sincere—he genuinely cared about Edith's health—but
he also really wanted to talk to her about Altrude.[1] Did she love him?
Was he too old for her? Was she seeing anyone else? Had he missed his
chance by not coming to Maine? Eventually he must have noticed
Edith's patience for the conversation wearing thin. He began to add
new topics: the ongoing conflict in Europe, the implications for the
U.S., how lonesome and shattered the president was. Again and again
he talked of his pity for Helen Bones, Woodrow's frail cousin who had

been left to shoulder all unavoidable First Lady responsibilities after Ellen's death. Margaret had done a bit but hated every minute that took her away from her fledgling singing career.* After her mother's death she wrote with bitterness to her sister Jessie, "I have practically no time to myself except to practise [sic] a little, because of my duties to my guests, some of them are most difficult to please, as you know. My evenings are given up entirely to them."[2] So Helen stepped in. The gossip columns occasionally linked Cary and Helen romantically.[3] As Edith well knew, the rumors were unfounded—he only had eyes for Altrude. But Cary was fond of Helen and worried she was "desperately lonely as she had no intimate friends in Washington."[4]

And now the man had gotten it into his head that she, Edith, should make friends with sad little Helen. He was sure they'd like each other. Edith could encourage her to take a break, maybe hike through Rock Creek Park, give her a little time away from her duties in the fresh autumn air. Edith was unconvinced. "My dear Doctor," she told him, "I am not a society person. I have never had any contacts with official Washington, and don't desire any. I am, therefore, the last person in the world able to help you."[5] Cary kept trying. Edith wouldn't need to participate in official society doings—the White House was in mourning, so there wasn't any entertaining going on. Helen just needed a friend. Edith finally put him off by nominating Altrude for the job instead. After all, if Altrude visited the White House regularly, Cary could arrange to see her more often. That seemed to work—Cary gave up his campaign.

Or so Edith thought. But then one day Cary just showed up at her

---

* This career never really took off. You can hear a recording of Margaret singing the national anthem in 1915 here: en.wikipedia.org/wiki/File:MargaretWoodrowWilson-TheStarSpangledBanner .org. She has a serviceable soprano, although her decision to jump the major fourth on the final "free" was probably a mistake.

house with Helen Bones and Nell Wilson McAdoo in a White House car. The weather was perfect, and they were all going for a ride in the park. Wouldn't Edith join them? He knew she was trapped: Edith was far too polite to refuse the president's daughter's company.

Somewhat grudgingly, Edith admitted she liked Helen and Nell. They were both "full of charm, easy to know, and thoroughly unspoiled."[6] Another ride followed a few days later. As Cary had predicted, Helen and Edith genuinely enjoyed each other's company. Throughout the fall and winter of 1914, they met up several times a week, often taking Edith's little electric to Rock Creek Park to "tramp along the lovely bridle paths then return to my house to have tea and sit before the fire in my library and talk."[7]

Inevitably, some of that talk strayed to "Cousin Woodrow," as Helen called the president. Helen described how Woodrow's parents had taken her in as a girl after her mother died, raised her as their own, and sent her to school. She was devoted to Woodrow and worshipped him personally as an older brother and politically as the champion of peace and justice. She called him "Tiger," an unexpectedly playful nickname. It was not a reference to the Princeton mascot but rather because, pathetically caged in the White House, her cousin "reminded her of a splendid Bengal tiger she had once seen" pacing in a zoo.[8] Edith still professed herself not much interested in the presidency or the man who filled it, but she appreciated that Helen's confidences gave her "a very intimate insight into the man whom the world judged cold, or a human machine, devoid of emotion."[9]

The president did have emotions, and at that moment they could be described only as depressed. "At heart he was desperately lonely," Cary Grayson wrote in his memoir. "It may be asked why I did not arrange to fill the house with company. I did what I could but Mr. Wilson had never been a man to find solace in crowds."[10] What Woodrow wanted was a wife. He wrote agonized letters to his female friends, desperate for a woman to confide in. To Nancy Saunders Toy he complained, "I have not yet learned how to throw off the incubus of my grief and live as I used to live, in thought and spirit, in spite of it. Even books have grown meaningless to me. I read detective stories to forget, as a man would get drunk!"[11] To his daughter Jessie Wilson Sayre: "I find that the only way to sustain a broken heart is to try to do what she would have done. So long as I act in her spirit and, as nearly as I can, as she would have acted I experience a sort of sweet relief and happiness that helps to carry me through the day."[12] Inevitably, he also reached out to his old friend Mary Peck. "I have never understood before what a broken heart meant, and did for a man. It just means that he lives by the compulsion of necessity and duty only."[13] Of course, as conditions in Europe deteriorated, necessity and duty were very demanding priorities for the president of the United States. Officially, the U.S. was neutral in the European war— Woodrow had issued a formal proclamation of neutrality two days before Ellen's death. He urged Americans to embrace neutrality on an individual level too, although he acknowledged that since so many Americans descended from the warring populations, it was natural to choose sides. Don't give in to the temptation, he warned in an August address to Congress. "We must be impartial in thought as well as in action, must put a curb upon our sentiments as well as upon every transaction that might be construed as a preference of one party to the struggle before another."[14] This injunction did nothing to countermand the president's reputation for lack of emotion. As ambassador to the United Kingdom Walter Hines Page wrote to his brother, "a government can be neutral, but no *man* can be."[15] Author Edith Gittings Reid protested that this was just another misinterpretation of her friend

Woodrow Wilson: "It was shouted all over the world in derision that he had asked the country to be neutral in thought as in deed. He asked nothing so absurd; for to be neutral in thought would be not to think at all. But he did ask them to be 'impartial,' which meant the use of the highest type of intellect there is, that of the judge, not the advocate."[16]

Americans' opinions of the president were put to the test that fall; 1914 was a midterm election year. With the ratification of the Seventeenth Amendment in 1913, this was the first time senators would be elected directly by the voters instead of by state legislatures. Woodrow was concerned it would be a referendum on his presidency, despite his name not literally being on the ballot. If voters were considering their president, the reviews were mixed. The Democrats picked up four seats in the Senate but lost sixty in the House. Still, they maintained healthy majorities in both chambers, and it looked like the party was outgrowing its East Coast roots and building support in the West. The electorates in western states were growing as their legislatures enfranchised women, so solid returns from that region boded well for the 1916 general election, when Woodrow's name really would be on the ballot.

But the election returns provided little solace to the exhausted and lonely president, who felt abandoned and unappreciated. Perhaps that is why, just a week and a half later, Woodrow lost his famous emotional control and got visibly angry in public, something he prided himself on avoiding. Like many other Black leaders, newspaper editor William Monroe Trotter had supported the president in the 1912 election, believing his progressive rhetoric extended to civil rights. But then several cabinet secretaries, including Postmaster General Albert Burleson and treasury secretary William McAdoo, moved to segregate their departments, demote Black professionals, and bar Black federal workers from government dining rooms and bathrooms. The president fully supported these initiatives. Trotter wrote angry editorials and organized a petition signed by twenty thousand Americans. But the presidential response was the patronizing equivalent of a pat on the head. So in November 1914, Trotter sought an appointment at the White House to register his displeasure in person. When Trotter and his delegation described the stories of humiliation they had heard from Black civil servants, now demoted to positions as janitors and forced to use broken basement bathrooms, the president was unmoved. He blamed Trotter and his fellow activists for any unhappiness the segregation caused. "If you take it as a humiliation, which it is not intended as," he said, "and sow the seed of that impression all over the country, why the consequences will be very serious."[17] Trotter did not back down, reminding Woodrow of the promises of the 1912 campaign, when candidate Wilson had assured Black voters they could "depend upon you for everything which would assist in advancing the interest of their race in the United States."[18] That's when the president lost his temper. He did not like direct criticism from anyone, and certainly not a Black man. He told Trotter his tone was offensive and he had "spoiled the whole cause for which you came." As he showed the delegation out, he huffed, "If this association comes again, it must have another spokesman."[19] Trotter went to the press, and condemnatory editorials appeared in both the Black and white papers.

But Trotter's pleas and the bad press apparently did nothing to persuade the administration to be more receptive to the needs of Black Americans. Three months later, in February 1915, the White House hosted a motion picture screening for the first time. The film was *The Clansman*, later renamed *The Birth of a Nation*, a sweeping, three-plus-hour epic of unapologetic white supremacy and race-baiting. A White House statement later claimed the president "was entirely unaware of the character of the play before it was presented and has at no time expressed his approbation of it."[20] But Thomas Dixon, who wrote the novel upon which the film was based, was an old colleague of Woodrow's from graduate school. Dixon made much of the appearance of a presidential endorsement. To this day, the film is credited with inspiring the revival of the Ku Klux Klan.

AS 1914 TURNED TO 1915, the president continued to play golf whenever he had the time. White House usher Ike Hoover didn't even think he liked golf very much. It was just an excuse to get out of the house. "He would play at all hours, sometimes as early as five in the morning and sometimes late in the afternoon. Good or bad weather was just the same to him. When there was snow on the ground, he would have the balls painted red and find amusement in driving them around on the ice and snow."[21] His game never improved much—even the loyal Cary Grayson admitted he "had taken up the game too late to become an expert player and his eye trouble was an additional interference."[22] But the president didn't seem to care—the score was never the point of the exercise. When there wasn't time for golf, Woodrow enjoyed driving around Washington in the White House Pierce-Arrow. This car, with presidential seals on the doors and Secret Service escort in front and behind, became a familiar sight in town. Always a creature of habit, Woodrow wasn't looking to explore new neighborhoods or see new sights, preferring to travel the same comforting roads over and over. "Methodically he arranged his various rides and numbered and named them to suit his fancy: 'Number one ride,' 'Southern Maryland ride,' 'Norbeck ride,' 'Potomac ride.' No change from a previously arranged route would be permitted."[23]

If his existence was somewhat dreary, the public accepted it as the appropriate fate for a recent widower trying to lead the nation through complex times. He had cultivated his image as an intellectual uninterested in the frivolities of social life, and now he was living it. Not everyone expected him to continue this monkish existence forever. On one of his regular automobile rides, Cary saw Edith and waved to her as they drove by. "Who is that beautiful lady?"[24] the president asked. Cary took it as a good sign that Woodrow had noticed something other than work and golf. Perhaps he was coming back to life, at least a little. In the fall of 1914 the always-irreverent Ellen Maury Slayden wrote in her diary that she told Robert Lansing's wife she expected Woodrow to remarry, and soon. Mrs. Lansing was scandalized. "'He wouldn't *dare* marry again while he is in the White House; public opinion would not permit it.' I reminded her that the public was having to reconcile itself to some worse things about him than marriage, and we argued the matter until we ended by betting five pounds of Huyler's—the usual stake these days—with Mrs. Scott the witness on the condition that she will get some of the candy. My bet is that he will marry again before leaving the White House."[25]

But who would be the bride? By early 1915, Washington gossip columnists were openly speculating about the president's hypothetical love life. The old rumors resurfaced about Mary Peck, who had resumed using her maiden name, Mary Hulbert, following her divorce. Woodrow continued his correspondence with her throughout 1914 and 1915, and she visited the White House at least once. The subject of those letters, more often than not, was the increasingly disastrous financial circumstances of Mary's son. She wrote to fret, or to ask for help, connections, or money. Instead of a vivacious, unconventional friend who encouraged Woodrow to take himself less seriously, Mary had become a needy acquaintance, slightly embarrassing. Even she acknowledged their temperaments would never suit. At his most pe-dantic he "was warranted to drive certain temperaments to the verge of consideration of brutal murder."[26] Besides, the public would not accept a divorced First Lady. Mary was never really in the running.

In February a *Town Topics* column suggested, "Rumors of a White House wedding that will surpass all others that have taken place there in recent years are beginning to circulate in New York society."[27] The president was apparently courting Daisy Harriman, one of the few prominent suffragists who had supported him in 1912 and whom he had appointed to the United States Commission on Industrial Rela-tions. The column went on to say, "In Washington it has been thought generally that if the President ever made another marriage it would be with the amiable Mrs. Peck," but "the appearance of a rival may de-moralize the prognostications of the Capital gossips." The anonymous writer approved of the president's rumored choice, confirming that Daisy Harriman, a blue-blooded New York Knickerbocker, "would make a White House mistress who would bring back much of the so-cial prestige it had lost during the present administration." The White House did not comment. The president continued to play golf and take drives, without female companionship.

If the president longed for a second marriage, the same could not be said of Edith. She did have the occasional suitor, but none she was will-ing to sacrifice her independence for. She simply did not pine for a soul mate the way Woodrow did. She was content with her family, her busi-ness, and her friends. She was happy to make time for a new compan-ion like Helen Bones, but as far as she was concerned, her life was full enough.

On a clear day in March, Edith and Helen went for one of their regular treks through Rock Creek Park. Early spring rains had left the bridle paths muddy, and by the time the women finished their walk their boots were filthy. Bewilderingly, this was the one day Helen insisted they take their tea at the White House, instead of in front of Edith's cozy fire. Edith was appalled. She could not possibly make her first visit to the White House with muddy boots; she "should be taken for a tramp."[28] But meek Helen was oddly persistent. Woodrow and Cary were out playing golf, and no one would see them. The tea was already ordered. Edith still refused. Helen appealed to her manners, which was usually a successful tactic with Edith. Helen felt terrible that she had never reciprocated all of Edith's lovely invitations. Surely Edith must understand Helen's need to be the host sometimes, not always the guest? For a little added guilt, she claimed her desolate cousin Woodrow had specifically asked her to bring friends to the lonely White House. Edith knew she was beat. She accepted Helen's invitation, after first extracting a promise they could take the elevator straight to the upstairs family quarters and not run into anyone.

It was a setup, of course, most likely coordinated by Helen and Cary. Helen and Edith drove to the White House and went straight to the elevator, muddy boots and all. On the second floor, the elevator doors opened to reveal Woodrow and Cary, still in their golf clothes and just as muddy as the women were. Everyone laughed, while an embarrassed Edith congratulated herself on having had the foresight to choose a well-tailored black suit and flattering hat that morning. "The two gentlemen, I am sorry to say, were not so well attired. Their golf suits . . . were *not* smart."[29] The four agreed to have tea together and "had an hour of delightful talk."[30] Helen Bones quietly congratulated herself on the success of the meeting. As she said later to Ellen Wilson's sister Margaret, "I can't say that I foresaw in that first minute what was going to happen. It may have taken ten minutes."[31] They invited Edith to stay for dinner, but she deemed it wiser to decline, promising to return for dinner soon when she wasn't so disheveled.

That dinner invitation came on March 23. Edith was the belle of the ball—no muddy boots this time. Ike Hoover was clearly impressed. "Mrs. Galt looked young and handsome and was dressed to perfection down to the last detail. A single purple orchid, pinned high on her left shoulder, set off the picture. She was just the type a man of the President's keen discernment would admire. When she spoke her voice was soft and musical, with a Southern accent. Her every characteristic was pleasing beyond measure."[32] Hoover wasn't the only one taken with Edith. As she walked in, doorkeeper Pat McKenna turned to Secret Service agent Edmund Starling and pronounced, "She's a looker." "And he's a goner," confirmed the president's valet, Arthur Brooks.[33]

He was, indeed, a goner. For months, Brooks had been trying to convince the president to pay more attention to his clothes, get better tailoring, or at least make sure his tie didn't clash with his suit. The president was indifferent, at least until Edith complimented his new dinner jacket, and suddenly "he was sold on the notion that clothes make the man. From then on, he was a willing fashion plate."[34] He began to invite Edith to whatever he could—tea, dinner, long drives in the car. On April 14, he invited her to join him at the Washington Senators' opening game, where he tossed out the first ball. With the great Walter Johnson pitching, the Senators beat the Yankees 7–0. On April 28, he sent her a note, the first of many. "My Dear Mrs. Galt. I have ordered a copy of *Round My House* through the bookseller, but while we are waiting for it I take the liberty of sending you a copy from the Congressional Library. I hope it will give you pleasure—you have given me so much!" He went on to invite her for a drive or a visit that very evening and signed the note "Your sincere and grateful friend,

Woodrow Wilson."[35] Edith wrote back right away, thanking him for his thoughtfulness but declining the invitation, as she had promised to spend the evening with her mother. She signed her note "Faithfully and proudly your friend, Edith Bolling Galt."[36]

That spring Woodrow never went to Edith's house—presidential protocol discourages accepting private invitations. So almost all of their time together took place at the White House. After dinner, family and friends would conspire to give them time alone. "They would often retire to the President's study," explained Ike Hoover, "and the rest of the company would find amusement in other parts of the house."[37] On April 30, the party included Cary and, for the first time, Altrude. Cary desperately wanted to make a good impression on Altrude, and for her to make a good impression on his boss. Planning to escort both women to dinner, Cary drove first to Edith's house, where he found her resplendent in a black silk dress. Gold slippers peeked out from under the hem, the perfect complement to the corsage of gold roses from Woodrow. Edith was all serene beauty—an invitation to the White House no longer held any anxiety for her. Together Cary and Edith drove to pick up Altrude. She was most definitely not serene. Neither was she dressed and ready to go. The president had sent her a corsage of pink roses, which didn't go with her dress at all. At the last minute, she had decided to change her clothes to suit the flowers, and now she was in a tizzy of nerves and silk and indecision. Cary's distress did nothing to help—the president could never abide tardiness, and Altrude was sure to make them late. Calm Edith stepped in, helped Altrude choose a gown, and convinced her to get in the car dressed but not accessorized. They could add the finishing touches on the ride over. Shoes and jewelry and perfume went on in the back seat of the car, as did the troublesome corsage. The evening was a triumph.

But it ended earlier than usual, as Woodrow and Helen were leaving early the next morning for the baptism of Jessie's new baby in Williamstown, Massachusetts.

They returned to Washington on May 3, and Edith received an invitation to the White House for May 4. It would be a larger dinner party than usual—Woodrow's sister Annie Howe was visiting, along with her daughter and baby granddaughter. The evening was lovely, warm enough to serve coffee outside on the South Portico. But almost as soon as the dinner party stood up from the table and walked out the door, all the other guests magically floated away, suddenly very interested in the gardens and lawns. Edith turned to find Woodrow right next to her in the moonlight. His gaze was ardent and "the very world seemed tense and waiting."[38] He had begged the others to leave them alone, he admitted, because he had something he desperately needed to confess. He loved her. He wanted to spend the rest of his life with her. At his grandson's baptism he had told all three daughters and Helen how he felt about her and that he planned to propose. They were all on board. Would she marry him?

Edith was gobsmacked. They had known each other six weeks and had rarely been alone together. Woodrow had buried Ellen just nine months earlier, after thirty years of a loving, happy marriage. Edith was taken wholly unprepared. "I said the first thing that came to my mind, without thinking it would hurt him: 'Oh, you can't love me, for you don't really know me; and it is less than a year since your wife died.'"[39] That wasn't important, Woodrow insisted. In his strange world of the White House, in his unique role as leader of the nation, time didn't matter so much as depth of feeling. He knew what he was asking of her. He knew the public life of First Lady held no appeal. But he could not in good conscience keep seeking her company without her knowing how he felt and what his intentions were. He wanted to marry. Would she have him?

She would not. Edith told him if it had to be yes or no, right that instant, it would have to be no. But couldn't they stay friends and get to know each other better? Would he give her time to see if her feelings could catch up to his? Yes, he said, he could give her that time. He would spend it convincing her how deeply devoted he was, how sincere in his adoration of her. "I will be patient, patient without end," he wrote to her, "to see what, if anything, the future may have in store for me."[40] He was fifty-eight years old, sixteen years older than Edith, and acting like a teenager with his first crush. She was his favorite topic, his foremost thought. "The President was simply obsessed," wrote Ike Hoover. "He put aside practically everything."[41] No matter what else was going on, he found time to write to her, sometimes several letters a day. She always wrote back promptly, if not quite at the same length. They used Helen as a go-between so no one would get too curious about a constant correspondence running between Twentieth Street and the White House.

Reading private letters long after the writers' deaths can shed light on the character of historical figures in a way public documents can't. Edith's letters are charming. She was usually chatty and full of news, talking about her day, what she wore or read, whom she saw for lunch. She especially delighted in telling Woodrow about the praise she heard of him from those who did not know their personal connection. She often rendered these accounts in dialogue, like little one-act plays. "What fun it has been to hear everyone talking of you," she wrote one night in May. She recounted how her butcher asked, "Well, Mrs. Galt have you read the President's speech made in Philadelphia? He is the greatest man this country has ever produced and he is going to stay right where he is for another four years."[42] She thought it was hilarious when friends speculated on the president's romantic life. She wrote that her friend Mrs. Rose thought Woodrow "so charming and attractive she knew women would fall in love with you—but adding, in a comforted tone, that of course 'with all he has on his mind he can't give his thought to any women.'"[43]

If she was intimidated by the contrast between her informal education and his PhD, she did not let it show. She did not put on a pose of intellectual depth to impress him or pepper her letters with scholarly references and allusions. The one time she did quote poetry, she admitted it was something she had learned by heart as a child.[44] She fussed over Woodrow a bit, asking if he was eating well and getting enough sleep. She was occasionally sentimental, but usually in reaction to something Woodrow had written, not on her own initiative. Her letters were a delightful mix of news, advice, and affection. In the beginning of their correspondence, the only reference she made to her feelings was to insist that she didn't have any. She claimed to "pride myself on my coldness and unresponsiveness."[45] She welcomed Woodrow's attempt to "quicken that which has lain dead so long within me" but, sensing that he would fail, pleaded, "If I am dead (as I believe) you will not blame me for seeking to live even if it means pain in your own tender heart when my pulse refuses to be in unison with yours."[46] It's hard to understand her agenda here. Edith was clearly not cold or unfeeling; she cared deeply for her family, was always quick with a compliment or a laugh. Perhaps it was just romantic love or sexual intimacy that she felt incapable of. She had never been deeply in love with Norman Galt. Was she simply applying the brakes on a romance that was moving into sticky emotions too quickly? Unlike in her memoir, in her letters she was curating her image for an audience of one. And for whatever reason, she wanted Woodrow to think of her as antiromantic, at least at first.

By contrast, Woodrow's letters were, from the very beginning, fervent—at times even racy. A glance at the many pages of formal stationery and neat, steady handwriting gives no hint of the deeply emotional content. On May 5, the morning after Edith rejected his proposal, he wrote, "Every glimpse I am permitted to get of the secret depths of you I find them deeper and purer and more beautiful than I knew or had dreamed of."[47] He called her his queen, his dear heart, his little girl. He gushed over her "wonderful personal charm" and her "sweetness and intelligence and power to comprehend and sympathize and love."[48] He told her of his fantasies, his "dream that her dear, beautiful form is close beside me and that I have only to stretch out my arms to have her come to them for comfort and happiness and peace, my kisses on her lips and eyelids."[49] He swore she could stand with "any one of the great women the world has loved and been ennobled by."[50] She was his "adorable sweetheart," his "precious darling," his "Beloved." He held nothing back. One June day Edith attended a ladies' tea at the White House (they were still keeping up the pretense that she was simply Helen's friend), and the president admitted to sneaking into the Green Room, where "from behind the lace curtains, [I] feasted my eyes on the loveliest person in the world,—with, oh, such a longing to go to her and take her in my arms and cover her with kisses, whispering in her ear every sweet secret of deepest love!"[51] He thanked her for choosing a seat where he could spy on her undetected; he even suspected she was clever enough to have done so on purpose.

He had written very romantic letters to Ellen when they were first courting in 1883. But then he was a twenty-six-year-old graduate student, insecure and shy, desperate to impress. The many love letters he wrote Edith, as a middle-aged world leader, provide the most intimate perspective available on this famously reserved man. And what sort of person do the letters reveal? Yes, he was the kind of man who would hide behind the White House curtains to watch his girlfriend, and not be embarrassed to admit it. But some of his public persona comes through as well—the respected scholar is there on every page. Unlike Edith, he regularly copied out whole stanzas of poetry, and he recommended Edith read Matthew Arnold and Robert Browning. According to Ike Hoover, he was not above calling the Library of Congress to find an impressive quotation.[52]

He returned again and again to the idea that he needed Edith to do his best work. "A man is not sufficient by himself, whatever his strength and courage," he wrote. "He is maimed and incomplete without his mate, his heart's companion, the dear one to whom he is lover and comrade."[53] It was her love and support that helped him lead the nation. "You are not only the Darling of my heart but the source of all serenity in me and of the happiness that frees the faculties of a man for action."[54] In July he wrote that "I cannot work at my best . . . unless my heart is satisfied and at ease." He was "a man of affairs, who finds you a woman fit to be a man's counsellor."[55] It was almost her patriotic duty to love him.

The letters do not, it must be said, contain any evidence of a sense of humor. While Edith's letters were sometimes playful or funny (at one point she went to Princeton and saw his official portrait there, which Edith found "perfectly awful! If you looked like that I could not love you"[56]), Woodrow's were always earnest. He was not given to wordplay or witty observations. Those who knew him well insisted the prim president had a lighter side. But the examples of levity even his friends gave show his humor was at best corny and at worst offensive. He had a few silly limericks that he recited over and over with a sly smile—although they never got any naughtier than the one about the old monk from Siberia who eloped with the Mother Superior. He got a huge kick out of "darkey stories"—exaggerated anecdotes that mocked Black people's ignorance or laziness. According to his daughter Nell, when friends from New Orleans visited, "Father could hardly wait for them to take their hats off before insisting that they sit down at once and tell him all their latest 'darkey stories.' 'I've told all I know,' he said. 'Please give me a new supply.'"[57] He did not leave these stories out of his letters for fear Edith would take offense—she indulged in the occasional racist joke herself. But his letters were deadly serious.

And they were, eventually, remarkably indiscreet about official business. The night he first proposed marriage, Woodrow was already mixing romance and politics. He must have confided in Edith his frustrations with his secretary of state, William Jennings Bryan. When Bryan was nominated for the job, no one expected the administration to face many major decisions in foreign affairs. The fact that the liberal Bryan was an evangelical pacifist was not considered much of an obstacle. But now Europe was at war. And it was becoming increasingly clear that this was no time for a peace-loving secretary of state. Woodrow's letters immediately following his proposal are restricted to romance, but Edith tried to steer them back to politics. "I did want to ask you more about the resignation of W.J.B.," she wrote on May 6, "but saw the subject troubled you so would not let myself discuss it. I think it will be a blessing to get rid of him and might as well frankly say I would like to be appointed in his place." She went on to vent the strong opinions for which she was known: "I know how you feel about being loyal to this person, but if he deserts you now he is entitled to small courtesy or consideration and I would not hesitate to put myself on record if he does so scurvy a thing."[58] This letter is remarkable for many reasons. She had just turned down a marriage proposal from the president. His letters were full of promises to be the kind of man worthy of her love. And here she is, suggesting herself for secretary of state at a time when women couldn't even vote nationwide. And even though she was joking (she went on to promise to let him do all the work and said she only wanted the job so she could have daily conferences with him), it is an amazingly confident statement. She claimed she knew little of politics and cared even less, but she did not hesitate to pronounce judgment on "scurvy" Secretary Bryan. From the very beginning of their correspondence, she was letting him know she wanted to be taken into his confidence and would clearly voice her opinion.

Woodrow had the chance to take her up on the implied offer just two days later, when a German submarine torpedoed the RMS *Lusitania*, killing 1,198 people, including 128 Americans. The outcry was immediate and loud. Telegrams poured into the White House, demanding action against Germany. Newspaper editorials turned "Lusitania" into a battle cry. Even loyal Colonel House, who had been sent to London to urge peace among the combatants, cabled, "We can no longer remain neutral spectators."[59] William Jennings Bryan urged moderation. The Germans had warned American citizens not to sail into the war zone on Allied ships. Shouldn't Americans take some responsibility for their actions? And if the president felt he must condemn the Germans, shouldn't he criticize the British too? Their shipping blockade was also a violation of international law. Woodrow retired to his study to think. He would not be rushed. Neither, it seems, did he seek much counsel, including Edith's, at first. He drafted a letter to the Germans more or less by himself. But if he didn't pursue Edith's input, he did turn to her for comfort. "I need you," he wrote on May 9. "I need you as a boy needs his sweetheart and a strong man his helpmate and heart's comrade." He asked her to "think of me tonight. I shall be working on . . . our note to Germany. Every sentence . . . would be freighted with greater force and meaning if I could feel that your mind and heart were keeping me company."[60] Two days later he wrote, "I have needed you tonight, my sweet Edith! What a touch of your hand and a look into your eyes would have meant to me of strength and steadfastness as I made the final decision as to what I should say to Germany."[61]

The president finished his draft of the letter and sent it to his cabinet for comment. Bryan wanted the more aggressive language toned down but was overruled. The letter went out across the Atlantic dated May 13, 1915, condemning submarine warfare and reasserting the right of Americans to travel freely. Bryan signed it but made it clear he did so with a heavy heart. It was the opening salvo in a war of paper that would last almost two years.[62] On May 14, Woodrow took a break from the drama to sail the *Mayflower*, the presidential yacht, up to New York to review the Atlantic Fleet. He invited Edith to join the party. As they headed down the Potomac River on a clear, silver night, Edith and Woodrow found themselves alone at the rail. In her memoir, Edith did not recall this as a romantic moment, although it is hard to imagine the lovesick president would not have taken advantage of moonlight and solitude to restate his devotion. Edith remembered that night because Woodrow sought her advice about Bryan. The secretary of state felt he could not support the increasingly likely possibility of U.S. involvement in the European war. He wanted to resign. "Good," responded Edith. "I hope you can replace him with someone who is able and who would in himself command respect for the office both at home and abroad."[63]

The next morning the *Mayflower* sailed into a violent storm, and everyone on board was terribly sick, including the crew. Even the Secret Service went down. The president "didn't have any more protection than a silk hat in a high wind!" recalled agent Joseph Murphy.[64] Edith and

Woodrow found themselves the last sailors standing, with a rare chance to be truly alone. Some combination of moonlight, confidence, intimacy, and surviving seasickness seems to have wrought a change in Edith. After this trip her letters were much more affectionate. The day after they returned she gushed, "Oh! To be with you tonight my precious one, to put my arms around you and hold you close and tell you how long the day has been without you."[65] In her memoir Edith confessed, "Even now it is impossible to analyze those days of doubt as to my own feelings, for not to have loved and honored Woodrow Wilson when once privileged to know him is incomprehensible. When he offered me his love so royally I confess my amazement that I ever hesitated."[66]

But their romance was not all smooth sailing from then on. Just a week later, something seems to have happened when they went for a nighttime ride. Perhaps eager Woodrow took things too far in the privacy of the back seat. Edith balked. The next morning she wrote to him, apologizing for "the pain I caused your own big, tender heart."[67] Woodrow replied that he had spent "an almost sleepless night of agonizing doubts and fears." He begged her, "For God's sake try to find out whether you really love me or not."[68] Clearly the man who had promised to be "patient, patient without end" was reaching the limits of his tether. He canceled his appointments and took to his room. But the next morning he emerged with a bright new outlook. "After many, many hours of a deep depression and exquisite suffering, which brought on a sort of illness which I could not explain to the doctor and for which he could do nothing, the light has again dawned for me and a new certitude and confidence has come to me."[69] He would no longer doubt himself, or her, he told Edith. He was confident in his love and hers; he was done talking it all to death. "Henceforth, we are not going to *discuss* our love, but live upon it, and grow in it."[70]

One way Woodrow lived upon his love was to involve Edith more closely in his work. The Germans responded to the first *Lusitania* letter with no regret or apology, claiming the ship was armed and carried Canadian troops. Neither was true. (It would turn out that the *Lusitania* did carry some 4,200 cases of rifle cartridges and 1,250 cases of shrapnel-laden artillery shells, but this was entirely legal under U.S. neutrality law.)[71] The president was not at all satisfied with this response. "The German note must be answered and answered very soon,"[72] he wrote to Edith on June 1. But he wasn't just keeping her up to date this time. As he drafted a second letter to Germany, he asked her to serve as his editor. He even seems to have invited her to his White House office to do so. She was delighted. "I was so genuinely pleased that you said you wanted me to read your answer to Germany," she wrote on June 3. "And it was the greatest delight to be in your chair surrounded by all the work-a-day things that come in such daily touch with you—and have you there opposite me, reading what is to be such pregnant history, and letting me share in the vital things that are making you famous."[73] As for the note to Germany, she was not impressed. "There was nothing of *you*, yourself in it and therefore it seemed flat and lacking color." Like all good editors, she tempered her criticism with praise, telling him the first *Lusitania* note was "so splendid that it will go ringing down the ages. And this new one must be an echo, only in reiteration of principles and you must put some little of your *splendid* self in it."[74] Woodrow took her comments to heart. Two days later he wrote, "I worked for you all last evening, too, till late bedtime,—revising the reply to Germany. I have simplified it and, I believe, strengthened it in many ways, and hope that I have brought it nearer to the standard my precious Sweetheart, out of her great love, exacts of me."[75]

This second *Lusitania* letter was the final straw for William Jennings

Bryan, who quit the administration very publicly and critically. Woodrow was ambivalent. He was happy to be able to replace Bryan with Robert Lansing, a man who was more supportive of the possibility of war, but he was also wary of the reaction. "I'm afraid, my dear one, that many consequences will spring out of Mr. B's action which will be very serious to the country and to the administration," he confided to Edith. "The newspapers do not express the real feeling of the country for that strange man, and he is evidently going to make a determined effort to direct public opinion in this German matter. He suffers from a singular sort of moral blindness and is as passionate in error as in the right causes he has taken."[76] Edith was not so subtle. "Hurrah! Old Bryan is out!" she crowed. "I know it is going to be the greatest possible relief to you to be rid of him. Your letter [to Bryan] is *much* too nice—and I see why *I* was not allowed to see it before publication."[77]

Edith was much more flattered by Woodrow's reliance on her judgment than she ever was by his ardent confessions of love. In one of her very first notes she reminded him "what unspeakable pleasure and privilege I deem it to be allowed to share these tense, terrible days of responsibility."[78] The letters about world affairs were Edith's favorites. The mushy love talk was all well and good, but that was not the way to Edith's heart. What she really wanted was to be Woodrow's trusted confidant, someone whose advice he sought and respected. Finally, she told him so. "Much as I love your delicious letters, that would make any woman proud and happy," she wrote, "I believe I enjoy even more the ones in which you tell me of what you are working on—the things that fill your thoughts and demand your best efforts, for then I feel I am sharing your work."[79] Woodrow took the hint. He wrote to her of the "delicate and ticklish" situation in Mexico,[80] where Venustiano Carranza's government was mired in internal opposition and increasingly strained relations with the U.S. Woodrow was also planning for the 1916 election, now only a year and a half away. He was deeply unhappy with William McCombs ("the most unconscionably jealous and faithless and generally impossible person"[81]) and was maneuvering to oust him as chair of the Democratic National Committee. Edith wanted to hear all of it. "I am always with you," she wrote, "and love the way you put one dear hand on mine, while with the other you turn the pages of history."[82]

That summer, the letters between Woodrow and Edith paused for a couple of weeks. They had no need to write—they were actually staying in the same house for the first time ever. As in previous summers, the first family rented Winston Churchill's house, Harlakenden, in Cornish, New Hampshire. Edith was invited, ostensibly as Helen's guest, staying from late June through early August. The president would come and go from Washington as he could. And now, for the first time, the newspapers began to speculate about the elusive Mrs. Galt. A rather restrained wire story was picked up in several outlets around the country. Under the headline CHUM OF WILSON'S COUSIN, the brief article explained only that Mrs. Galt's first husband owned a jewelry store and that she was born in Wytheville. Almost apologizing for even that much information, the article went on to explain "the friends of the presidential household are more or less in the national eye, and so Mrs. Galt, who has always shunned social publicity, has come in to sudden prominence as one of the few familiar guests at the White House."[83] It was hardly front-page news: the *Montrose (MO) Recorder* placed it alongside a piece about a man who could talk to animals but not people, while *The Davey (NE) Mirror* ran it under recipes for summer drinks, including a horrifying concoction called "Grape Nectar." The more widely read gossip paper *Town Topics* was slightly bolder: "A conspicuous figure in society lately is Mrs. Norman Galt, of Washington." It misidentified her as a cousin of the president and "an intimate of his daughters" who was "staying at present with the Wilson family at Harlakenden House."[84] *The Stockton (CA) Evening Mail* broke the wink-wink barrier entirely. Under the headline PRESIDENT TO WED ONCE MORE? ASK GOS-SIPS, it quoted the Washington correspondent for *The Oakland Tribune*, who described Edith's many charms and assets: "The Galts, albeit 'in trade,' have always had a prominent place in the best society of Washington. . . . The marriage would be approved at Washington. It would bring an element in society, now aloof from the White House, in closer touch and it would help to restore an old time social condition in Washington. It would, too, bring into the White House a hostess of poise, graciousness, and social experience."[85]

If the happy couple knew about this coverage, they did not let it concern them. They were too busy being happy, and taking advantage of having more than an evening together for the very first time. Despite four months of courting and the president's steadfast certainty, they didn't actually know each other very well. Now they had the chance to truly share their days. (And maybe some nights, if you interpret Woodrow's euphemisms a certain way. There was a particular piece of furniture, "that dear lounge," that made him sentimental to the point of tears. "For there my darling had wholly surrendered her dear heart to me and endowed me with a love that makes me sure of every sweet and sacred and precious thing that my heart can desire.")[86] Even the less sentimental Edith remembered that time with a romantic aura. "Whenever my thoughts turn back to that wonderful summer," Edith wrote in her memoir, "there seems about it all a halo of gorgeous color from the flowers, and music made by the river where nearly every day we walked when the President was there."[87] Family members and Secret Service agents joined them during the day, but the evenings were theirs alone. Yet it wasn't shenanigans on the dear lounge that Edith recalled fondly. It was being involved in the work of the nation. "With the curtains drawn to shut out the cold night air, we would gather before a fire, and together read the latest dispatches sent from Washington, from Europe, from Mexico, from everywhere. The President would clarify each problem for me, and outline the way he planned to meet it. Or if, happily, nothing was pressing, we sometimes read aloud, and discussed the things we both loved."[88]

Edith described their romance as blossoming into full flower amid the beauty of a New Hampshire summer. From the vantage point of Secret Service agent Edmund Starling, the blossoming was not quite so full. Starling traveled with the president back and forth to Washington often, for "whenever it was at all possible he was at Harlakenden House, and the romance prospered. At least it seemed to prosper. What was going on in the lady's mind nobody knew but herself. What was going on in his mind was obvious. He was in pursuit. She was retreating, but how rapidly and with what purpose in mind, no one knew."[89] Edith explained her ambivalence this way: "Those days in Cornish had brought the banishment of any doubt of my love for Woodrow Wilson, but had not overcome my reluctance to marry him while he was in the White House."[90] She told Woodrow she would marry him only if he lost the 1916 election. He seems to have only heard the promise and not the *if*; from then on he treated their marriage as certain. He told his daughters they were engaged. He reported to Edith that all three were sincerely delighted at the prospect. (This was not strictly true. Jessie called Edith "a funny person" for whom "no hints take."[91] Nell complained about her "awful"[92] family. But for the most part they were glad to see their father happy.) Edith's hesitation was genuine, however. Not only was she reluctant to take on the role of First Lady, but she "had a sort of stubborn pride to show the world it was the man and not the President I loved and honored."[93] So soon after Ellen's death, Edith was worried she'd be publicly derided, if not exactly as a gold digger (she owned a successful business; he owned absolutely nothing), then at least as the boldest kind of social climber. And she had built an independent life for herself—one that was hard to give up. She had quite a lot to lose, and she knew it.

No matter how happy she was at Harlakenden, in early August she left for a previously scheduled visit to her friends the Roses in Geneva, New York. The president stayed in New Hampshire without her. He hated it. The second she left, Woodrow missed her so desperately he decided he couldn't possibly wait for the mail to have any word from her—a day without communication was simply too long. He wasn't entirely sure of her schedule but remembered she planned to stay overnight in Troy on her way to Geneva, and he convinced Margaret to call up every single hotel in Troy to see if he could find Edith. When he couldn't reach her, he started calling her friends' house in Geneva, only to discover they had no telephone. Desperate, he resorted to a telegram but was frustrated again. When he finally admitted defeat and went back to letter writing, he complained to Edith he "was unable this morning to obtain any assurance that the telegram had been delivered. Is Mr. Rose at outs with the telephone and telegraph companies?"[94] Edith took pity and diligently wrote every day while they were apart.

The letters from the month after their time together at Harlakenden show a couple relaxing into the kind of easy companionship that generally follows the "whirlwind" portion of a whirlwind romance. Woodrow, now fully aware of the romantic potential of flirting-by-policy-analysis, told Edith all about the debate over war preparedness, challenges with control of Haiti (that "dusky little republic"[95]), the prospects for peace in Mexico. "Whatever is mine is yours," he wrote to her in Geneva, "knowledge of affairs of state not excepted."[96] She wrote to him for advice about her niece Elizabeth, daughter of her brother Rolfe, who announced her intention to marry a Panamanian diplomat named Jorge Eduardo Boyd. Rolfe and his wife, Annie, were absolutely undone by this news, plotting all sorts of farcical schemes, including Rolfe faking a fatal illness, to stop the wedding. To her credit, Edith thought they were mad and couldn't understand their objections. She reserved particular disdain for Annie's brother, "who is a doctor (and a jackass, I think),"[97] who had suggested he drug Elizabeth and drag her home unconscious. Edith wrote directly to Elizabeth, offering her support and friendship. Woodrow had no advice for Edith but praised her level head ("you always *think a thing straight*"[98]), sympathized with her concern, and thanked her for confiding in him. He did make some discreet inquiries about the character of the proposed groom and reported back that "he is very handsome, well educated, of an excellent family which is not very popular because considered aristocratic."[99] In another letter Woodrow offered his own opinion of the case: "It would be bad enough at best to have anyone we love marry into any Central American family, because there is the presumption that the blood is not unmixed; but *proof* of that seems to be lacking in this case . . . and even if it be so, we must not turn away from and abandon the girl, who is of *our* blood."[100] Elizabeth and Jorge married on August 18.*

When she wasn't recounting family mini dramas, Edith insinuated herself further as Woodrow's confidant. It was a position she guarded

---

* There is an amazing footnote to this story. In 1921, Elizabeth and Jorge would go on to have musically talented identical triplet daughters, who performed as the Boyd Triplets in the forties and fifties. In 1965, they renamed themselves the Del Rubio Triplets after the blond hair dye they all shared. In the 1980s, when they were in their sixties, the triplets became a camp hit on TV shows like *Pee-wee's Playhouse*, performing covers of "These Boots Are Made for Walking" and Devo's "Whip It."

jealously. She started to quietly undermine Woodrow's closest advisers. She was only beginning to learn to judge the value of the advice they gave—more pointed criticism on that score would come later. At this stage, her opinions were based on personality. She didn't like Colonel House. "I know I am wrong," she ventured in a letter, "but I couldn't help feeling he is not a very *strong* character. . . . He does look like a weak vessel and I think he writes like one very often."[101] She also failed to warm to Joe Tumulty, whom she found "common," which was more or less code for "Catholic."[102] Woodrow defended both, without contradicting Edith. With a gentle "you are a little hard on my friends, you Dear" he explained that Tumulty's "lack of our breeding" was an asset to him. "An administration—an office—manned exclusively by 'gentlemen' could not make the thing go for a twelvemonth." Moreover, the president continued, "he is only technically common, not essentially." As for House, "about him you are no doubt partly right. You have too keen an insight and too discerning a judgment to be wholly wrong, even in a snap judgment of a man you do not know." Woodrow praised House's loyalty and prudence. "But," he admitted, "you are right in thinking that intellectually he is not a great man."[103] For the besotted Woodrow, even Edith's baseless criticism was just more evidence of her perfection. "You must remember, dear little critic, that Sweetness and power do not often happen together. You are apt to exact too much of others because of what you are yourself and mistakenly suppose it easy and common to be."[104]

While they were apart, Edith still clung to her condition that she would marry Woodrow only if he lost the 1916 election. She could imagine abandoning her hard-fought independence for the life of a respected, retired private couple in Washington. She could not yet reconcile herself to life as First Lady, in the glare of the nation's spotlight.

As long as she did not see Woodrow face to face, her resolve held. Then September came, and they both returned to Washington. She crumbled as soon as she saw him. At dinner her first night back, she told him so. Win or lose, she said, she would be his wife. The need for secrecy was over. Finally, their relationship could be conducted out in the open, at least among family and friends. The Wilson daughters and Helen Bones already knew, and Cary and Altrude had both guessed. Now Edith told her mother and her brothers and sisters. Bertha and Mrs. Bolling were invited to the White House to meet the groom. Usher Ike Hoover watched the scene with amusement. "The approval of these two relatives meant as much to this great man as it would have to the plainest of everyday citizens. He was no more the President but a prospective son-in-law and brother-in-law to them. As for them, they must have been delighted at the prospects. Their departure was like the triumphant march of a powerful army which had just come through battle and come out victorious."[105] The household staff was less enthralled. Lillian Rogers Parks, daughter of housekeeper Margaret Rogers, claimed, "The White House was in an uproar. The servants were upset. Some of the more dignified and conservative ones were saying it was too soon, it was almost indecent for a man to be courting a woman before his wife had been dead for a year."[106] Woodrow had a private phone connection installed between the White House and Twentieth Street. But the ability to speak privately did not slow down their daily exchange of mail—their letters just became a little shorter. Woodrow's brief notes were regularly accompanied by "big envelopes"[107]—packets of White House letters and draft legislation and diplomatic correspondence, often with marginal comments from the president. Edith liked to keep up with Woodrow's work, and reading the primary sources was the best way to stay informed. He was happy to comply, security issues be damned. Romantic Woodrow also sent daily flowers. He knew of Edith's particular fondness for orchids, which she often wore pinned to her belt or her shoulder. For the lovestruck president, this was more evidence of her exceptionalism. "You are the only woman I know who can wear an orchid. On everybody else, the orchid wears the woman."[108] Ike Hoover sweated over the orchid supply. "Many are the worries that attended the getting of these orchids, for they are scarce always and during this time seemed scarcer than ever. But they must be had, and the flower shops were put to a test to furnish them."[109]

As Washington returned to business after summer vacation, the president was busier than ever, but he always made time for Edith. "The weight of public matters rests rather grievously upon me this morning," he wrote on September 13, "but there is one resource for me always: I can turn to you (what would it not be worth to me if I could *go* to you) and all the burden will fall away with the realization of your love and vital, comprehending sympathy."[110] According to Secret Service agent Starling, he did go to her, as much as he could. "Now that he was free to visit the little house on Twentieth Street the President did so frequently. . . . Almost every night we took him to see her, then waited outside the house until he reappeared. That was never before midnight, and on Sundays the vigil was frequently from 1 p.m.—after church—to 1 a.m. We didn't mind. We were all romantic, and we were glad the boss had made good."[111] The agents tried their best to chase away reporters and photographers, but inevitably gossip about the couple spread. "Back in her Twentieth street home in Washington is Mrs. Norman Galt," reported *Town Topics*. "And very much in the public eye because of the attention of President Wilson, who is a constant caller and frequent host of parties at which Mrs. Galt is the honored guest." Newspaper columns like these were exactly why Edith worried people would paint her as a social climber. "Her marriage to Norman Galt, of Washington, was a distinct social step downward, for during her husband's lifetime she made no progress socially. Now, a widow, she has a rosier outlook." The anonymous writer would neither confirm nor deny rumors of an engagement. "A certain little circle is confident that Mr. Wilson will marry Mrs. Peck, while another set know positively that he will lead Mrs. Norman Galt to the altar. It is also said that his children know of and have accepted this fact."[112] Woodrow knew what made Edith skittish and was terrified the attention would cause her to apply the brakes. "I must beg you, my sweet Darling, not to attach too much importance to Washington gossip, or to what anyone is saying. If we keep within bounds, as we shall, and give them no proofs that they can make use of, we can and should ignore them." Having just won her promise of marriage, he was desperate that she not pull back in the face of public scrutiny. Once again he reminded her how vital she was to him, and by extension to the nation. "I am absolutely dependent on intimate love for the right and free and most effective use of my powers and I know by experience—by the experience of the past four weeks—what it costs my work to do without it to the extent involved in entire separation from you. And so we are justified in taking risks."[113] When Edith suggested they write to each other less frequently, Woodrow objected. "The mails, sent through the Post Office, tell no tales to gossips, and we've got to risk the gossips anyway, if we are not to long ourselves sick."[114] The letters continued.

If, as *Town Topics* suggested, Margaret, Jessie, and Nell had accepted their father's engagement, not everyone was delighted. Hoover thought that Woodrow's family "felt he was traveling a little too fast, that they were being subordinated with too much of a rush."[115] And then there were the political considerations. William McAdoo, the president's treasury secretary, son-in-law, and heir apparent, was particularly worried a marriage might cost the Democrats the election. The voters wanted a proper wartime leader who had no time for anything but the desperate business of global peace, not a lovesick schoolboy. Plus, more and more women were voting, especially in the crucial western states, and they might read the president's quick remarriage as dishonor to Ellen. Colonel House agreed, as did Joe Tumulty. They urged delay. But the president would not hear of waiting a full year to marry. Now that he finally had Edith's promise, he wanted to secure her commitment as soon as possible. His advisers tried to dispatch Josephus Daniels, secretary of the navy, to encourage the president to wait. Daniels declined. In his inimitable way, he explained he wanted no part of "the difficult and perhaps dangerous high and exalted position of Minister Plenipotentiary and Envoy Extraordinary to the Court of Cupid on a mission in which neither my heart nor my head was enlisted and in the performance of which my official head might suffer decapitation."[116]

Unable to find a credible messenger and too cowardly to confront the president himself, McAdoo, probably with House's help, cooked up a preposterous scheme. He knew about Woodrow's long correspondence with Mary Hulbert Peck. It had surfaced as a potential issue in the 1912 election, when McAdoo ran the campaign. He knew from his wife, Nell, that the letters had continued since, and that Woodrow had sent Mary thousands of dollars to bail out her profligate son. And there is where the plot departed from the facts entirely. On September 18, with all the appearance of a concerned friend, McAdoo privately told his boss he had received an anonymous letter from Los Angeles. The letter supposedly reported that Mary, in a jealous pique, was showing Woodrow's intimate letters around town. She bragged about the money he sent. And most crucially, she threatened to go public with the whole affair if Woodrow and Edith announced their engagement. In light of all this, McAdoo advised, they had much better wait till after the election.

If McAdoo and House expected Woodrow to prioritize winning reelection over his desire to marry Edith immediately, they had badly misjudged their man. Woodrow believed McAdoo entirely but knew Mary well enough to doubt she was behind the rumor at all. Instead, he suspected Republican dirty tricksters had concocted the whole thing. Even if his letters to Mary did go public, he was confident there was nothing truly damning in them, just the mild embarrassment of overly eager affection. His only thought was for Edith. The whole potential scandal, even if it ultimately amounted to nothing, would humiliate her by association, through no fault of her own. Woodrow couldn't bear it.

With a shaky hand, he dashed off a note, begging Edith to let him come visit her at Twentieth Street that night. "There is something, personal to myself, that I feel I must tell you about at once," he explained, but gave no more detail. Edith wrote back immediately, curious and concerned. Of course he was welcome to come. She would expect him at eight.

Exactly what Woodrow told Edith that night is not recorded. He seems to have confessed all about his friendship with Mary and conceded that if Edith wanted it, he would release her from their engagement. She seems to have forgiven the Mary affair, which, after all, occurred before they had met, but did not give him a final decision on the wedding. Both spent a sleepless night. At dawn the next day, they wrote each other letters. Woodrow, addressing "My noble, incomparable Edith," confessed himself more in love than ever. "My love, my reverence, my admiration for you, you have increased in one evening as

I should have thought only a lifetime of intimate, loving association could have increased them." His affectionate friendship with Mary, platonic as he swore it had been, was a small mistake in a lifetime of propriety. Still he felt it left him "stained and unworthy." He once more gave Edith a way out. "Surely no man was ever more deeply punished for a folly long ago loathed and repented of—but the bitterness of it ought not to fall on you, in the prime of your glorious, radiant womanhood." Finally he begged for the right to keep loving her. "I know I have no rights, but I also know it would break my heart and my life if I could not call you my Darling and myself Your own Woodrow."[117]

In her letter, Edith apologized for being unreasonable and said the morning had chased away her hurt feelings. She was all in. "This is my pledge, dearest one. I will stand by you—not for duty, not for pity, not for honor—but for love—trusting, protecting, comprehending love. And no matter whether the wine be bitter or sweet we will share it together and find happiness in the comradeship."[118] Woodrow wrote back immediately confirming he had received her letter with tremendous joy and pledging to be the man she deserved.

And that, for the moment, was that. Woodrow prepared a statement in case the Mary letters really were published. But of course it was never needed, since the whole rumor of exposure was entirely fictional.

Fictional, too, was Edith's retelling of this episode in her memoir. For reasons known only to herself, Edith created a much more dramatic narrative of the night in question. In this version, it was Cary Grayson who came to Edith's house that night. The president was too upset to speak or write and sent Cary to tell Edith the whole sordid tale. She listened to him, silent and uncomprehending. When he had finished, she begged for time to think and sent Cary back to the White

House to tell Woodrow to expect her letter in the morning. She sat up all night fretting, but with the sun dawned clarity. "I saw things in their true proportions. It was our *lives* that mattered, not politics, not scandal. If I did not care enough for the man to share his misfortunes, his sorrows, then it was a futile love!"[119] She wrote the letter pledging to stand by him and sent it off. But instead of an immediate note of acknowledgment and thanks, Edith claimed she received no answer, that day or the next. Humiliated and hurt, she began to worry that her letter had gone astray. On the third day, Cary came again, but now "grave anxiety marked his chiseled features."[120] He begged Edith to return with him to the White House, where the president lay very ill. "If you could see him you would not hesitate. He looks as I imagine the martyrs looked when they were broken on the wheel. He does not speak or sleep or eat."[121] She rushed to Woodrow's bedside and clasped his cold, lifeless hand. Presumably her very presence revived him, for here she skips ahead in the story three months, to their cozy honeymoon suite at Hot Springs, Virginia. There Woodrow pulled out her letter from that fateful morning. "The seal was unbroken, the envelope worn on the edges from being so long in his pocket." He could not bear to read it at the time, he confessed, convinced she was ending their affair. Now happily married, they would read it together, and he would always remember how she "came like an angel of light to heal my wound."[122]

Why would Edith embroider a story with fabrications that can easily be fact-checked? Woodrow's second letter from that morning clearly states that he received and read her letter. Of course, those letters had not been published at the time of her memoir; they were held, by her request, until fifteen years after her death. So maybe she simply thought her version of events would be the only one. But other sources did exist. There is no record, for instance, of Woodrow's illness in either the

White House ledgers or the diaries of the staff. Edith herself visited the White House in the days she claimed to be waiting in vain for an answer—a fact that *was* recorded in the ledgers. If she was trying to play up her importance to the president by painting him as lost without her, she didn't need to invent a tale—his over-the-top devotion is written in every one of his letters and confirmed by everyone who knew him. Perhaps she simply enjoyed a good story well told and was not interested in the truth getting in the way of a good plot. Or maybe, and this seems most likely, she was setting the stage for Woodrow's ultimate collapse in 1919 and her own reaction to it. It would serve her well later if she introduced the idea that stress and self-doubt critically damaged Woodrow's health, and her own steadfast support was the best medicine.

Regardless of how it happened, this incident brought Edith and Woodrow even closer. All talk of postponing the marriage was abandoned. It was time to announce their engagement to the public. But first, Woodrow had to write to a few friends and relatives who shouldn't hear the news from the newspaper. He wrote to Ellen's family and some of his own relatives. He told Ellen's old friends Lucy and Mary Smith. And he told Mary Hulbert Peck. She must have held out some tiny hope that she would be the second Mrs. Wilson, for her answer was bittersweet. "I have kissed the cross. We are very very glad you have found happiness and that you had time to think of us in the midst of it. . . . I wish you will have all the happiness that I have missed. I cannot wish you greater."[123] Finally, that duty done, the president typed up a draft of a press release announcing his engagement to Edith Bolling Galt. She read over his shoulder. "I am glad that I paused there," she wrote in her memoir, "for that serene evening in the study, with the fire crackling on the hearth, and the blinds drawn, was the last quiet time we were to have together in the White House for so many months and years to come."[124]

The announcement went out on October 6 and dominated newspapers the next day. *The Atlanta Constitution* was typical. Under the headline WHITE HOUSE FIANCE WEARS HAPPY SMILE; TO BUY RING TODAY, the paper reported, "Telegrams came to the white house in such numbers that an extra force of operators and clerks was needed to handle them."[125] Altrude's odious cousin Pat cabled her the smug message, "KNEW THOSE BELLS WOULD RING WOODY DIDNT HAVE A CHANCE."[126] Somewhere, Ellen Maury Slayden presumably collected on her five-pound box of candy. The papers were desperate for any detail about the elusive Mrs. Galt, who had captured the president's heart so fast. They clocked what she wore, where she ate, what baseball team she supported. Much was made of her descent from Pocahontas. In the absence of facts, they made things up, much to Edith's amusement. *Town Topics* smugly poked fun at the inventions of other publications. One column claimed Edith "was amazed recently to discover that she was a superb musician and a good water-color artist. Mrs. Galt does not pretend to excel in music and she never laid a claim to a talent in art. Nor is her sister, Miss Bertha Bolling, a musical genius, and the role assigned her of playing the wedding march for the Presidential nuptials caused the Bolling family almost fatal attacks of hilarity."[127] The *Town Topics* columnists were throwing stones from their glass house, however, as they not only published that Edith was Woodrow's cousin but also entirely invented that Woodrow and Norman Galt had been classmates at Princeton. Reporters constantly speculated on the timing and the venue of the wedding. An addendum to the engagement press release announced it would not be at the White House but would be "solemnized within the next two months, before the convening of congress in

December, either in Mrs. Galt's home or in a church."[128] The anonymous columnists at *Town Topics* did not approve. "President or no President, a true lover, who occupies a handsome house, ought to desire his wedding to be held in it. President or no President, he ought to desire to bestow upon the lady of his choice all the honors, splendors, and ceremonials that he can give her only once in his lifetime."[129]

Not at all coincidentally, on the same day the White House announced the engagement, a second press release explained that the president would be traveling to his home state of New Jersey to cast his vote for statewide women's suffrage. It was a cynical move; Woodrow had actively obstructed federal suffrage, hiding behind the excuse that it should be left up to the states. Now he made a big show of voting for suffrage in New Jersey, where it never stood a chance of passage. He wanted the few women who could vote to see him as an ally when the 1916 election rolled around. He even wanted them to think his new bride had changed his mind. As Cary wrote to Altrude, who supported the cause, "in the morning the President is going to Princeton to vote on women's suffrage. Miss Edith is getting the credit for bringing him over to votes for women. The joke is that she is against it: but she is too good a diplomat to say anything on the subject these days."[130] Despite her independent spirit and the fact that she ran a successful business, Edith was indeed against the vote for women. It was an opposition that would only grow more forceful when suffragists started holding Woodrow personally responsible for their disenfranchisement.

But that was all in the future. For now, Edith enjoyed being a bride-to-be. She and Altrude traveled to New York "on a quest for the royal trousseau."[131] She was made an honorary member of the Princeton class of 1879. She joined Woodrow at the Army-Navy football game at the Polo Grounds. By tradition, the president watches the first half of the game from a box on the Army side, then is escorted over to the Navy side at halftime. As Edith and Woodrow crossed the field, "there was a perfect ovation. Everyone seemed to be our friend."[132] Meanwhile, White House usher Ike Hoover was tasked with planning the wedding. They had settled on December 18 at Edith's narrow house on Twentieth Street. The guest list was limited to forty people, just family and a few very close friends, like Cary and Altrude. "Even that number would tax the capacity of the two small rooms where the ceremony was to be held," fretted Hoover. "Fifteen or twenty would be a crowd."[133] Hoover arranged to have all the furniture removed from the first floor rooms and built a gorgeous bower of ferns, heather, and roses. Edith's favorite orchids tumbled over mantels and mirrors. Two ministers would officiate, Dr. James Taylor from Woodrow's Presbyterian church, and Dr. Herbert Smith of Edith's Episcopal one. Smith was Edith's second choice. She had originally booked Bishop Lucien Kinsolving, son of the man who had married her parents. She reminded the bishop that the guest list was very tight and his wife would not be invited to attend. The bishop said he understood. But two days before the wedding, he announced she was coming after all. They were heading to England together the following week, and it would cause his wife "much chagrin to acknowledge to her titled friends that she had not been asked to the marriage of the President where her husband had officiated."[134] The bishop was certain this plan would be okay with the generous bride.

It was not okay. The bride's generosity did not extend to grasping strangers who only wanted to boast of their attendance. Edith fired off an angry letter, excusing the bishop of his promise to perform the ceremony. Then she called Woodrow and told him what she had done. He urged her to take a deep breath and think it over before she sent the letter. "No," she responded, "this letter goes to him right now. I will postpone our wedding rather than be bludgeoned into a thing of this kind."[135] The bishop was out. Happily, Dr. Smith agreed to step in.

The wedding day dawned cold and clear, with the previous day's light snow still dusting the ground. Edith wore a black velvet gown and a velvet hat rimmed with goura feathers. Naturally, she added a corsage of purple orchids. Woodrow wore the traditional cutaway coat, striped trousers, and top hat. The ceremony went off without a hitch. And if the guests were uncomfortably crowded in the narrow rooms, no one complained. Secret Service agent Edmund Starling concocted an elaborate scheme to keep reporters and curious members of the public from following the newlyweds to their honeymoon. He worried it was "a perfect occasion for cranks and emotionally unstable persons, and we couldn't risk it."[136] He let a White House car be seen earlier in the day driving luggage to Washington's Union Station. He made sure not to tell anyone the train's destination—not the crew and not even his fellow agents, who were told to pack for a two-week stay in any climate. While the wedding ceremony was going on, the empty train slunk out of Washington and into a siding at the edge of the freight yards in Alexandria. No one in the crowd gathered at Union Station noticed or cared—they knew the president and his bride were not aboard. When the ceremony ended, Woodrow and Edith were whisked into an unmarked car and driven by an erratic route to Alexandria, where Starling was waiting by the private train. It took less than a minute for the couple to switch from car to train and the train to pull out of the siding. Only then was it revealed that the destination was Hot Springs. In the wee hours of the morning of December 19, Starling discovered the dignified president, still in his formal clothes, dancing a jig and kicking up his heels in the narrow corridor.[137]

From the Hot Springs station, a limousine took the newlyweds to the Homestead resort. "The mountains were white with snow," wrote Edith, "and the air from them crisp and biting; but it came to me as a real touch of welcome from *home*, for my whole early life had been spent in that stimulating climate."[138] They didn't let the cold keep them from daily rounds of golf. In the afternoons they went for long drives. One day they took a hike that left their boots somewhat muddy, and Edith had a loose shoelace. Starling dropped to his knee to tie it. Edith lifted her skirt enough to show her ankle. The president was not amused. He stared straight ahead, "his nose pointing and his jaws working—tell-tale signs of his anger." He didn't speak to Starling for two weeks.[139]

Edith and Woodrow enjoyed their first Christmas together at the Homestead, where the management installed a great glowing tree in the dining room of their suite. All seemed joyous and hopeful as they rang in 1916 together. They were in love, they were married, and they were cocooned alone in a beautiful place. But their idyll couldn't last. Two days later, Joe Tumulty wired with the news: without warning, a German U-boat had torpedoed the British steamship SS *Persia* off the coast of Crete. Of the 501 passengers and crew, only 167 survived. "In view of critical situation here arising out of *Persia* case think it would be unwise for you to prolong your vacation,"[140] the telegram said. The next day, they packed up and headed back to Washington. It was time for Woodrow to resume the presidency and Edith to make her debut as First Lady.

Chapter Five

THE FIRST LADY IN WAR

1916–1918

Really, Edith thought, the role of White House hostess was absurd. It was a completely unworkable mix of inscrutable rules and constant public attention. The worst was the ridiculous yet apparently sacred ritual of "behind the line" at White House receptions. While guests stampeded the food tables out in the dining room, she and Woodrow, Vice President Marshall and his wife, and the cabinet secretaries and their wives stood for hours in the Blue Room, behind a red rope, shaking hand after sweaty hand. For reasons Edith did not care to understand, it was considered a great honor to stand in the shadows behind this receiving line and watch the common people go by. Those who were invited "behind the line" were smug. Those who were excluded schemed and lied for the privilege of crossing the red rope. The jockeying became so physical that "the poor women in the line were constantly buffeted about and the trains of

their dresses used as rugs."[1] Edith lasted exactly one reception following this nonsensical custom. Then she abolished "behind the line" forever.[2] The coveted space was filled up with ferns and palms instead.
She didn't care that it was White House protocol—she was First Lady
now, and she got to make the rules. And while she was on the subject,
wasn't the title "First Lady" a little silly?[3] She didn't serve the nation;
she served her husband. She much preferred "Mrs. Woodrow Wilson."
That was who she had agreed to be when she finally accepted Woodrow's proposal, and she performed that role to the exclusion of all else.
As White House seamstress Lillian Rogers Parks observed, "no outside
hobbies did she have, no painting, no designing of gardens. She centered her full and complete attention on her husband, and even went
golfing with him. The poor President could not even turn to golf to get
away from the womenfolk."[4]

But the pressure to entertain was constant and intense. Before the ink
was dry on the marriage license, newspapers claimed, "The Washington
social world is greatly pleased at the news. It is hailed as signifying the
reopening of the White House for official and social functions."[5] And
while everyone understood the first family did not entertain while still in
mourning, that excuse expired with the presidential marriage. For the
upcoming winter after the wedding, "things are expected to be decidedly
different,"[6] threatened one gossip column. Edith realized that after a
quiet year, the pent-up demand for White House parties in general, and
the desire to see and judge her in particular, would lead to huge crowds
at every event. She would definitely need help. Unfortunately, the formidable social secretary Belle Hagner had announced her own engagement
just after Woodrow and Edith did. Edith fretted Belle's marriage would
leave the White House without a social secretary. But Belle recruited her
friend Edith Benham as a replacement. The papers approved. "A more

suitable person for this difficult position is not to be found in Washington. It was a prudent choice and shows that the future Mistress of the White House possesses discriminating judgment."[7]

Traditionally, the Washington social season started in January with the diplomatic reception at the White House, followed by receptions for the judiciary, Congress, and the army and navy. That first event was, to put it mildly, ill-advised in 1916. As Benham wrote in her memoir, "there could be no Diplomatic Reception with the members of the Embassies of the warring countries pitchforked together into the Green Room."[8] The usual huge reception was replaced with two smaller diplomatic dinners, one for the Allies and their friends and one for the Central Powers. These were not mere parties. They were occasions of tricky diplomacy for the neutral U.S. "The balance had to be very finely kept," wrote Benham. "One dinner could not be more important than the other."[9]

While she rearranged the social calendar, Edith rearranged the president's routine. First she replaced Ellen's prim twin beds with the huge bed made for Abraham Lincoln. Then she set up a schedule. Edith and Woodrow would wake at six and serve themselves coffee from a thermos left outside their door. If the weather allowed, they would golf for an hour, then return to the White House for breakfast at 8:00 a.m. sharp. Together they would retire to Woodrow's study to see what business had accumulated overnight. Usually this was a stack of military commissions that had to be signed by the president. They were left in what Edith ominously called the Drawer, and Woodrow would sign as many as he could, with Edith standing by blotting and sorting, until stenographer Charles Swem arrived at nine. Edith would leave them to business while she conferred with the housekeeper and tackled her own mail with Edith Benham. These hours constituted a crash course in how to be First Lady. She planned menus and responded to invitations. She had her official portrait painted by Adolfo Müller-Ury. She caught on quickly. "Daily I learned new things, for instance that when the President dines out—which he does officially only with the Vice President and members of the Cabinet—the hostess submits in advance a list of prospective guests for White House approval. At first it gives one a funny feeling to tell a lady, in effect, whom she can and whom she cannot invite to her table—but I discovered that they were quite used to it, and after a while so was I."[10]

Most days, Edith and Woodrow would have lunch together, then receive guests or attend meetings until dinner, where they were usually joined by friends and family. If they didn't have theater tickets or some other obligation, they went back to the study after dinner. This was when Edith resumed her role as confidant, editor, and adviser. Woodrow would talk through the day's business, read her what he had written, and ask for her help encoding the more delicate messages. There was never any question of keeping political details from her—Woodrow had come to rely on Edith as much as, if not more, than any man in the administration.

In May of 1916, Altrude and Cary finally stepped off their romantic roller-coaster ride and got married at St. George's Chapel in New York. Altrude had not planned on having any attendants but at the last minute asked Edith to step in as matron of honor. "Fortunately I had worn a pale gray taffeta, and a big gray hat made of tulle; so I did not mar the effect of the white decorations, and the bride's white loveliness, by having dark clothes."[11] Everywhere they went together Edith was photographed, stared at, and gushed over in the local press. Any fear that his marriage would hurt Woodrow's popularity seemed entirely unfounded.

By the summer of 1916, Edith and Woodrow's attention turned to reelection. Still bruised from the bitter divisions of the 1912 campaign, the Republicans nominated an inoffensive moderate named Charles Evans Hughes. Hughes had served as a Supreme Court justice since 1910 and had therefore made no political statements of any kind for six years. Woodrow was scrupulous in his belief that no campaign business should be conducted from the White House. He also returned to the tradition, upended by Teddy Roosevelt, that the campaign would not begin until he was formally nominated on September 2. So on September 1, he and Edith, along with Helen, Altrude, Cary, Joe Tumulty, and various campaign staff, repaired to the Jersey Shore. A committee of prominent New Jersey citizens offered the first family use of an opulent fifty-two-room mansion called Shadow Lawn. Edith found it appalling. In her description it sounds spectacularly gaudy: The central staircase was "wide enough for an army abreast," until it divided into two sections that rose "in opposite directions as if each was ashamed of the other." The billiard room sported "lights hidden behind armor." The only book in the elaborate library was a New York telephone directory. The whole monstrosity boasted "much crimson as to curtains and walls." Worst of all was a white marble statue in the vast entrance hall. "It must have weighed a ton, or we would have had it removed. So we draped it as much as possible."[12] Happily the house also included "acres of porches" where Edith and Woodrow could turn their backs on the excess and face the Atlantic.

They used Shadow Lawn as a home base for the next two months as they traveled and campaigned together. Kentucky to dedicate a shrine at Lincoln's birthplace. Atlantic City for a charity concert. Omaha for a speech and a visit to the swine show, where Edith marveled over a pig that weighed 1,115 pounds. A detour to Columbia,

South Carolina, for the funeral of Woodrow's sister Annie Howe. Chicago, Buffalo, Cincinnati, Indianapolis—there was never any question but that Edith would go everywhere Woodrow went. She shook all the appropriate hands (she was admired for her "pump-handle handshake," a welcome departure from the "languid three-finger" gesture of more fashionable ladies).[13] She charmed the right journalists. She wrote dutiful thank-you notes to all their hosts. "Some enthusiasts described her carriage as queenly," reported the *Town Topics* columnist after a successful political dinner. "I am not familiar with the carriage of queens, but she seemed to me to be a well-gowned American woman, who knew what to do and did it with ease and grace and common sense."[14] She might not have embraced the title "First Lady," but she played the role admirably. Campaigns are exhausting and difficult even for seasoned professionals in landslide races. Edith was a rookie, and the 1916 presidential campaign was a toss-up.

It has now become conventional wisdom that Woodrow's reelection slogan was "He kept us out of war." But the president thought that a dangerous motto and never used it himself.[15] He knew how precarious the situation in Europe was, and how little control any president had. There is a famous story, possibly apocryphal, that he admitted to Josephus Daniels that "any little German lieutenant can put us into the war at any time by some calculated outrage."[16] Even if the anecdote is not genuine, the sentiment behind it certainly was. Woodrow believed neutrality was America's best play, for the moment. But he did not fool himself that it was a position he could guarantee. Still, the rallying cry "He kept us out of war!" was shouted by other Democrats on campaign stumps all over the country throughout the fall of 1916.

On October 15, the traveling Wilsons found themselves back at Shadow Lawn to celebrate Edith's birthday. *The New York Times* duly reported that the president gave his wife a handsome diamond-and-platinum brooch along with her birthday cake, but snarked that "the number of candles it bore was a profound secret."[17] It was not a secret—Edith was forty-four. She had been married for less than a year. Even as she adjusted to the hectic schedule and constant crowds, she continued to hope for a private life. Quietly, she began to plan for their retirement after the White House. As soon as early March, she imagined, they could be leading the privileged, sophisticated life of an urban couple with means. On the Sunday before Election Day, Woodrow found Edith daydreaming in a sitting room at Shadow Lawn. She admitted that she had been mentally mapping out their postelection lives as private citizens. "What a delightful pessimist you are!" he exclaimed. "One must never court defeat. If it comes, accept it like a soldier; but don't anticipate it, for that destroys your fighting spirit."[18]

What Woodrow couldn't admit was that he was anticipating his own loss just as much as Edith was. And he was making his own plans, which did not require Edith to wait until March for the life she imagined. With literal life-and-death decisions pummeling the presidency every day, the time between the election and the inauguration would be critical. Woodrow figured if the nation wanted Charles Evans Hughes in the driver's seat, they should have him as soon as possible. The law of succession dictates that if the offices of president and vice president are vacant, the secretary of state is next in line. So if he lost the election, Woodrow decided the best course of action would be to ask Vice President Marshall and Secretary Lansing to step down, appoint Hughes to State, and then resign himself. It is possible Colonel House was the original brain behind this idea, but the president embraced it willingly. And though he did mention it to Lansing, he does not seem to have shared this radical plan with Marshall.[19] But he nurtured it in his mind as a secret compact between himself and the voters.[20] Publicly, he maintained confidence in his victory.

On Tuesday, November 7, Woodrow and Edith drove to Princeton to vote. Or rather, Woodrow voted and Edith waited in the car. Predictably, women's suffrage had failed in New Jersey. Edith lingered outside the enginehouse that served as a polling place, casually flirting with some starstruck students—she mused later that it was the closest she ever came to casting a presidential ballot at the polls. In 1920, once the Nineteenth Amendment was ratified and women's right to vote was recognized nationally, Edith voted absentee in New Jersey. For all successive presidential elections, and she would live to see ten more, she once again lost her right to vote,[21] since she was a resident of Washington, DC. Citizens of the capital would not gain presidential voting rights until the 1964 election, three years after Edith's death.[22]

From Princeton they drove back to the shore and sat around the overdecorated rooms of Shadow Lawn awaiting their fate. Cary, Helen, Margaret, and Jessie's husband, Frank Sayre, joined them. The mood was oddly subdued, the house unusually quiet. Woodrow had declined the telegraph company's offer to run special wire to the house. They'd get the news from Tumulty in Washington, he decided, whenever there was news to give. They ate, they talked, they attempted to play a game of twenty questions. No news arrived. Finally at 10:00 p.m. the phone rang, startling them out of their torpor. It was a friend of Margaret's, and he was offering condolences. Apparently *The New York Times*, which had promised to beam a white light from its building if Wilson won, had instead flashed red, for Hughes. Margaret was indignant. How dare the *Times* concede to the Republicans this early! The polls were still open in the West! Woodrow called Tumulty for confirmation. It was true, Tumulty admitted, barely able to form the words.

The election was lost.[23] Edith professed herself disappointed but not shocked. "I had long been secretly preparing an armor against the arrow of defeat," she admitted. "This armor met the test."[24]

The president, faced with the end of his political career and the repudiation of his leadership, did not display Margaret's resentment, Tumulty's gloom, or Edith's resignation. He said calmly that it was too early to send a congratulatory telegram to Hughes, but he would do so in the morning when things were settled. Then he drank a wholesome glass of milk, put on his pajamas, and fell soundly asleep.[25]

The rest of the party stayed awake, pacing the vast halls of Shadow Lawn. At 4:00 a.m. Margaret talked to Democratic headquarters in New York and learned the tide might be turning in their favor. But it was a thin straw to grasp. Dawn brought the morning papers, full of Hughes's victory. Two old friends from Princeton were expected for lunch, but they arrived late and shamefaced. The meal was awkward, the guests embarrassed. Finally they blurted out that they had planned this lunch expecting to be the first to congratulate their buddy on his reelection. They had arrived at Shadow Lawn on time, they admitted, then hidden in their car for half an hour, unable to face their friend in his defeat. The president found this hilarious. No one else could muster a sense of humor. The day ended as it had begun, uncertain and bleak.

On Thursday, they had to move out of Shadow Lawn and Woodrow had to resume the presidency, still not knowing whether he was a lame duck. Edith and Woodrow decided to squeeze in one more round of golf before they left town. According to Agent Starling, "the President seemed as calm as ever, and played just as poorly."[26] They were setting up on the eighth tee when Cary ran up to them, equal parts excited and nervous. It looked like California had gone for Wilson. Victory might be around the corner, he suggested, but nothing was official yet. Edith and Woodrow said goodbye to New Jersey and boarded the *Mayflower* for a trip up the Hudson to Rhinebeck, New York, where they would catch a train to Williamstown, Massachusetts. They were due at the christening of Jessie's daughter Eleanor.[27]

They woke early on the yacht on Friday, November 10, and were immediately handed a sheaf of wireless messages. They were filled with news of victory in the western states. It was finally over. Woodrow had been reelected for a second consecutive term—the first Democrat to do so since Andrew Jackson in 1832. Edith had been less than enthusiastic about returning to the White House and even allowed herself to imagine "personal freedom for my dear one, and for myself, which the relinquishment of this burden would bring."[28] But after days of uncertainty, she was relieved to see the "suspense and strain"[29] of limbo resolved. And she was proud that the voters had "stood by my husband."[30] She rallied herself for four more years in office.

As final returns came in from across the nation, it became clear that the Democrats had lost seats in both the House and the Senate but maintained razor-thin majorities in both. And for the first time in the nation's history, a woman was elected to Congress: Republican Jeannette Rankin of Montana. At the time, women were able to vote in just twelve states—all but one of those in the West. Woodrow won ten of them. Senator Gore of Oklahoma credited that risky antiwar slogan. "The women voters of the West," he concluded, "elected Wilson on the peace issue."[31]

For women in the rest of the country, 1916 was a terrible election for suffrage. Every state that had the issue on the ballot voted it down. And now Woodrow Wilson, who had continued to oppose a federal amendment enfranchising women, was back in the White House. So as 1917 dawned, the activists in the National Woman's Party decided to try something new: they would picket the White House. No one had ever done such a thing before, certainly not women. But every day, no matter the weather, the women were out there at the north gate, purple, white, and gold sashes in place, calling themselves "Silent Sentinels." They were there to hold Woodrow personally accountable for their lack of voting rights. One banner asked, "Mr. President what will you do for woman suffrage?" And another: "Mr. President how long must women wait for liberty?" And the worst: "He kept us out of suffrage." Every time she looked out her window, every time she and Woodrow drove out to play golf, there they were. Edith was incensed. "Those detestable suffragettes"[32] were rude, and unladylike, and had the nerve to criticize her husband in public.

So why wasn't Edith—financially independent, car-driving, business-owning, world-traveling Edith—a suffragist herself? She never gave any public statements on the issue. Like so much else about Edith, it feels like a contradiction, leading others to speculate wildly different motivations. Some scholars have concluded she actually did support the cause, that her distaste was for the picketers' tactics, not their goals.[33] After all, plenty of mainstream suffrage supporters found the radical fringe of the movement uncomfortable and counterproductive. At best, this is wishful thinking. In addition to Edith's open contempt for the activists, there is Cary Grayson's letter of October 1915, stating, "The joke is that she is against it."[34] There is her own statement in her diary[35] that the only speech Woodrow ever gave that she actually disliked was one supporting suffrage.[36] Even *The New York Times* reported, "Mrs. Wilson has never been partial to the cause, and up to the time of her marriage to the President was counted among the anti-suffragists of the district."[37]

Others have rooted her opposition in class—that the suffragists were just too tacky and vulgar to support.[38] In 1913, the guards at the

Tower of London, alert for militant suffragists, had found her suspicious. That must have been an unsettling novelty for a well-dressed white woman like Edith and would reinforce her desire to dissociate herself from women who deserved such attention. The rudeness she perceived on the part of the White House picketers in 1917 would underline that snobbery. "Nice girls" didn't march in the street. Of course, if she wanted examples of wealthy, well-bred, high-society suffragists, she didn't have to look further than own dear friend Altrude Gordon Grayson. Daisy Harriman was right there on the picket line,[39] and she was a blue-blooded Knickerbocker. The National Woman's Party was in large part funded by the fortunes of Alva Belmont, the society widow of two prominent men. Nor were administration wives shy to join the ranks—the wives of Wilson's postmaster general, his attorney general, and the secretaries of both the interior and agriculture were all suffragists.[40] Even within the president's own family, Margaret and Jessie described themselves as supporters. If Edith needed social cover to join the cause, she could have found plenty of it.

More likely, Edith, like millions of American women, truly wasn't convinced the act of voting was appropriate for women. The antisuffrage ranks included plenty of garden-variety sexists—men who thought women were too stupid or fragile to handle the vote. And there were powerful industries, including the liquor lobby and anyone who employed child labor, that feared the economic impact of women voters and funded antisuffragist propaganda. But there were millions of American women who not only did not want to vote themselves but also feared their enfranchisement would upend the social order. This line of thinking dovetails with the cult of True Womanhood in which Edith was raised. The public sphere was properly the sphere of men. Women should be proud of their role behind the scenes in the domestic sphere and not dirty their hands with the sordid business of men, except as private advisers. Or as the Georgia Association Opposed to Woman Suffrage put it, "we do not want to go into politics, we do not wish to do a man's work, but to prepare by thought and conservative living to help them when they ask us to do so."[41] This is how Edith could, with a straight face, maintain she was "not political,"[42] even as she attended congressional sessions and edited diplomatic correspondence. She rationalized she was simply studying up to be the best helpmeet her husband could ask for. She was not the First Lady; she was Mrs. Woodrow Wilson.

Without public statements it is impossible to confirm, but it seems likely Edith evolved from distrusting votes for women entirely to her husband's position of leaving the matter up to individual states while opposing a federal amendment. This was a popular stance in the South, where it was often simply racism, thinly veiled. Or not veiled at all. As antisuffragist Dolly Lamar warned the Georgia state legislature in 1914, woman suffrage would include two million Black women. "Is there any doubt as the party with which they would affiliate?" she asked the audience of white male Democrats. "If the Republicans get in control again we will have the negroes put into office over our heads."[43] For Edith, whose whole childhood played out under the shadow of Reconstruction, this would have been a powerful argument. But like so much else concerning Edith, this is just speculation.

By the spring of 1917, suffrage and all other domestic issues had to take a back seat to the war in Europe. As battle after bloody battle resulted in millions of casualties, Woodrow desperately played for peace as long as he could. Convinced that "both sides have grown weary of the apparently hopeless task of bringing the conflict to an end by the force of arms,"[44] he drafted a "peace note" to both the Allies and the

Central Powers. He encouraged both sides to clarify their goals, hoping the process would force them to realize a negotiated peace was closer than they imagined in the heat of battle. Colonel House and Secretary Lansing both objected to the peace note.[45] House expected the Allies to bristle at the suggestion that their war aims were anything other than to stop German imperialism and slaughter. Lansing thought the gesture was far too friendly to Germany. Woodrow sent it anyway. House, as was his habit, seethed privately. But Lansing issued a public statement suggesting the U.S. needed to know the combatants' positions because it was close to joining the war, undermining the president's staunch support of neutrality. Woodrow was furious that his own secretary of state had contradicted him so publicly. He stopped just short of demanding Lansing's resignation. It was becoming increasingly clear that, war or no war, Woodrow was not particularly interested in advice or opposing viewpoints on matters of state.[46] Across the Atlantic, the peace note was ignored by both sides.

Well then, Woodrow decided, if the warring parties would not offer a plan for peace, he would offer one of his own. On January 22, 1917, he addressed the U.S. Senate and outlined his vision for "peace without victory." A lasting peace, he said, was one between equals, not the forced concessions of the victor over the vanquished. The best way to ensure this peace, he elaborated, was a covenant of cooperation, a "League of Peace."[47] The speech was the public debut of his vision of international unity that would become the League of Nations. Edith, watching from the gallery, was enraptured. She wrote in her diary that his message "is so just and conclusive that more and more I feel that he is inspired and that he must attain all he is striving for, for the good of the world."[48] Woodrow was the savior, and she was his guardian angel. The praise rolled in, with one senator calling the speech "the most startling and honest utterance that has fallen from human lips since the Declaration of Independence."[49]

Not everyone was so transported. Alice Roosevelt Longworth had long criticized the administration policy of "watchful waiting." ("No atrocity could stir him to action," she lamented. "He just wrote notes—and then more notes.")[50] For her, peace without victory was a meaningless platitude and "nothing more than a continuation of cowardly temporizing."[51] Senator Lawrence Sherman of Illinois quipped this hopeless quest would "make Don Quixote wish he had not died so soon."[52] Others suggested Woodrow was under the delusion that he was president of the whole world. Senator Henry Cabot Lodge, in a preview of criticisms to come, said all the speech offered were "collections of double-dealing words under which men can hide and say they mean anything or nothing."[53] In Europe the reviews were even harsher. Ambassador Page in London reported the British were not interested in peace without victory. Their goal was a defeated, humiliated Germany. Germany resumed its campaign of unrestricted submarine warfare soon after Woodrow's speech. Peace seemed further off than ever.

Still, the president remained desperate to avoid U.S. involvement. On February 3, 1917, he severed diplomatic ties with Germany. But he continued to urge neutrality for the U.S., hoping against hope that Germany would not engage in direct confrontation. That hope was short-lived. In February, British intelligence passed along an intercepted telegram from the German foreign minister, Arthur Zimmermann, to his ambassador in Mexico. The U.S. would be likely to enter the conflict after submarine warfare resumed, Zimmermann explained. If Mexican president Carranza allied himself with Germany now, he'd be on the winning side when the Central Powers inevitably prevailed. As a reward, the Mexicans could expect "generous financial support and an understanding on our part that Mexico is to reconquer the lost territory in Texas, New Mexico, and Arizona."[54] This was it, a direct provocation that Woodrow could not downplay. He asked Congress to authorize legislation arming merchant ships and began to plan for the war that now seemed unavoidable.

But first he had to mark his second inauguration. March 4 was a Sunday that year, so Woodrow, who always tried to hold the Sabbath sacred, took the oath of office in a quiet private ceremony. In freezing, stinging rain, suffragists circled the White House with signs and banners. Woodrow and Edith ignored them. There was a more formal inaugural ceremony the next day, with a little more pomp, but no one really had the heart for it. Woodrow gave a brief, grave speech. "United alike in the conception of our duty and in the high resolve to perform it in the face of all men," he said, "let us dedicate ourselves to the great task to which we must now set our hand."[55] Edith was right there with him—the first First Lady to sit next to the chief justice during the speech and the first to stand behind the president when he took the oath of office.[56] "I stole a look at Mrs. Wilson," admitted agent Starling. "With shining eyes she watched her husband, proud of him, her head held high, little smile on her lips."[57] Two days later, Woodrow came down with a wretched cold and took to his bed. The armed ship bill was filibustered to death in the Senate, so the president sought advice about whether he could skip congressional approval and arm merchant ships through executive order. The matter was urgent; American vessels faced constant deadly threat from German U-boats. But the president was bedridden and under strict medical orders to rest and recover. So for the first time, he asked Edith to act as his agent. Her role was to keep unwanted visitors out and conduct essential meetings in Woodrow's place.[58] On March 8 she met with Secretary

Daniels to discuss arming ships, as well as resolve conflicting promotion schedules between the navy and the reserves. The matter was top secret, to the point that the president told Lansing, "I should feel justified in ordering a court martial for disobedience to such an order."[59] But there was never any suggestion that Edith be excluded from the inner circle. This visibility was unprecedented. Many First Ladies had advised their husbands about world affairs in private, but Edith was the first to have a literal seat at the table.

When he was feeling better, the president convened his cabinet secretaries and asked if they thought the U.S. should join the war. Since the sinking of the *Lusitania* two years earlier, these men had represented a continuum of viewpoints, from bellicose McAdoo to pacifist Daniels. But now they were unanimous.[60] One by one, they told their president the time had come to act. He thanked them and adjourned the meeting. None of them knew what he would decide—the president was perfectly capable of opposing his entire cabinet. For the next few days, Woodrow tried to get away from the White House to think and plan. He and Edith played a lot of golf and took a lot of car rides. When he wanted to talk to one of his cabinet secretaries, he walked to their offices, with Edith in tow. White House clerk Thomas Brahany observed it was "the first time in history that a President's wife has accompanied the President in a purely business call on a Cabinet Officer."[61]

Behind the scenes, Edith helped the president conduct the vital, secret business of preparing for war. But publicly, she continued to play the role of domestic perfection the nation expected. The president began to prepare a statement to Congress. He did so alone, on a typewriter, at a little table on the South Portico of the White House. When the clock ticked past midnight and the air grew chilly, Edith brought Woodrow milk and biscuits[62] and wrapped a coat around his shoulders as he wrote, the fate of the war in his tired hands. He stayed up all night. When word of this little family tableau was printed in the paper, the White House "was deluged with letters from grocers and biscuit manufacturers, asking what brand of biscuits Mrs. Wilson had put on his table that historic morning, and saying that if it were theirs please might they advertise to that effect."[63]

On April 2, a special session of Congress convened at noon. All day the president waited to hear if they were ready for his speech. He tinkered with the wording, read a draft to Edward House, made a few small changes. Finally at 8:30 p.m., it was time to tell the world what he had decided. A well-behaved crowd had gathered outside the Capitol. Inside, the gallery was packed. Woodrow repaired to a side room and Edith found seats in the front row with her mother and Margaret. The president solemnly walked up to the podium. Everyone in the crowd rose to their feet. "We will not," he told the expectant crowd, "choose the path of submission."[64] And then the famous line: "The world must be made safe for democracy." Deafening applause followed. He had done it. He had urged the nation to go to war. Three days of pro forma congressional debate followed, but the war resolution was passed on Sunday, April 6, with overwhelming majorities in both chambers. Jeannette Rankin was one of the very few members to vote against it. The official war resolution document was brought to the White House once Edith and Woodrow returned from church. The president sat down to sign it right there at the usher's desk, instead of going upstairs to his own study. But this desk didn't have a pen. Edith quickly handed him hers, a lovely gold one that had been a present from him. She moved to watch over his right shoulder. Starling stood behind his left shoulder. "Carefully the President read the tragic document, his jaw set, his countenance grim. Then, with a firm, unhesitating hand he wrote 'Woodrow Wilson.' When it was done he rose from the chair, returned the pen to Mrs. Wilson, excused himself, and went with the ladies into the corridor and to the elevator."[65] America was officially at war.

Edith's public role immediately shifted from society hostess to war-time role model. "The First Lady finally got interested in some activity other than being a companion to her husband,"[66] snarked White House seamstress Lillian Rogers Parks. Edith joined the cabinet wives in sign-ing a public pledge to "reduce living to its simplest form and to deny ourselves luxuries in order to free those who produce them for the cul-tivation of necessities. We have decided to omit the usual entertain-ing and to eliminate largely our social activities to enable us to give more time and money to constructive preparedness and relief work."[67] Edith had brought her own sewing machine from the Twentieth Street house when she married Woodrow, much to the amusement of the White House staff. Now she set up a little seamstress unit in a room next to Helen's, where she and the other women of the White House sewed pajamas, sheets, and pillowcases for the Red Cross. *Town Topics* reported that a "charming domestic scene is sometimes discernible through the trees in the south garden when Mrs. Wilson sits knitting and the President holds her yarn."[68] All over Washington, women fol-lowed Edith's example and sewed, gardened, cooked, and knitted for the war effort. Most were enthusiastic, if not always talented. "I do my knitting by proxy," Ellen Maury Slayden claimed, giving all her yarn to her mother. "There is no use in adding mine to the other horrors of war, and Mother's is so beautiful."[69] Like homes all over the nation, the White House proudly boasted a window card from the Food Adminis-tration, announcing that the first family had pledged to follow food conservation guidelines.[70] *The New York Times* reported that "all who pass by may see the red, white, and blue emblem hanging in the third window from the right of the portico."[71] This promise meant "meatless Mondays" and "wheatless Wednesdays," which the president's kitchen strictly observed. On days they did eat meat, Edith served "cheaper cuts" to save money. The recipes were printed in the paper, allowing Americans enjoying their oxtail soup and chopped beef au casserole to feel they were doing a small part for the war effort.[72] *The Washington Post* approved: "Mrs. Wilson and Miss Margaret Wilson, the unmarried daughter of the President, are setting an example in the domestic economy to which they ask the women of their country to subscribe, by paying personal attention to the management of the White House."[73] As the war continued, the fuel conservation board instituted "gasless Sundays" as well. Following this restriction proved a little harder. It was not difficult to find a horse-drawn buggy to take Woodrow and Edith to church, according to Agent Starling, but finding an appropriate vehicle for the Secret Service was a challenge. "Eventually we set off in an old-fashioned Surrey, with plenty of fringe on top, most of it frayed."[74]

A group of political wives led by Eleanor Roosevelt (her husband, Franklin, was assistant secretary of the navy) set up a Red Cross canteen not far from the freight train depot. They did not have to wait long for customers—they were called on almost immediately to serve coffee and sandwiches to men arriving for the officers' training camp at Fort Myer.[75] Edith Benham was proud of the role she and Margaret played there. "I think that both she and I shone as floor scrubbers and dishwashers. Later Mrs. Wilson herself joined up with this canteen, carrying to the troop trains trays of cigarettes, picture post cards and other articles."[76] All wore the same striped blue-and-white uniforms, navy hats, and large bib aprons, and after hot hours of service the women were often reduced to identical sweaty, exhausted drones. One particularly warm day Edith was recognized by one of the soldiers, who rounded up a dozen friends to come meet the First Lady. One young man took a skeptical look at the tall, tired woman and declared himself unconvinced. "You don't think I look the part?" Edith asked. "I certainly do not," he replied. Edith looked down at her bedraggled uniform and was forced to agree with him. "But when you come back from France," she told him, "if you come to the White House I will do my best to 'look the part' and give you such a warm welcome it will convince you."[77]

And then there were the sheep. At first, the sheep seemed like another visible way to set an example of frugality and collective responsibility. The flock of eighteen Hampshire sheep took on the job of trimming the White House lawn, saving manpower and encouraging Americans to keep livestock. But the sheep, as sheep do, had reproduced. "Twins and three others born to bring flock up to 25," exclaimed *The Washington Post*.[78] And now they were becoming a bit of a burden. They nibbled on the bushes and flower beds, requiring some careful fencing. The White House staff hated them and took to referring to Edith as "Little Bo Peep" backstairs.[79] To be fair, their enmity was earned: the alpha ram, Old Ike, who had developed a taste for chewing tobacco, was notorious for headbutting the staff.[80] Neighborhood dogs occasionally slipped the fence to chase the sheep around the White House grounds. They were scared of the cars that drove down Pennsylvania Avenue, and several had developed "the dips" from their fright. Edith came across one sickly lamb and carried it into the White House kitchen, where it had to be revived with some of the president's secret stash of whiskey. The press started to poke fun at the enterprise, with *The Washington Post* running the headline WILSON'S SHEEP SCARED BY AUTOS.[81] But they were hugely popular. Tourists would stand at the White House fence for hours to watch them graze, and photos of the sheep graced newspapers across the world. They even marched in a commemorative parade marking "Be Kind to Animals Week."[82] Inevitably, the sheep had gotten very woolly. They had actually started woolly—the farmer who sent them to the White House acknowledged that under normal circumstances he would have sheared them first. But he knew the optics were important, and "as they would look something like picked chickens if shorn, I gave instructions not to shear them, but to trim them up so they would look nicer."[83] After a few weeks, it was clear a nice little trim would no longer suffice. Edith brought someone from the Department of Agriculture in to shear them, and now she had almost one hundred pounds of rather stinky wool. Together with the Red Cross, she hit upon a scheme that would vindicate the sheep project in the eyes of its detractors. The sheep had been "the subject of a good deal of joking," admitted Starling, "but Mrs. Wilson had the laugh on all of us later when the sheep were sheared and she divided the wool equally between the 48 states, each of which auctioned off its portion for a good sum."[84] The states engaged in friendly competition to bid up the prices, but it was the non-states that really put the total over the top. The territories of Alaska and the Philippines each raised close to $6,000 (worth over $120,000 today) for less than two pounds of wool. It remains the most expensive wool ever sold by weight.* Together wool from the White House sheep raised over $50,000 for the Red Cross. "I feel the sheep . . . need no apologies from me," wrote Edith, "and certainly did their bit to help win the War."[85]

---

* A shadow box of some of this precious wool is one of the odder artifacts on display at the Woodrow Wilson House in Washington, DC.

Another public war job that fell to Edith was renaming seized German ships. Edith readily agreed to this task when the chairman of the shipping board asked, having no idea of the scope of the responsibility she was signing up for. Soon she received a list of the ships needing new names, along with the tonnage of each vessel. There were eighty-eight of them. A very few were actually named after U.S. presidents and could retain their titles. Edith crossed them off her list with relief. A couple more just needed a simple respelling, so the *Amerika* became the *America*. The president contributed a few ideas: The very biggest ship, the *Vaterland*, became the *Leviathan*. The tiniest on the list was rechristened the *Minnow*. But not only did the rest need entirely new names, but the names couldn't duplicate any other vessel. Edith discovered she had to consult five different Lloyd's Registers to make sure she wasn't repeating an existing name. It was much harder than she had anticipated. "I started to use the names of American cities, rivers, lakes, mountains and so on, and was surprised to find that most of them had been previously used."[86] So she hit on the idea of using Native American names. She swore this was not a recognition of her own Indian descent but simply a quest for variety. And while the Indian names were unique, she worried many of them were too long and hard to spell. With much trial and error, she found new names for all eighty-eight ships and sent the list off to the shipping board with a sense of a job well done. They sent back a new request—could she please find names for the new vessels being hastily built in America's shipyards? There were hundreds of them. "I sent to the Library of Congress for Indian dictionaries and pressed my brother Randolph into service. We tried for short and pretty names, and exhausted the supply very soon. After struggling with the jawbreakers I would get up a list of a hundred names. Randolph would go to work with Lloyd's and scratch out forty as already used."[87] Still, she plugged away at list after endless list. Secretary Daniels was impressed. "When women decide to become cabinet officers," he told her, "the Secretary of the Navy's portfolio should be assigned to you."[88] In August 1918 Edith was given the honor of christening the 7,500-ton freight steamer the *Quistconck*, the first ship to come off the ways in the new Hog Island shipyard, now the site of Philadelphia International Airport. "The name Quistconck is the ancient Indian name of the place now occupied by the shipyard," *The New York Times* reported. "The name was selected by Mrs. Wilson."[89]

As her public stature grew, Edith reinforced her importance behind the scenes. Only a few days after the declaration of war, she felt sick enough to spend the day in bed. The president was lost without her. He sat by her bedside and read her a draft of an appeal he planned to make for the cooperation of American industry. When she reminded him he had entirely left out the railroads, he was embarrassed. "My brain is just too tired to act," he told her. Edith was vexed. Without her to share his stress and cajole him into relaxing, she was worried his health would crack under the strain. "After that experience I needed no one to tell me what my most important war-work would be,"[90] she declared. There would be no more days off for Edith. No matter what else was going on, her first responsibility was to keep Woodrow healthy and sane. She encouraged him to imagine a time when they could escape the burdens of the White House and take a real vacation together. Woodrow began to wax nostalgic about traveling Europe by bicycle. As a student he had loved to wheel along back roads with no set agenda, stopping at farms and churches and taverns as he wished. He was so fond of this long-ago trip, he still wore a holey brown sweater he had purchased at the time. Perhaps after the war they could tour the countryside together? But Edith didn't know how to ride a bicycle. She had skipped right over that trend among fashionable urban ladies and went straight to driving a car instead. A deficiency easily remedied, insisted her husband, who ordered her a shiny new Columbia bicycle and encouraged her to learn to ride it. But where could she possibly do that without attracting the notice of the soldiers, suffragists, and sheep watchers who crowded the White House fence line? It was Woodrow who suggested clearing a space in the White House basement. "My husband and a couple of the Secret Service men used to go down with me at night. I fell off several times and nicked the enamel of the new wheel. Though I did not master the cycling art we made up for that in laughter and had such hilarious good times that it was genuine recreation for all involved."[91]

More successful was a suggestion of Cary Grayson's: horseback riding. Cary, an excellent horseman himself, had recommended it before, but the president always demurred. Now the doctor appealed to Edith, and she told Woodrow that *she* wanted to take up horseback riding. Woodrow agreed immediately. Without a moment's hesitation, Agent Starling was sent to Front Royal, Virginia, to find two safe horses for the president and First Lady. "For him we chose a particularly gentle but good-looking light bay named Arizona. . . . The President liked him and rode him with the vigor of a cowboy breaking a bronco, but with none of the skill."[92] Edith, surprised by the speed and strength of Woodrow's enthusiasm, rushed to cobble together appropriate riding clothes. She borrowed Margaret's breeches, Nell's coat, and Altrude's boots. When it became clear the rides would become a regular thing, Edith invested in her own riding habit. It was the only new item of clothing she bought in that summer of public self-denial.[93] She rode sidesaddle, and they usually contented themselves with a stately walk around the bridle paths of the Ellipse, just south of the White

House. But occasionally they took longer rides through Rock Creek Park. One memorable day the president, feeling cocky, challenged Starling to a race. Starling's competitive instinct kicked in, and before he thought too hard he was in the lead. This was a stupid move both personally and professionally. The president did not like to lose, and Starling was supposed to keep his charge in sight at all times. Before they reached the designated finish line, where Edith waited, better sense prevailed. Starling managed to rein in his horse while hiding the fact that he was doing so. Woodrow and Arizona pulled ahead to victory.[94]

As the war raged on, and American soldiers and sailors trained to ship overseas, Washington society tried to figure out how to act. Strangers poured into the city, newcomers with government jobs or aspirations of one, often without family or community ties. "From every state the war workers, civilians and men in uniform, flocked to the capital," wrote hostess Dolly Gann. "Financier and clerk, employer and laborer, general and lieutenant and enlisted man—all of them arrived in such numbers that there were not enough hotels, rooming houses, and barracks to hold them, nor enough business buildings to give them office space."[95] And although the official parties of federal Washington had ceased, these temporary workers found plenty of entertainment. "Among them was a large element of youngsters who labored through long, hard hours and then drifted into dissipation as a relief from the day's grind. This class of war workers danced furiously and drank aplenty, in spite of the prohibition laws that were unforced for them in Washington and nearby Baltimore."[96] The more permanent private citizens of the capital did their entertaining much more quietly. "It isn't good form for patriots to give parties," explained Ellen Maury Slayden. "And while, no doubt, some are given in stealth, they must lack zest when they cannot be blazoned in the society columns."[97]

The lack of official entertaining did not mean the White House was quiet. Throughout the summer and fall of 1917, diplomats, industrialists, cabinet officers, reporters, and opportunists flooded in, all with vital official business. Fifty-eight-year-old Theodore Roosevelt arrived to ask permission to raise a private regiment and go fight. His offer was politely declined. Investment whiz Bernard Baruch came to voice his concerns about the nation's lack of preparedness. The president was so impressed he appointed Baruch to the Council of National Defense.[98] Woodrow and Baruch would remain lifelong friends. Colonel House was in and out between trips to Europe. Edith's opinion of the man had not improved since House had tried to delay her marriage, and she wished he would stay away. At one point, she suggested he might be sent to London as official ambassador. House declined—he believed he'd be more effective if he was able to move back and forth among allies and enemies without official standing. Edith's opinion of House took another hit one day that fall. The administration was considering annexing the nation's railroads in order to streamline the wartime delivery of goods and soldiers. House arrived at the White House to discuss the proposal with Woodrow. Being told the president would be meeting with the War Cabinet for hours, he decided to approach Edith instead. He disagreed strongly with the president's plan, he said, and gave a point-by-point criticism. But he didn't want to blindside the man as soon as he walked in the door. Would Edith please mention his concerns and give Woodrow time to think about it before they discussed the matter at dinner? Edith was confused but did as he asked. When the hour for discussion rolled around, Woodrow said he understood House had qualms, and he was eager to hear them. But as Edith sat aghast, House declared he had changed his mind completely and was now all in favor of the plan. "I sat down and re-read the entire paper before dinner, and agree with every word of it." Edith felt she had been set up. "I do not like people to change their minds so quickly, and was never able to forget this little scene."[99] Her distrust of House took firm root.

The president used his State of the Union address in December of 1917 to urge war against Austria-Hungary in addition to Germany. But he continued to believe that the U.S., with no territorial stake in the war, held the moral position to dictate fair and lasting terms of peace. As 1918 began, he concentrated his work on a speech that would lay out, point by point, a road map for world peace and the rebuilding of a postwar world. As he refined and numbered his aims, this document would become the Fourteen Points speech. The fourteenth point returned to his concept of an international association to guarantee "political independence and territorial integrity to great and small States alike"[100]—a League of Nations. Woodrow delivered the speech to Congress on January 8, 1918. "No public utterance Mr. Wilson had ever made was received with such general acclaim," gushed Edith. "For me, the burdens of the War seemed lighter after that."[101]

But the war would continue for another ten months. Dramas large and small played out in the White House. The president, inspecting a tank, grabbed hold of a red-hot pipe and burned away the flesh of his right hand. For weeks, he signed letters and bills with his left.[102] There was a tussle with the insurance company, which refused to pay, since he was evidently ambidextrous and therefore not incapacitated.

The French ambassador sent Edith a note saying his government wished to give her a personal present, a small piece of Gobelins tapestry. She thanked him and agreed that when the parcel arrived from France she would invite the ambassador to tea so he could present the gift in person. When the day arrived, both giver and recipient were shocked to discover the tapestry was enormous—easily eighteen by fifteen feet. Edith was embarrassed. The gift was far too extravagant to be a personal present. Perhaps the French government meant it for the White House, and it would remain there regardless of occupant? No, the French insisted, it was absolutely *not* meant to be left in the White House. If Edith did not personally accept the gift, the French would take it as a personal insult from an ally. Edith dutifully acquiesced, and the giant tapestry hangs today in the house she and Woodrow retired to in 1921. It is so big the bottom third is folded back under itself.*

In early August, the White House hosted the wedding of Alice Wilson, the daughter of Woodrow's younger brother. The bride had originally planned a big wedding in Baltimore, but Uncle Woodrow convinced her to move it to his house to ensure he could attend.[103] It was brutally, unceasingly hot, and the president suggested the men wear their white summer clothes instead of swaddling themselves in stiff black tailcoats. No dice, said the mother of the bride—formal dress was required.[104] The family were sticklers for tradition; many wartime brides shunned music by German composers, but Alice stuck to Mendelssohn. As the bride posed for photographs on the South Portico, the heat and humidity coalesced into a violent storm and the sudden wind wrapped poor Alice's veil around a column. Everyone untangled the bride and rushed inside, and the ceremony continued without further incident. The worst of the weather swept through, and "the coolness which follows such storms made us all feel that life was still sweet and worthwhile."[105]

---

* It was apparently a tradition to weave "mistakes" into tapestries to provide the owners with entertainment for their guests when asked to spot the error. Edith's tapestry, which depicts Cupid and Psyche, includes a Cupid with, intentionally, two right feet. The error is easily spotted if you look at the angel's big toes.

Meanwhile, the nation's suffragists were finally starting to see some progress. New York, the most populous state in the union, enfranchised women in 1917. More and more antis in the Democratic Congress began to worry that millions of new female voters would all register Republican if they didn't do something to change their party's reputation. The Susan B. Anthony Amendment had been introduced in every Congress since 1878, but it passed the House of Representatives for the first time in 1918. The Senate was slated to take up the issue at the end of September, just weeks before the 1918 midterms. The president, as good as anyone at counting votes, finally decided the time was ripe to support the federal amendment. He took the further step of going to the Senate to make a speech urging passage of the amendment. It was unprecedented—by tradition, the president did not address Congress in order to influence a vote on pending legislation. But these were unusual times, or so he reminded the Senate. "I regard the concurrence of the Senate in the constitutional amendment proposing the extension of the suffrage to women as vitally essential to the successful protection of the Great War of humanity in which we are engaged,"[106] he declared. It didn't work. Suffrage lost in the Senate by two votes.

And now the midterms were upon them. One night near the end of October, Woodrow indulged in his usual habit of reading Edith a statement he had been drafting. It was a bald appeal for the voters to return a Democratic Congress on Election Day. "If you approve of my leadership and wish me to continue to be your unembarrassed spokesman in affairs at home and abroad," the statement read, "I earnestly beg that you will express yourself unmistakably to that effect by returning a Democratic majority to both the Senate and the House."[107] Edith thought this was a terrible idea. "I would not send it out," she

told him. "It is not a dignified thing to do."[108] Woodrow was not particularly proud of the statement himself, but he felt he owed it to congressional Democrats fighting for their political lives. The statement
went out on October 24. It was a disaster. Even his supporters accused
him of "ineptitude and lack of tact."[109] His opponents were positively
gleeful. "That appeal was for us a welcome blunder on the part of
President Wilson," crowed Alice Roosevelt Longworth. "We delight-
edly seized on it as meaning that 'politics is adjourned'—one of the
President's phrases—was definitely out the window."[110] The final week
of the campaign turned into a gloves-off fight. The Wilson Democrats
will give you a weak negotiated peace, the president's opponents insisted to a war-weary electorate, while a Republican Congress will deliver the unconditional surrender America deserves. When the votes
were counted on Tuesday, November 5, the Republicans had taken
control of both the House and the Senate.

Chapter Six

THE FIRST LADY IN PEACE

1918–1919

J ust two days later, on November 7, 1918, whistles and sirens and bells began to ring all over the nation. Word spread with lightning speed: Germany and the Allies had signed an armistice. The war was over. Americans flooded into the streets, dancing, cheering, singing, and throwing their hats in the air. Hearing the jubilant crowds on the South Lawn of the White House, Edith urged Woodrow to come outside and greet the people. But he refused. He knew the truth—no armistice had been signed. The Germans were just setting off on their way to meet the Allies, but the deal was not done. Celebrations were premature.

Finally, word came on November 11 that the guns had been stilled. Effective officially at the eleventh hour of the eleventh day of the eleventh month, the World War was over. Edith and Woodrow looked at each other in stunned silence, unable to fully grasp the news. Eventually, the national jubilation caught up with them. Together they reviewed a parade of war workers and then drove out Pennsylvania Avenue to watch the people celebrate. They were immediately recognized, and joyful citizens swamped their car. The Secret Service agents were totally overwhelmed. Finally a group of soldiers formed a circle around the car, locked arms, and slowly escorted them back to the White House. But they were too keyed up to go to bed, and the president wanted to keep the party going. Coincidentally, the Italian embassy was hosting a ball to celebrate the king of Italy's birthday. "Filled with enthusiasm the President decided to go to it," recalled Agent Starling, "so we all climbed in to white tie and tails and accompanied him."[1] Edith and Woodrow pulled up to the party unannounced at 11:00 p.m. Edith was exhilarated. "The ball, colorful with uniforms, was in full swing when our surprised hosts rushed down to receive us. The President toasted the health of the King, and we stayed for about an hour. The day had been so crowded with emotion that we were too excited to sleep when we got back to the White House. So kindling up the fire in my room we sat on a big couch and talked until the early hours of the morning."[2]

NOT EVEN A MONTH LATER, Edith and Woodrow set sail for Paris so the president could personally attend the peace talks. This decision was not universally admired. For one thing, it had never happened before. President Roosevelt briefly visited Panama to inspect construction progress on the canal. President William Howard Taft had spent an afternoon in Ciudad Juárez, part of an exchange of visits across the border with Mexican president Porfirio Díaz. But the length and scope of this foreign visit was wholly unprecedented.[3] There was no system in place to manage the government in the president's absence, which promised to last for months. Vice President Marshall reluctantly agreed to preside over cabinet meetings but insisted his presence was ornamental. "I am here informally and personally," he told the secretaries. "I am not undertaking to exercise any official duty or function."[4]

Beyond simple logistics, they had to consider the optics of the trip. Supporters and detractors alike worried that if Woodrow dirtied his hands with the messy business of treaty negotiations, he would lose his moral high ground. Far better to stay unsullied in America and offer disinterested advice from a safe distance. Colonel House was a strong proponent of this view, although he admittedly wanted the seat at the negotiating table for himself. House couched his caution as coming from Americans in France, who, he claimed, were "practically unanimous" in their belief that Woodrow's presence "would involve a loss of dignity and your commanding position."[5]

Woodrow was unmoved. He never really considered any other course of action. This was why he had urged U.S. involvement in the war—so that America had a right to participate in constructing a just peace and a postwar world. If his beloved League of Nations stood any chance of acceptance, it would be because he personally ensured its inclusion in the treaty process. He was always going to go to Paris. The only question was who would go with him. Colonel House, of course. And Secretary of State Lansing. Woodrow didn't always trust Lansing's judgment, but excluding him would be a profound breach of protocol. Since Woodrow had never served in the armed forces himself, he needed at least one member of the team with military experience. He chose General Tasker Bliss, the army's chief of staff. Finally, he was persuaded to include a Republican. After all, any negotiated treaty would have to be approved by two thirds of the

Republican-controlled Senate, and Woodrow needed to at least pretend to make a show of bipartisanship. But he really didn't want someone who would disagree with him—he'd get enough of that from Lansing and his foreign counterparts. So Henry White was added to the delegation. Republicans in the Senate, including Henry Cabot Lodge, denounced the appointment as cosmetic. White, who had served as an ambassador and statesman in the Roosevelt administration, was considered a Republican in name only.[6]

One person whose presence was not debated, at least not in the White House, was Edith. It seems to have never occurred to Woodrow to leave her behind. If he was going, and he was certainly going, she would be there by his side for every step. Her foreign travel was even more unprecedented than Woodrow's—no sitting First Lady had ever gone abroad. The president's critics found Edith's inclusion ridiculous. Author H. G. Wells suggested she would lend a "social quality, nay, almost a tourist quality" to the proceedings.[7] None of it mattered. On December 4, 1918, the American delegation, including the president and First Lady, boarded the *George Washington* (one of the few seized former German ships Edith did not have to rename) bound for France. Beyond the official delegates, the American contingent was purposefully huge; some 1,600[8] experts, researchers, and clerical staff made the trip to Paris, along with an estimated five railroad cars' worth of documents.[9]

After the stress of the election and the tension of the armistice and the flurry of preparation for departure, the journey itself was a mini vacation for the first couple. "The ship was steady but slow," recalled Edith, "giving us ten full days aboard, which I loved, for I felt better with every new day. It was a real holiday, life-giving to my husband, though he worked every morning."[10] Afternoons were for strolls around the decks, and evenings were for movie screenings and sing-alongs in the ship's several theaters. On December 13 they arrived at the port of Brest, on the western tip of Brittany. The streets were crowded with locals dressed in traditional Breton clothing, shouting "Vive Vilson!" as they passed.[11] The delegation took a train to Paris, where a much bigger celebration awaited. American and French dignitaries rode in a triumphant procession of horse-drawn carriages, through the Arc de Triomphe and all the way up the Champs-Élysées. Edith, who had been to Paris many times before, had never seen it like this. "Paris was wild with celebration. Every inch was covered with cheering, shouting humanity. The sidewalks, the buildings, even the stately horse chestnut trees were peopled with men and boys perched like sparrows in their very tops. . . . Flowers rained upon us until we were nearly buried."[12]

The parade ended at the Palace Murat, where Edith and Woodrow would be staying. They had only a second to take it in before it was time to dress for a formal luncheon. That's when the first of many little issues of etiquette and protocol emerged. Apparently, the French wore long, tight-fitting frock coats to formal affairs, while the Americans wore cutaway coats with tails. Happily, the ever-resourceful valet Arthur Brooks had brought coats of several styles to prepare for any eventuality, and Woodrow was able to appear at lunch properly attired. Then came the formal process of escorting the ladies to the table. Edith, paired with French president Raymond Poincaré, found it all hilarious. "Instead of a perfunctory escort, such as is our custom when a gentleman takes a lady in to dinner or to lunch, the French take the office seriously. When the arm is offered and accepted, the lady finds a viselike hold fastened upon her, which apparently nothing but death can relax before the goal at the table is reached." The situation was made more absurd by the fact that Edith was a full head taller than Poincaré, so she "felt like a big liner with a tiny tug pushing her out from her moorings." Finally, the table came in sight and, "mowing down waiters as we went, we arrived breathless and panting. This was my first experience, but as time went on I got so expert that I felt I could qualify for a football rush."[13]

Edith was forced to become expert in many new things, and very quickly. She was occasionally included in official ceremonies more than she anticipated. When Woodrow was awarded the "freedom of the city" of Paris, their hosts also presented Edith with a gift, a huge Lalique brooch depicting eight doves of peace.* Edith was surprised but schooled her features and gave proper thanks.[14] The president spoke no foreign languages. "To know English properly," he claimed, "has kept me so busy all my life that I haven't had time for anything else."[15] Edith had learned some French from Grandmother Bolling. But her grandmother was self-taught, and her pronunciation was eccentric, to say the least. Still, it fell to Edith to make polite noises in their hosts' native language. It was Edith who sat next to prickly Madame Poincaré and smoothed over issues of precedence. And it was Edith who sat by the bedsides of wounded soldiers, forcing back her tears to bring joy and warmth to hospital wards.

After just a week in France, the pomp and circumstance started to wear on Woodrow. He wasn't there for parties and ceremonies; he wanted to get the negotiations started. His hosts wouldn't even consider it. There was an upcoming parliamentary election in Great Britain, and Prime Minister David Lloyd George couldn't possibly come to France while his political fortunes were at stake. And also, didn't the

---

* René Lalique was a master of publicity. This Art Deco brooch had originally been described as depicting pigeons on a laurel branch. Lalique rechristened the pigeons doves and the tree an olive branch and insisted it was a symbol of international peace. The Lalique "peace brooch" is now in the collection of the Smithsonian's National Museum of American History.

Americans want to make formal visits to the royal families of England and Italy to thank them for their alliance and lay the groundwork for further cooperation? Woodrow had not planned on making either of those trips, but it was clear there was nothing for him to do in Paris until the slow gears of diplomacy clanked a little closer to actual treaty negotiations. So on the day after Christmas, Edith and Woodrow crossed the channel to England.

In London, their train was met by King George and Queen Mary, who escorted them to Buckingham Palace for a state visit. The royals didn't let on that this visit came as a surprise to them—evidently Lloyd George had extended the invitation without consulting Buckingham Palace.[16] Every day was crowded with official visits and ceremonies and grand dinners. It was in these set pieces of social niceties where Edith's skills proved invaluable. According to her secretary, Edith Benham, she didn't mind sitting next to the dowager Queen Alexandra, who was totally deaf and kept up a running monologue. She easily flagged down a palace servant to ask what the etiquette was on gloves at dinner. She was happy to sign Princess Victoria's autograph book, with no self-consciousness or doubt. (When she signed her full name, Edith Bolling Wilson, the princess was amazed that she had more than one. "I could not determine whether that stamped me in their eyes as three times more royal or deducted in like proportion from my social status,"[17] quipped Edith.) The president, acutely aware of his status and nervous about putting a foot wrong, was uneasy and dull in these circumstances. His self-consciousness was particularly awkward in England. "He is shy," explained Benham, "and has to be met more than half way, and the English are shy, too."[18] Whereas Edith, who had marched unprepared into almost every circumstance of her life, blithely expected her humor and confidence would carry her through. And she was right; the English were totally charmed by Edith. One night at dinner, someone asked her if she was a Quaker. Edith, surprised, said she was not. "Oh, I thought you were," said the woman, "because you wore no tiara." Instead of blushing, Edith laughed. "I would wear one," she joked, "but you see my husband can't afford to give me one."[19] Later they discovered this visit was also unprecedented. Not only were women never invited to state dinners, but they also did not stay at Buckingham Palace. "I didn't realize at the time I was assisting at a precedent-making affair," recalled Benham. "Mme Poincaré and the wives of the other French presidents were never invited to Buckingham, and to royalties it was often intimated their wives were not wanted and they were left at home."[20] They returned to Paris to discover the prominence of Edith in the visit to London was the gossip of French society. It made the American papers too. "Since there are no precedents by which to go, new precedents are being created by the king," reported *The Washington Post*. "And Mrs. Wilson is being received with the same royal honors as if she were a crowned head."[21]

Their return to Paris was brief, for Edith and Woodrow were expected at another royal visit in Rome. It was another week of state dinners and troop reviews and ceremonial gift exchanges. Edith loved Rome, where "the sky was a dome of sapphire pouring golden sunshine over a radiant world."[22] They took a side trip to Milan, where they were invited to a gala performance of *Aida* at the fabled La Scala opera house. But it was a Sunday, so the president declined. He never went to the theater on Sunday. His hosts were appalled by this circumspection. Every seat was full, and people had come from all over the country to pay their respects to the man they hailed as a savior. Finally an enterprising Italian diplomat hit upon a solution. Would the president and First Lady come to the theater for a concert of sacred music? They found they could not refuse. When they got to the theater, under much bowing and flag-waving, the company performed two perfunctory sacred pieces and then launched into *Aida*, as planned. "It was such a magnificent spectacle I have always been glad they did it," admitted Edith. "Secretly, I think my husband was too; and he made no comment regarding the elastic fulfillment of their promise."[23]

From Italy, they returned to Paris, where Woodrow fervently hoped the peace process could begin in earnest. He naively expected the whole thing could be wrapped up in time for the closing of the sixty-fifth Congress on March 4. He never fully grasped that these ceremonial visits were a vital part of diplomacy. But Edith did, and she knew she was making history. As a justification for devoting a whole chapter of her memoir to this time, she wrote, "These two journeys—to England and to Italy—were experiences that come to few Americans. Fate having chosen me for such a Cinderella role, I have tried to picture it for others, in an endeavor to make a return for this great privilege which was mine."[24] Now, of course, foreign travel and state visits are a standard part of the First lady's portfolio. Successive presidential administrations have realized the value of these junkets; the First Lady is flatteringly famous and important but remains outside the nitty-gritty of official diplomatic relations. At cultural events, national anniversaries, state weddings and funerals, and international summits, the First Lady regularly represents the U.S. around the world. But Edith was the first. She did not necessarily set out to break the mold of her predecessors' role. But by refusing to leave her husband's side, she set the precedent of international visibility for the president's spouse.

On January 12, 1919, Woodrow held his first formal meeting with the men who would become known as the Council of Four: Lloyd George, Italian prime minister Vittorio Orlando, and Georges

Clemenceau of France. If Woodrow hoped to finally get down to business, he was disappointed. The pace of conversation was glacial, stopping for argument about whether to open the window and a lengthy interval for tea. On January 18, the peace conference officially commenced. The American delegation had already been in Europe for over a month.

Now Woodrow was busy with negotiations and meetings every day, and Edith was on her own. She visited soldiers and hospitals, theaters and churches, French war industries and tourist attractions. She paid social calls to diplomats, philanthropists, and aristocrats. One elderly French duchess, who had turned her grand home into a hospital, refused to receive Edith as she had no title or aristocratic lineage. Edith didn't mind—she had plenty of other hospitals to visit. But a Serbian diplomat who knew Edith pretty well from his days in Washington took it upon himself to inform the duchess that Edith was actually royalty, and presented a newspaper clipping tracing her descent from Princess Pocahontas. Suddenly, the duchess was desperate to have Edith visit. When the Serbian friend related the whole episode, Edith laughed and threatened to tell the lady that her mother resided in the ancestral palace. Mrs. Bolling lived at the modest Powhatan Hotel in Washington, named after Pocahontas's chieftain father.[25] When she wasn't out calling on eccentric aristocrats, Edith hosted teas for the household staff: the guards, chauffeurs, telephone operators, messengers, stenographers, and soldiers who served the president and his wife at all hours of the day and night.[26] She particularly loved those occasions, although she did worry the soldiers' hobnail boots would damage the ancient floors of the Palace Murat.

In addition to her public duties, Edith continued as a behind-the-scenes adviser to her husband. As other members of the U.S. delegation realized she had the president's ear, they used her as a back channel to get information directly to him. Edith enjoyed this role and welcomed the confidences of those she felt were sympathetic to her husband.[27] Henry White confided to her that Secretary Lansing was miffed that whenever the American contingent met at the Hôtel de Crillon, they gathered in House's suite, not his own. It was a small oversight, White admitted, "but Lansing is a small man, and sometimes personal vanity makes or mars the success of large affairs."[28] Edith dutifully relayed the information to Woodrow, and the hotel conferences were moved.

Trickier was the question of who was talking to the press. The newspapermen liked to go to Colonel House, knowing they would get a colorful quote. Woodrow found this completely innocent, but Edith suspected the colonel was inflating his own importance. Regardless, the members of the press were getting different stories from different sources, and that had to stop. The president decided to deputize journalist Ray Stannard Baker as his press liaison. Every night at seven, Baker would report to the Palace Murat to hear the news of the day. Sometimes he had to wait an hour or more for the president to finish the day's conferences. But eventually Woodrow would emerge and update Baker on what had been achieved and what remained unfinished. Edith always tried to be present for these updates, as a way of making sure she had all the latest information. Baker "kept up a continual fire of questions and was never satisfied until he had each point clarified. So it was a stimulating half hour."[29]

Edith also continued her vigilance over Woodrow's health. With no possibility of golf or horseback riding, Edith begged her husband to walk when he could. At the very least, she hoped he would walk from the Palace Murat to the conferences every day. He did not love this idea. "The President hates to walk," observed Benham, "and is like a bad child in trying to find excuses not to walk to the Quai d'Orsay, where the Conferences are held, or to walk at other times."[30] He was working eighteen-hour days, with the highest possible stakes. Edith worried every day that he would collapse.

By mid-February, it was clear that nothing would be wrapped up by early March. But Woodrow had to get to Washington to preside over the closing of Congress and be available to sign any last-minute legislation. So he set a new goal. If he could secure the agreement of his colleagues that the League of Nations would be included in the final treaty, he could take that assurance home with him in March and report to the Senate. Then he could return to Paris armed with the senators' concerns and questions and make sure they were incorporated into the final agreement, smoothing the way for ratification. He decided to make a formal plea for the league to the full peace conference on February 14. Then he and Edith would board a ship back to America to attend the closing of Congress. They would be home just a week, then head back across the Atlantic. On the night of Woodrow's speech, Edith was desperate to watch. This seemed impossible—the meeting was for members only, and any outsider, particularly a woman, would be glaringly conspicuous. Edith decided to appeal to Clemenceau directly. As it happened, Cary Grayson also wanted to eavesdrop on the proceedings. Together they were given permission to hide in a curtained alcove at the far end of the Room of the Clock, where the meeting was to take place. They could watch from there, as long as they arrived before the delegates, stayed perfectly still and silent, and waited to leave until the room was totally empty. Edith and Cary readily agreed and secreted themselves behind the curtain well before the meeting began. When Woodrow stood up to speak, they dared to part the curtain just enough to watch. Edith forgot the heat and her tense stiffness as her husband addressed the crowd. "It was a great moment in history, as he stood there—slender, calm, and powerful in his argument."[31] And he carried the day—the delegates voted to include the League of Nations in the treaty. Woodrow and Edith sailed home that night, confident that his precious league would go forward with international support. In theory, Secretary Lansing should have led the American delegation in the president's absence. But before he left, Woodrow asked faithful House to play that role instead. House agreed without hesitation, eager to assume the authority he had wished for.

The journey home was uneventful. Edith and Woodrow headed back to the White House, where they hosted a dinner for senators who wanted to learn more about the league. Republicans William Borah and Albert Fall refused to attend, saying nothing could induce them to support the League of Nations. Henry Cabot Lodge showed up but sat brooding and silent, refusing to engage. Frank Brandegee of Connecticut, another anti, took the role of challenger, peppering the president with questions and criticisms. Woodrow, confident in his righteousness and believing the American people were behind him, prepared to return to France. The opposition senators began eviscerating the league in the press before he even got on the boat.

Woodrow and Edith returned to France on March 13, not quite a month after they had left. The date was not a coincidence—the president had a surprising superstitious streak and believed the number thirteen to be good luck.[32] Colonel House met them in Brest. According to Edith, she was left to "do the courtesies to the French people" while House caught the president up on all that had happened in their absence. When the meeting finally ended sometime after midnight, Edith went to check on her husband. "The change in his appearance shocked me. He seemed to have aged ten years, and his jaw was set in that way it had when he was making a superhuman effort to control himself." Alarmed, Edith begged him to tell her what was wrong. "He smiled bitterly. 'House has given away everything I had won before we left Paris. He has compromised on every side, and so I have to start all over again and this time it will be harder, as he has given the impression that my delegates are not in sympathy with me."[33] While dramatic, Edith's retelling of that meeting may not be strictly accurate. For one thing, House sent regular cables to Woodrow while they were apart, so the status of negotiations should not have been a complete shock. But even accounting for Edith's dislike of House, it is true that he never regained his role as the president's most trusted adviser. As Agent Starling described it, "the Colonel through weakness had betrayed his trust and given in to the foreign delegates, and this, to a man whose only weakness was that he would give in to nobody, was unforgivable. From the time of our second arrival in Paris the President had little use for Colonel House's opinions or advice."[34] Ike Hoover agreed that House had lost the president's confidence. But from his vantage point, it looked like House had been the victim of jealous rumors, which the insecure president was only too willing to believe. "The President was very serious, very conscious of his influence, very intent on his purpose, and very egotistical about his new position in world affairs. He was jealous of his power and responsibility," Hoover wrote. "So it was that these innuendoes about Colonel House took root, grew as time went on, and finally terminated in the complete alienation for the two men."[35] The next few months in Paris would be the last they ever saw each other.

Edith saw this night as a turning point not just in her husband's friendship with House but also in his health and hopes for the nation. "I look back on that moment as a crisis in his life," she wrote in her memoir, "and feel that from it dated the long years of illness, due to overwork, and that with the wreckage of his plans and his life have come these tragic years that have demoralized the world."[36] The first signs of illness came just a few weeks later. On April 3, Woodrow succumbed to a violent coughing spell in the middle of a meeting and had to excuse himself. Cary discovered he was running a fever of 103 and had intense body aches and diarrhea in addition to the uncontrollable coughing.[37] The doctor put his patient to bed, now in a new mansion lent to Woodrow and Edith for the remainder of the talks. At first reluctant to make any public statement, Cary finally released the news that the president was suffering from influenza. It might not have been the strain called "Spanish flu," which had ravaged populations worldwide the previous year, but it could have been a variant, as that virus mutated several times. It was serious enough to keep Woodrow in his bedroom for four full days. He did not fare well when he was isolated from the action. Convinced his adversaries were taking advantage of his incapacity to steamroll his priorities, the president threatened to storm out of Paris and even went so far as to order that the *George Washington* be readied for his imminent departure. This seemed to light a fire under some of the slower-moving negotiators, who rushed to appease Woodrow as best they could. It was a bluff, but an effective one. "Mr. Wilson did not want, or intend, to leave Paris if there was still a fighting chance for terms he could sanction," explained Edith. "So the order regarding the *George Washington* was rescinded, and, as soon as the Doctor was willing, the President resumed his work."[38]

The next few weeks were grueling. The president met with everyone, at all hours—not just the Council of Four but also delegations from Syria, Dalmatia, Albania, Greece, Portugal, Serbia, and Armenia.[39] Edith and Cary were both concerned for his health. Edith stayed close to home, always available if there was the slightest chance he would get a break or take a walk.[40] And although Woodrow seemed to recover from the most acute symptoms of his illness, he continued to exhibit cognitive changes. Much has been made of the president's health in Paris, with a lot of speculation and retroactive diagnosis. Was it a neurological impact of the flu virus? Encephalitis? A small stroke? The early signs of dementia?[41] The medical records from this time no longer exist, if they ever did.[42] Whatever the cause (and given his history of hypertension and his subsequent collapse, a stroke seems the likeliest explanation), those around the president began to notice odd behavior. "The President was sicker than the world ever knew, and never afterwards was he more than a shadow of his former self," recalled Ike Hoover. "Even when conscious, he was unreasonable, unnatural, simply impossible. His suspicions were intensified, his perspective distorted."[43] Agent Starling agreed. "He never did regain his physical strength, and his weakness of body naturally reacted upon his mind. He lacked his old quickness of grasp, and tired easily."[44] Even loyal Ray Stannard Baker felt his hero was changed. "More than once, there in Paris, going up in the evening to see the President, I found him utterly worn out, exhausted, often one side of his face twitching with nervousness."[45] This famously rational man began to behave erratically. He became convinced that everyone in the house was a spy, that the servants all secretly knew English and were reporting on his every move. More strangely, he developed a preoccupation with the furniture in the house. He raised a fuss if anything was moved.[46] One day he became fixated on the colors of the chairs and convinced Cary to help him rearrange everything so the red chairs were all together on one side of the room, the green ones on the other, with a purple one in the center.[47] Edith did not detail these oddities in her memoir but did note that her husband neither slept nor ate well, and she was constantly alarmed by the strain he was under. Her vigilant care for her husband was needed more than ever. As Benham wrote to her fiancé, "probably no one will realize fully if the President's work does come to anything, how much Mrs. Wilson has done to make it possible. She is the most wonderful wife in the world, to a man who needs love and care more than any I have ever seen. Without it I don't believe he could live—certainly his work would be greatly crippled."[48]

Eventually, even the most contentious details of the treaty were hammered out, and a 214-page agreement was set before the Germans on May 7. While they took time to digest this document and request changes, Edith and Woodrow accepted an invitation from the king and queen of the Belgians.* Edith, now wholly accustomed to royalty, liked Queen Elisabeth immediately. "I found her easy to know, with a keen interest in affairs, a splendid sense of humor, and a happy way of telling of the things she had done and seen during the War, so that much of the sorrow of those awful days was touched lightly."[49] Unaffected, informed, funny, and able to keep a positive outlook—it was a description that might be used for Edith herself at her best. The trip was a success, and they returned to Paris to discover the Germans had agreed to sign the treaty. No one got everything they wanted, and the president had made many compromises, but his beloved League of Nations remained in the final version. The official signing ceremony was set for June 28 in the Hall of Mirrors at the Palace of Versailles. This time Edith did not have to spy on the proceedings from behind a curtain; she and the other wives were invited as distinguished guests. The

---

* According to the Belgian constitution, the monarch is most properly referred to as "King (or Queen) of the Belgians" rather than "of Belgium" to underscore primacy of constitutional rule.

paperwork duly completed, photos taken, celebratory dinners eaten (Edith wore black charmeuse and the huge Lalique peace brooch), and exhausted farewells made, they headed home on June 29. Other than the brief week in March, they had been gone for seven months. The journey back on the *George Washington* would be a chance to rest and regain strength for the fight ahead. The domestic front of the treaty war awaited them in Washington.

Chapter Seven

THE STROKE

1919

They all knew the train trip was a terrible idea. Everyone could see the president was struggling. Cary Grayson worried four hot weeks sardined in a train car, making daily speeches and shaking thousands of hands, might literally kill him. Joe Tumulty agreed: "Indeed, it needed not the trained eye of a physician to see that the man . . . was on the verge of a nervous breakdown."[1] Edith was frantic, and the relentless summer weather wasn't helping. "Anyone who knows the heat of Washington in July and August can picture the way energy is sapped, with no strain needed to add to that of the weather," Edith wrote in her memoir. "The increasing demands on my husband's brain and body exacted a toll which pyramided, while I looked on with an anxious heart."[2] But Woodrow was stubborn. "I feel it is my duty," he insisted, "and my own health is not to be considered when the future peace and security of the world are at stake."[3] When he raised the stakes that high, it was hard for anyone to argue.

For a few weeks, it looked like it might not come to this. The Wilsons returned from Europe on July 8, 1919. The leisurely journey on the *George Washington* had restored their spirits almost back to normal, and the cheering crowds that met them in New York made up the last difference. Feeling triumphant, they hopped a train back to Washington. The crowd there was a little less enthusiastic, at least according to Alice Roosevelt Longworth, who admittedly hated Woodrow and didn't have nice things to say about Edith, either. "There was very little cheering," she recalled, "such as there was had a treble quality, as women predominated." She followed the motorcade from the train station to the White House, where she "stood on the curbstone to see the Presidential party pass, fingers crossed, making the sign of the evil eye, and saying 'a murrain on him, a murrain on him, a murrain on him!'"[4] But she didn't need to call a biblical plague down on Woodrow. He was already cursed with the Senate Republicans.

On July 10 Woodrow hefted the brick of a treaty, including his beloved League of Nations, and drove it down Pennsylvania Avenue to the U.S. Senate for ratification. He was not interested in their opinion on the deals he had made in Paris; he wanted a simple vote of yes or no. He made it clear that revisiting the terms of the agreement was not just an insult to him; it was no less than a repudiation of God's plan. "The stage is set, the destiny disclosed," he told the Senate. "It has come about by no plan of our conceiving, but by the hand of God, who led us into this way. We cannot turn back. We can only go forward, with lifted eyes and freshened spirit, to follow the vision."[*][5] The anti–League of Nations Republicans found this holy rhetoric ridiculous. "Soap bubbles

---

[*] This quotation, too, became one of the four engraved in the Wilson Bay at the Washington National Cathedral.

of oratory and a soufflé of praises," sniffed Connecticut senator Brandegee. The math looked dicey for the president. Treaty ratification required a two-thirds majority, or sixty-four of ninety-six votes. There
was a core group of about fifteen Republican senators, including Brandegee, Borah, and Fall, who opposed anything Wilson promoted on
general principle. Indeed, this group of "irreconcilables" made plans to
fight the treaty tooth and nail before it even existed.[6] Another thirty-
four Republicans considered themselves "reservationists"—those who
might be persuaded to accept the treaty with some changes. Of this
group, a subset identified themselves as "mild reservationists" whose
support might be more easily secured. And then there was Henry Cabot
Lodge of Massachusetts, the Senate majority leader. Lodge was the
sneakiest form of opponent, an irreconcilable who masqueraded as a
reservationist. It didn't help that the men personally loathed each other.
As Lodge told fellow Wilson antagonist Teddy Roosevelt, "I never expected to hate anyone in politics with the hatred I feel toward Wilson."[7]
As he admitted to another senator, instead of a "direct frontal attack,"
Lodge pretended he reasonably wanted some revisions before he could
support the treaty, thereby fighting its ratification by "the indirect
method of reservations."[8] He even made sure these were branded as the
"Lodge reservations." He knew the president's pride and personal ani-
mosity meant he would never be induced to accept a treaty modified
by "Lodge reservations." To Woodrow, the league was the only way to
avoid another war on the same scale, the only outcome that would make
the American sacrifice worthwhile. To Lodge, the league was nothing
less than an existential threat to the power and sovereignty of the United
States. There was, it seemed, no middle ground. Throughout July and
August, the two tangled daily, without approaching any sort of compromise. Meanwhile, Woodrow's health continued to deteriorate, and even

sympathetic observers knew he wasn't at his best. He stumbled over his words, forgot key details, and made uncharacteristic errors. He was hitting diminishing returns lobbying the Senate—no more minds would be changed in Washington.

Which is why the foolhardy train trip was back on the table. The president was absolutely convinced that the American people, especially those in the West who had supported him in the 1916 election, wanted the treaty ratified with the League of Nations and without the Lodge reservations. If he could speak to them directly, their enthusiasm for his ideals would convince the stubborn senators to see the light and switch sides. A White House staffer drew up a possible schedule. It was brutal: four weeks, ten thousand miles, and twenty-nine cities, all in a train car that promised to bake like an oven in the August weather. The president was all in. At the last minute his friend Bernard Baruch begged him to cancel. But the president was dead set on his martyr's course. "What is one life in a great cause?"[9] he asked. The combined forces of Edith, Cary, and Tumulty could not convince him to reconsider. They all realized the best they could do was join him for the journey and hope to save him from the very worst of his own self-destructive tendencies.

The ill-fated train set out from Washington's Union Station on September 3, 1919. It was exactly the rolling circus Edith had dreaded: in addition to the porters and personal servants, there were staffers, Secret Service agents, photographers, telegraphers, movie camera operators, and dozens of journalists. It was clear this journey would not involve a single opportunity for peace or rest. Cary was in anguish over his patient. "For him the journey was a prolonged agony of physical pain; for Mrs. Wilson and me an unceasing agony of anxiety."[10] From the very first moment, Woodrow was already behind schedule. "The pressure of work at the White House during the past few days gave the President no opportunity to prepare any of his speeches in advance," explained *The Washington Post*, "and he will speak chiefly from notes made during the trip."[11]

The first stop was Columbus, Ohio, where the newspaper reported that "the fighting temper of the President's appeal to the country was apparent."[12] Stops in Indianapolis, Saint Louis, Kansas City, and Des Moines all seemed to go relatively smoothly. But by day four in Omaha, journalists were starting to comment on Woodrow's growing weakness. "Although his voice is holding up well, it has broken once or twice during his addresses," an Associated Press dispatch revealed. "And to one audience he remarked that the circumstance was due to 'the remains of a Paris cold.'"[13] A hoarse voice was only the tip of the symptomatic iceberg. "The tour had not progressed far when serious headaches began to afflict my husband,"[14] admitted Edith. Even the distance between stops offered no chance to rest—local politicians came aboard at every station and insisted on bending the president's ear until the train pulled into the next town. Bismarck, North Dakota; Billings, Montana; Coeur d'Alene, Idaho—the whistle-stop tour covered thousands of miles and dozens of events. Edith herself seemed to draw crowds, although she never spoke a word. "Women predominate among the onlookers everywhere," reported *The Washington Post*, "and they are more interested in seeing the first lady of the land than they are in applauding the President." The *Post* reporter, part of the traveling journalistic contingent on the train, was amazed to discover the local coverage in the towns along the way was written by female reporters "telling their readers how Mrs. Wilson looks, how she travels, how she dresses, and whether or not all her hats and gowns are Paris creations."[15] Woodrow began to call Edith out onto the platform with him, joking that she was much better to look at than him.[16]

As the train rumbled on, the headaches got worse, to the point where the president was more or less blind when he was suffering the worst of them. Eventually he could no longer rely on the restorative power of his habitual heavy sleep, Cary recalled. "From the time we reached Montana the President suffered from asthmatic attacks and severe headaches, which seriously interfered with his rest. Frequently I was summoned during the night to give him necessary aid and to assist him in breathing. It was necessary for him to sleep a good part of the time sitting up, propped up with pillows in a chair."[17] But still the tour continued, through Tacoma and Seattle and Portland. On September 16 the train headed down the coast of California, home of irreconcilable Senator Hiram Johnson. Under the headline PRESIDENT NOW IN FOE'S STATE, the *Baltimore Sun* reported, "Thoroughly satisfied that the people of the Northwest Pacific Coast States are generally in favor of the League of Nations and want the Senate to ratify it without further discussion, President Wilson is speeding toward San Francisco tonight."[18] The schedule for Northern California was particularly crowded, with five major speeches booked over two days. "The weather was warm and enervating," recalled Edith. "These two days would have taxed the vitality of one who was rested and refreshed. My husband took them on top of twelve days and nights of travel, and twenty-odd speeches; and was worn out when he started." But the momentum of the train tour could not be slowed. Woodrow survived his time in the Bay Area only to head for Southern California to do it all again. "So on to San Diego and Los Angeles," Edith wrote, "with the Doctor and me trying to act as buffers. The crowds at every station, the local committees travelling from one stop to another, and politicians who must have 'just a word with the President,' rendered our efforts almost futile."[19]

Finally, there was a slow Sunday in Los Angeles with a decent window of unscheduled time when Edith thought her husband could finally relax and recharge, at least a little. Somewhat inexplicably, Woodrow took advantage of the quiet afternoon to invite Mary Hulbert Peck to lunch. Surely Edith would have preferred almost any other agenda. But if the legendary Mrs. Peck was coming to lunch, she couldn't possibly miss it. "Because of the work scandalmongers had done to make an intrigue of that friendship, I was glad to receive her," Edith claimed, "and show my disdain for such slander."[20] On September 21, Mary took the streetcar from her little house in Hollywood to meet the Wilsons at the Hotel Alexandria. She was escorted to the presidential suite, where Edith opened the door. The two women sized each other up. Edith thought Mary looked old, describing her as a "faded, sweet looking woman."[21] She wasn't the only one resorting to euphemism. Mary stopped just short of calling Edith fat. "Mrs. Wilson was not the least as I expected to find her from her photograph, the official likeness issued at the time of her engagement to Mr. Wilson. She was much more junoesque."[22] Agent Starling, admittedly half in love with Edith, was more direct. "The mysterious Mrs. Peck . . . turned out to be a drab woman of middle age, and how anyone could have cast her in a romantic role was more than I could imagine."[23] With Cary and Woodrow, they sat down to lunch. It was a simple meal accompanied by polite chitchat and was soon over. Their duty was done, Edith thought, and now the president could rest. But after lunch Mary planted herself in the suite's reception room and stayed. Delegations came to meet with the president, and every time he left the room, Edith expected their guest to excuse herself. Yet she lingered, making awkward small talk with Edith until Woodrow returned. "All through that afternoon we talked," recalled Mary fondly, while Edith "played well that most difficult role of being the third party to the reunion of two old friends endeavoring to relive the incidents of years in a single afternoon."[24] Edith described the day somewhat differently, damning Mary with bless-your-heart sympathy. "Poor woman, weighed down with her own problems of course she did not understand. Darkness had fallen when she finally rose to go."[25]

The exhausting tour schedule resumed the next day as the train headed back east. Reno, Nevada, on the twenty-second. Salt Lake City on the twenty-third, where the Mormon temple was so crowded and airless, Edith almost fainted up on the rostrum.[26] All the way to Cheyenne, Wyoming, by September 24, where Woodrow was in visibly terrible shape. "By now the President was on his last legs. Nothing but courage kept him going," recalled Starling. "In his speeches he had begun to repeat himself a little, and several times I noticed that he lost the thread of his thought and wandered into a new subject."[27] By the time they hit Denver on the twenty-fifth he was barely able to stay upright. He'd sweat through his clothes in a matter of minutes. At lunchtime, the train left for Pueblo. Grimly, the president addressed a fairgrounds crowd of some ten thousand people. Starling was convinced he wouldn't make it. "While he spoke I stood close behind him, afraid he might collapse at any minute. Much of his speech was mumbled; he mouthed certain words as if he had never spoken them before. There were long pauses. He had difficulty following the trend of his thought. It was a travesty of his usual brilliant delivery and fine logic. His voice was weak, and every phrase was an effort for his whole body."[28] But he made it through. Exhausted, shivering, blinded by a crushing headache, Woodrow stumbled back to the train, which swiftly pulled out of Pueblo. The next day he would have to do it all again four hundred miles east, in Wichita.

Cary Grayson was desperate to find some way to help his patient recover at least a little of his strength. About half an hour outside of Pueblo, he suggested stopping the train so he and Edith could take Woodrow on a walk in the fresh Colorado air. This they did, stepping along "at as brisk a pace as was possible without tiring the President too much."[29] Agent Starling followed them down a dusty country road along the Arkansas River, "the President walking slowly, lifting his feet that were once so light, as if they were weighted and shackled."[30] The cocky man who had raced horses through Rock Creek Park just a year before seemed very far away. Still, Edith was encouraged—the walk seemed to have refreshed her husband enough to leave him cheerful and hungry for a good dinner. Everyone retired to their respective berths early, hopeful that a good night's sleep would work its restorative powers.

But before the clock even struck midnight, Woodrow called out for Edith. She found him with his forehead pressed against a chair back, desperate for some relief from the unrelenting headache. He hadn't slept a wink and could find no position comfortable enough to even consider it. Edith called for Cary, and the two of them tried everything they could think of to help him sleep. Nothing worked. They sat up all night, Woodrow restless and suffering, Edith and Grayson anxious and frightened. The president finally drifted off around five o'clock in the morning. Edith stayed awake, watching him sleep. She held out a faint hope that he would wake up feeling better, but in her heart she knew he never would. As the train rumbled relentlessly east toward the rising sun, she made a decision. "The dear face opposite me was drawn and lined; and as I sat there watching the dawn break slowly I felt that life would never be the same; that something had broken inside me; and from that hour on I would have to wear a mask—not only to the public but to the one I loved best in the world; for he must never know how ill he was, and I must carry on."[31]

Edith's instinct had always been to protect her husband, and she had a lifetime of experience in "carrying on" in the face of setbacks. But her decision to keep the full extent of her husband's incapacity from almost everyone, including the man himself, would have fateful consequences for her, for him, even for the nation. The riskiness of her self-imposed position presented itself almost immediately, as the train slowed for Wichita. After just a couple of hours of restless sleep, the president got up and went to his private car to prepare to deliver that morning's speech. Edith knew he was far too ill to do any such thing but was hesitant to tell him so. She convened Cary and Joe Tumulty, and in hushed voices the three discussed how best to handle the situation. It was clear the rest of the train tour would have to be canceled. But how could they convince the president without revealing how sick he really was? They were still whispering among themselves when the president appeared, freshly dressed and shaven. His face, pale and haggard, wasn't quite right.[32] The left side of it had fallen, and only the right side responded when he tried to smile.[33]

His trio of protectors decided to take it in turns to convince him to stand down. First came a medical argument from Cary, who told him if he didn't cancel the trip, it might kill him. Woodrow batted this concern away the same way he had before the trip. If he died in service to world peace, wasn't that a worthy sacrifice? Joe Tumulty tried next, advocating the political viewpoint. Giving up on the trip did not mean giving up on the treaty, he insisted. The league's allies in the Senate could take over the fight for a week or two while the president recovered. But the president knew the Senate irreconcilables had embarked on a speaking tour of their own. If he left the battlefield now, they would win by forfeit. "Don't you see," he implored Tumulty, "if you cancel this trip, Senator Lodge and his friends will say that I am a quitter and that the Western trip was a failure, and the Treaty will be lost."[34] No one in the whole world thinks you are a quitter, insisted Tumulty. His arguments fell on deaf ears.

So it fell to Edith. It was her job to get him to see that making a martyr of himself would not help his cause. He owed it to his country and his family to live to fight another day, and "in justice to his cause he must stop for a while. I think it was about the hardest task that has fallen to my lot. At last, though, it was done."[35] The president accepted the truth. But with tears running down his cheeks, he admitted, "This is the greatest disappointment of my life."[36]

As soon as the president consented, the cancellation of the trip proceeded swiftly. Organizers in Oklahoma City, Little Rock, Memphis, and Louisville were informed the president would not be coming. The tracks were cleared and a pilot engine engaged to run the whole way from Wichita to Washington. Woodrow telegraphed his daughters the news so they wouldn't learn it from the papers. Then Tumulty released a statement to the press. It concealed more than it revealed. "The President has exerted himself so constantly and has been under such a strain during the last year and has so spent himself without reserve on this trip that it has brought on a nervous reaction in his digestive organs," the statement read. "Dr. Grayson therefore insists upon the cancelation of his remaining appointments and his immediate return to Washington, notwithstanding the President's earnest desire to complete his engagements."[37] The on-board journalists rushed to spread the news. WILSON ILL: CANCELS TOUR[38] blared one headline. PRESIDENT SUFFERS COLLAPSE;

CANCELS DATES[39] read another. Not a single report questioned the dubious diagnosis of "nervous indigestion." All assured their readers the president would be back in fighting form after a few days of rest.

The train sped back to Union Station, covering some 1,700 miles in forty-eight hours. All along the route, crowds gathered to watch the train roar through. It felt like a funeral cortege to Edith. Woodrow still couldn't sleep. Edith desperately tried to distract him with small talk and herself with knitting, but it was hard going. They both knew a few days of rest would not magically restore the president. But it was the best they could do.

The train pulled in to Washington on September 28, 1919. A crowd had gathered there, and Woodrow managed to tip his hat to them, thank the train staff, and wave to the journalists before climbing into his car for the ride back to the White House. Cary had prescribed complete rest, but the president was still unable to sleep and instead paced the halls, in too much pain to work or read. The original plan had been for him to finish the tour, then personally resume lobbying for the treaty in the Senate. Now Senator Gilbert Hitchcock of Nebraska took on that role. It was generally understood that the messy details of the ratification fight should be kept from the president in the meantime. In fact, no business was expected to come to him for now—it could all wait until he was feeling better.

So Edith was annoyed when British intelligence agent William Wiseman showed up at the White House, insisting on an audience. Edith had always disliked Wiseman and took some pleasure in turning him down. Whatever information he had, she said, she would take to her husband herself. If he came back in a few hours, she would deliver the president's response. "I was glad my husband decided his information was not important enough for further consideration," she wrote in her memoir, then followed up with this brazen statement: "That was the only instance that I recall having acted as an intermediary between my husband and another on an official matter, except when so directed by a physician."[40] This was, as it happened, demonstrably untrue. Soon enough, Edith was serving as her husband's intermediary full time.

Early in the morning of October 2, Edith crept out of bed to check on her husband. She had been doing this regularly since they had returned home—dozing for an hour or two, then peeking in on the president. This morning she found him sleeping peacefully, so she tiptoed back to her own room to try to get a little more sleep. Sometime after eight she checked in again. This time Woodrow was awake and trying in vain to reach a water bottle on his bedside table. His left hand was useless. He asked Edith to help him to the bathroom. His halting, painful steps made it clear his entire left side was paralyzed. Edith left him sitting in the bathroom and ran to summon Cary Grayson, taking care to use the phone in the hall that went directly to the ushers' desk, instead of risking the closer phone where she might be overheard by switchboard operators. She reached head usher Ike Hoover, who immediately dispatched a White House car to Cary and Altrude's house.[41] As she was hanging up the phone, Edith heard an alarming noise. She rushed back to the bathroom and found her husband unconscious on the floor.[42] He had suffered a massive stroke.

What happened next has been the subject of debate and speculation for the past hundred years. Hoover saw bloody cuts on the president's temple and nose and assumed he had hit his head on the bathtub plumbing when he fell.[43] Edith claimed he didn't even have a bruise and had slid smoothly sideways to the floor.[44] Edith insisted "an arm and one leg were useless, but, thank God, the brain was clear and untouched."[45] Cary told a similar story: "His body was broken, but his intellect was unimpaired and his lion spirit untamed."[46] Hoover thought that was nonsense. "He was physically almost incapacitated; he could articulate but indistinctly and think but feebly."[47] Even loyal Joe Tumulty described him as "weak and broken" and "hardly able, because of his physical condition, to discuss [treaty] matters with me."[48] But Hoover conceded, "The story of this, his last and lasting illness, is tragic. The whole truth, of course, can only be told by one person in all the world, Mrs. Woodrow Wilson the second."[49]

But Edith was not interested in telling the whole truth. Her entire goal, from the very beginning, was to protect her husband at any cost. So she lied when she could and told the truth when she had to. There was no way to pretend the president was perfectly well—he was bedridden and drifted in and out of consciousness. So she conspired with Cary to create a plausible story, one that would be given to the press, the public, Congress, even the president himself. Woodrow was very sick, but he would get better. His mind was as sharp as ever. He was absolutely in control of the presidency. He'd be back on his feet soon.

If anyone wanted to prove that story untrue, they would have to get through Edith to do it. And Edith was going to pretend everything was fine.

Chapter Eight

"STEWARDSHIP"

1919–1921

Everything was definitely not fine. The president was an invalid, bedridden, half paralyzed, and often incoherent. For days, his life hung in the balance. The press was told only that he suffered from "nervous exhaustion"; the words *stroke* and *paralysis* were never mentioned in the artfully vague White House bulletins. Faithful Cary Grayson attended his patient around the clock, and a few other specialists were called in to consult. In her memoir, Edith claims one of these specialists, Dr. Francis Dercum of Philadelphia, was the one who instructed her to keep her husband's presidency going. The president could recover, Dercum said, but only if he was entirely protected from anxiety or excitement. At the same time, he must not resign, for ratifying the peace treaty and seeing his dream of the League of Nations fulfilled provided the best incentive for recovery. In Edith's telling, Dercum proposed this solution to Edith: "Have everything come to you; weigh the importance of each matter, and see if it is possible by consultations with the respective heads of the Departments to solve them without the guidance of your husband. In this way you can save him a great deal. But always keep in mind that every time you take him a new anxiety or problem to excite him, you are turning a knife in an open wound."[1] The way Edith chose to characterize her own decisions after Woodrow's stroke is instructive. In her version, she was acting on expert medical advice. Keeping her husband in office while shielding him from stress was the only way he would recover. And his recovery was not only important to Edith personally; it was vital to the future of the nation, maybe even the world. Acting as the "steward," as she put it, of Woodrow's final years as president was nothing less than Edith's wifely and patriotic duty.

It is also interesting that Edith worked to convince her readers she was up to the task. She did this chiefly by emphasizing the support of the men in the room. "He [Wilson] has the utmost confidence in you," Edith recalled Dercum telling her. "Dr. Grayson tells me he has always discussed public affairs with you; so you will not come to them uninformed."[2] In these two sentences, Edith conveyed the endorsement of two respected doctors and the president of the United States. Had she been a different sort of First Lady, she implied, the sort who tended only to private affairs and did not participate on a global stage, the president and his advisers would never have trusted her in this vital role. At the same time, Edith downplayed her authority. "I, myself, never made a single decision regarding the disposition of public affairs. The only decision that was mine was what was important and what was not, and the *very* important decision of when to present matters to my husband."[3] Edith rode a seesaw between raised stakes and low impact. She claimed, in essence, that if her husband did everything a president is elected to do, he would die. If he resigned, he would die. If he died, world peace would never be achieved. And she would be an excellent gatekeeper and presidential proxy until he recovered. But at the same time, it wasn't that big a deal.

The only part of this stunning statement of rationalization that was undeniably true is the first one: if Woodrow did everything a president is elected to do, he would die. Even if his brain was as razor-sharp as before the stroke, and it certainly was not, his doctors were telling him not to use it. The president was not capable of doing his job. And ultimately, that was all that should have mattered. Perhaps he would eventually recover, perhaps not. But for now, and for a foreseeably long time, he did not have the abilities of the man who had been reelected three years earlier. And no matter how able a substitute Edith believed herself to be, no one had elected her to anything. Whether she had been urged to do so on medical advice or simply took the decision into her own hands, the fact remains that Edith decided to hide the extent of her husband's illness from him and from the public, and to protect him at all costs. She did not apologize. "Woodrow Wilson was first my beloved husband whose life I was trying to save, fighting with my back to the wall—after that he was the President of the United States."[4]

One might be forgiven for asking, where was the vice president, the person who actually *had* been elected to substitute for the chief executive? Certainly Secretary of State Lansing asked that question. According to Joe Tumulty, as the president lay prostrate in the massive Lincoln bed, Lansing broached the topic of having Vice President Marshall step in. The Twenty-fifth Amendment to the Constitution, which clearly defines the vice president's role if the president is incapacitated, did not yet exist. The question of presidential vacancy was covered only by Article II, section 1: "In Case of the Removal of the

President from Office, or of his Death, Resignation, or Inability to discharge the Powers and Duties of the said Office, the Same shall devolve on the Vice President."[5] This is the clause Lansing quoted to Joe. But the language was maddeningly vague. Would the vice president act as president only until the president recovered, or would he hold the office for the rest of the term? And how was "inability to discharge the powers and duties of the said office" defined? Most crucially, who was supposed to make that decision? The issue had come up in 1881, when President James Garfield was confined to bed as he gradually sickened from a gunshot wound and subsequent infection. In that case, Vice President Chester Arthur did not step in until the president died seventy-nine days later.[6] But that was the height of summer, when Congress was in recess and there was little pressing business before the federal government. This was October, and the Senate was debating a document concerning nothing less than global peace.

Lansing suggested that Joe himself, or maybe Cary Grayson, had the authority to certify the disability of the president. Both categorically refused to do so. "You may rest assured that while Woodrow Wilson is lying in the White House on the broad of his back I will not be a party to ousting him," bristled Joe. "He has been too kind, too loyal, and too wonderful to me to receive such treatment at my hands."[7] Like Edith, Joe and Cary were concentrating on how the president could best recover, not how the nation could best be governed.

To be fair, the vice president had no desire to take on the top job. With no clear mechanism or decision maker for declaring the president unfit, no vice president wanted to look like he was usurping power illegitimately. And Thomas Marshall, in particular, didn't have the stomach for real authority. He had been added to the ticket in 1912 purely to secure Indiana's electoral votes. And in the seven years since, he had done nothing to distinguish himself. A friendly, affable type who could be counted on to crack vaguely inappropriate jokes, Marshall had taken on a kind of court jester role. He claimed to enjoy the title "His Superfluous Excellency." He regularly told a joke about a man who had two sons: One went off to sea and the other became vice president. And neither son was ever heard from again.

In addition to being something of a clown, Marshall was particularly sensitive to accusations of abuse of power. When he was governor of Indiana, he tried to introduce a new state constitution to the legislature and asked that it be submitted to the voters for ratification. The Supreme Court of Indiana stepped in and blocked Governor Marshall and the legislature from putting the measure on the ballot. Marshall thought this was a clear violation of the separation of powers, and way beyond the court's prerogative. He sought to have the U.S. Supreme Court overturn the supreme court of his own state. He failed, and much to his shame, he gained the reputation of overstepping his own authority. In his retelling of this incident in his memoir (charmingly if enigmatically called *A Hoosier Salad*), he uses some form of the word *usurp* seven times in four pages. When the president left for Paris, Marshall made it exceedingly clear that he was never going to take on the role of acting president.

But still, he needed to know what was going on. If Woodrow really was at death's door, the man who might have to take his place at any moment would like a little chance to prepare himself. But he was stuck in an impossible position. "These were not pleasant months for me," he admitted. "The standing joke of the country is that the only business of the vice-president is to ring the White House bell every morning and ask what is the state of health of the president. . . . I was afraid to ask about it, for fear some censorious soul would accuse me of longing for his place. I never have wanted his shoes."[8]

So Marshall wasn't asking, and the White House wasn't telling. As Edith, Cary, and Joe closed ranks, it became clear that they would stick to the strategy of "no details, no explanations."[9] In the absence of facts, journalists and cabinet officers alike latched on to any crumb of news. Had the president suffered a cerebral hemorrhage? Was he insane? Was he actually dead? Alice Roosevelt Longworth watched Republicans gossip among themselves. "Fantastic rumors spread as to what was really the matter with the President. It was some time before we had any realization of the gravity of his condition. Some of the comments were noticeably lacking in the Greek quality of Aidos—the quality that deters one from defiling the body of a dead enemy."[10] Cary and the other doctors weren't answering any questions. Instead, they issued useless statements that expressed concern that the president's "nervous exhaustion" might progress to "nervous prostration" but said that for now they were "encouraged by his progress."[11] If the vice president, who was never a regular White House visitor, was seen heading for the executive mansion, rumors would abound that the president was dead or dying. So instead, the Edith/Cary/Joe conspiracy dispatched a trusted reporter, Frank Essary of the *Baltimore Sun*, to brief the vice president in secrecy.[12] How much they told Essary is unclear, but he was able to convey to Marshall that the situation was not as rosy as it was being portrayed in the press. Marshall was stunned. "If there were a soul so lost to humanity as to have desired his death, I was not that soul."[13]

But Marshall had no time to process the information. The White House needed him to turn on his vaunted charm and host the king and queen of the Belgians. This royal couple and their son had been aboard a ship heading to America when the president collapsed. When they arrived in New York and heard the news, they quickly downgraded their plans from a series of ceremonial visits to a little quiet sightseeing,[14] including a trip to California to see the movie studios. But now they were coming to Washington. They certainly couldn't stay at the White House. And while Vice President and Mrs. Marshall would officially be their hosts, they wouldn't stay with them, either. The Marshalls' home was far too modest for such distinguished guests (there would not be an official residence for the vice president until 1977). Instead, the royal family would be hosted by Assistant Secretary of State Breckinridge Long, who had a grand mansion on Sixteenth Street (now the home of the Mexican Cultural Institute).

Refusing royal houseguests was sure to fuel the rumors of Woodrow's incapacity. But it turned out to be a wise move. Just as the Belgians headed for Washington, the president's health took a dramatic turn for the worse. An inflamed prostate caused an obstruction in his urinary system, blocking elimination from the bladder. All noninvasive efforts to release the blockage failed, and an assortment of specialists told Edith her husband would be poisoned to death in a matter of hours. The only solution, they insisted, was surgery. Cary balked. He was certain his patient would not survive an operation. Surgery would be fatal. As the patient's temperature climbed, Edith wrestled with what to do. Ultimately, she trusted Cary. There would be no surgery. Instead, Edith sat by Woodrow's bedside, holding his hand, hoping the hot packs and other local treatments would work their magic. And then, miraculously, they did. Somehow "the tense condition relaxed and Nature again asserted her power over disease. The temperature receded, and the weary patient slept. The doctors went home to rest, and again peace descended upon my spirit."[15] Edith was more certain than ever that her husband would survive, if everyone followed her lead.

By the end of October, he was feeling well enough to receive the royal visitors. They would have to come to his bedroom, and the meeting would have to be brief. But still, the president would speak with someone outside his inner circle for the first time in a month. Edith welcomed the royal family to tea in the Red Room. Then she brought the king up to Woodrow's bedroom so he could personally present his gift—a hand-painted set of eighteen china plates, each decorated with a historic place in Belgium.* The president had been wrapped in his best silk dressing gown and propped up in bed. The two leaders greeted each other fondly and exchanged polite conversation, and Woodrow showed appropriate appreciation for the gift. Then it was over. Edith escorted the king back downstairs to his family. But before they left, the queen insisted that she also wanted to see Woodrow and introduce him to her son the prince. Edith could think of no way to refuse, so back to Woodrow's bedroom they went. They found him in bed, studying the intricate plates with a magnifying glass. He had exchanged the fussy dressing gown for his favorite old sweater, the one he still cherished from his student cycling tour of Europe. He apologized for his informal dress, but the queen laughed and apologized in turn for visiting unannounced. She introduced the prince. And then, finally, it was time to go. A flock of journalists met them at the door. Queen Elisabeth charmingly described how comfortable the president looked in his worn wool sweater. Edith was mortified. "The next day a long account came out in the papers, quoting what she said, only

---

* You can see these plates in the second-floor pantry at the Woodrow Wilson House in Washington.

using the word *torn* instead of *worn* sweater. By the next mail I began to get letters from old ladies telling me how shameful it was for me to allow the President to wear a torn sweater; that I could at least mend it—and some of the dear old souls even sent me gray wool to darn it with."[16]

But Edith did not have the time or desire to fret about old dears and old sweaters. After fifty-five days of debate, the Senate was getting close to a vote on the peace treaty. Their focus centered largely on the League of Nations, the covenant Woodrow saw as his legacy. Most controversial was Article X, which required league members to assist any other member nation in the event of an invasion or attack. Senator Lodge wanted the United States to have more autonomy under the agreement, more control over when and how to participate in its allies' conflicts and governance. In his view, Article X took the power of declaring war away from the U.S. Congress and gave it to an international body. The only way the Senate would ratify this treaty, Lodge swore, was if amendments were included specifically codifying the authority of Congress.[17] Many who were close to the president agreed. As senior adviser Bernard Baruch put it, "half a loaf is better than no bread." Edward House wrote directly to Edith: "You can never know how long I have hesitated to write to the President about anything while he is ill, but it seems to me vital that the Treaty should pass in some form. His place in history is in the balance. If the Treaty goes through with objectionable reservations, it can later be rectified. The essential thing is to have the president's great work in Paris live." Meanwhile, Senator Gilbert Hitchcock of Nebraska, who was leading the Democratic forces for ratification, looked desperately to the White House for direction.[18]

Edith was torn. She knew Woodrow had wanted the treaty ratified as written—no changes. The last time he had interacted with the public had been on his train tour, and he was convinced the cheering crowds he met there meant his league was both just and popular. But friends and allies with more knowledge of legislative realities were telling her that without at least some of the Lodge reservations, the treaty was facing certain defeat. Given the risks her husband had been willing to run to secure support for the treaty, Edith was sure even a rumor of its defeat would further damage his well-being.

Edith told the public the president made the final call. It's possible he actually did. She wrote in her memoir that she went into her husband's sickroom and told him a treaty vote was imminent. Kneeling by his bedside, she pleaded, "Won't you accept these reservations and get this awful thing settled?" According to Edith, Woodrow "turned his head on the pillow" and remained adamant. "It is not I that will not accept; it is the Nation's honor that is at stake. Better a thousand times to go down fighting than to dip your colors to dishonorable compromise."[19] Edith would never bring up compromise again. To do so, she decided, "would be manifestly dishonorable."[20]

Edith told Hitchcock to direct loyal Democrats to refuse all amendments. She gave him a letter she said was dictated by the president, which read in part, "I trust that all true friends of the Treaty will refuse to support the Lodge resolution."[21] It would have to be simply yes or no. On November 19, 1919, the Senate finally voted. First up was the ratification of the treaty with Lodge reservations. Having been told their chief steadfastly opposed this version, senators loyal to the administration voted against it. The vote was 39–55. All but four Democrats voted no, along with fifteen irreconcilables.[22] Next came the vote Woodrow had been waiting for: the treaty without reservations, the treaty he had hammered out in Paris with his own two hands. The vote was 38–53. Only one Republican voted yes. The treaty was defeated. Woodrow had gambled and lost. Longworth and other Republicans were jubilant and amazed the president had so badly botched his strategy. "Thanks to President Wilson, his followers in the Senate never wavered. They persisted in their refusal, in Mr. Wilson's refusal, to vote for the Versailles Treaty with the Lodge reservations, and so the Wilson Democrats and the irreconcilables saved the country from the League of Nations."[23]

When word of the loss arrived from the Capitol, Edith almost crumbled. How would she tell him? This was all he had fought for, what he had given his health and maybe his life for. If the treaty was dead, what motivation would he have to live on? Was she about to give him news that would kill him—if not on the spot, then slowly over the next months of depression and defeat? She steeled herself, then went to his bedside. Quietly she told him the terrible news. "For a few moments he was silent, and then he said: 'All the more reason I must get well and try again to bring this country to a sense of its great opportunity and greater responsibility.'"[24] The news had not done him in after all. But neither had it made him more open to compromise. The Senate never would ratify the Treaty of Versailles. When the League of Nations convened in 1920, the United States did not participate.

Despite its outsize importance to the White House, the treaty was not the only matter before the government in the fall and winter of 1919. Some legislation Edith simply ignored. Fully twenty-eight bills became law that session without the president's signature, since he didn't respond within the constitutionally required ten days.[25] That was fine when Woodrow would have supported the matters anyway. But then Congress passed the Volstead Act, a law meant to define and enforce Prohibition as set out by the Eighteenth Amendment. The president had told Joe

Tumulty more than once that it was "the wrong way of doing the right thing. You cannot regulate the morals and habits of a great cosmopolitan people by placing unreasonable restrictions upon their liberty and free-dom."[26] But he was in no shape to draft a statement, let alone deliver one. With Edith's approval, Joe wrote up a message supposedly from the president, explaining he was vetoing the Volstead Act, and why. They ran the draft by David Houston, the secretary of agriculture, and sent it on to Congress. Congress overrode the veto within hours. It's not clear whether Woodrow ever knew it had happened at all.[27]

Then there was that charade with the kidnapping of William Jen-kins in Mexico, which handed hostile Senators an excuse to come sniffing around. Edith and the others had pulled off that miracle visit when the "smelling committee" came calling, and knocked Senator Fall off his presidential-incapacity soapbox. But someone else was sure to demand a visit soon. Not everyone was satisfied with her insistence that she would convey their priorities to the president. They were right to suspect that many issues were not ever brought before Woodrow, and some were ignored entirely. As Edith wrote to Mrs. House, "we keep everything from him (which it is not important to have his advice about and which would annoy or distress him)."[28] Edith had not, for instance, mentioned to Woodrow that Colonel House, once his very closest adviser, had left Paris and was back in the States. House was appalled. He wrote to Edith, "The fact that you have not told him of my return indicates that he is either much sicker than I had thought, or that he laid more stress upon my remaining abroad than seemed to me possible."[29] Edith ignored him. Several of House's letters were among a pile of 1919 presidential correspondence sent to the Library of Congress in 1952. They were unopened.[30]

One of the more persistent callers was Sir Edward Grey, a British statesman who had been sent to Washington to advise in the treaty-ratification battle. His diplomatic priorities were twofold: to counter the American impression that Great Britain's role in the peace process had been selfish and greedy; and to do all he could to encourage the U.S. to join the League of Nations. He was a man Woodrow respected professionally and personally. He was also almost entirely blind. As a widower who lived alone, he was particularly dependent on ambassadorial staff to help him navigate unfamiliar settings. Generally, a new ambassador presents his credentials to the president in person. But Grey had arrived in the U.S. just as Woodrow collapsed and all official activity was suspended. It became clear that Grey would not be able to meet with the president for weeks, maybe even months.

Then came word from the State Department that the delay in recognizing Grey was not entirely because of Woodrow's illness. Apparently the president objected to one of Grey's staff members, Major Charles Kennedy Craufurd-Stuart. This man had served in the British embassy in Washington previously, and Grey had brought him back. But now the president insisted: if Grey wanted to serve as ambassador, he must send Craufurd-Stuart home.

Of course, the president was bedridden. He was being kept away from matters that were much more crucial than the staffing of one embassy. This seemed strangely personal and small-minded. What was the big problem with Craufurd-Stuart? He was a well-known bachelor about town, considered somewhat dashing and romantic. He was also a bit of a blowhard—the kind of dinner guest who tells vaguely insulting, slightly naughty jokes, sometimes at his hosts' expense. In 1918, he openly criticized Woodrow's mission to Paris, and particularly his decision to bring Edith with him. He insinuated that middle-class Edith wanted to hobnob with royalty for her own social gain. And at more than one party he cracked the same racy joke: "What did Edith Wilson say when the president proposed? She was so surprised, she fell out of bed."

In several retellings of what became known as the Craufurd-Stuart affair, Edith is cast as petty and thin-skinned, willing to thwart an important diplomatic partner for the sake of a personal grudge against his aide. She looks like she took advantage of her power to settle a personal score. And she probably did. But she was not the only person close to the president who had reason to despise Craufurd-Stuart. Bernard Baruch also wanted the man sent back across the ocean, and for reasons much more complicated than a boorish quip. Craufurd-Stuart dabbled in intelligence gathering, keeping tabs on Washington gossip and its implications for international security. The U.S. head of British intelligence was concerned about sensitive information leaking to Germany and asked Craufurd-Stuart to see what he could dig up. Craufurd-Stuart became convinced Bernard Baruch was the leak. Baruch had been romantically involved with a woman named Olive Moore, who then had an affair with the German ambassador. That alone made Baruch suspect. He next began a relationship with May Ladenburg, a rich and glamorous hostess whose father was German. That, along with a healthy dose of anti-Semitism, was enough to convince Craufurd-Stuart that Baruch was feeding secret information to his girlfriend, who was passing it on to the Germans.

What happened next has all the absurdity of a farce. British intelligence enlisted Alice Roosevelt Longworth, who had been to parties at May Ladenburg's house, to tell them where to plant listening devices that might catch the lovers in an unguarded moment. Longworth happily did so, excited at the chance to "look over transoms and peep through keyholes. Could anything be more delightful than that?"[31]

Her cousin Franklin Roosevelt, assistant secretary of the navy, prepared reports of fake naval maneuvers so they could feed Baruch false information and track any leak. It was all nonsense. The recordings of that night do not survive, but no charges were ever considered against Baruch or Ladenburg. In trying to clear his name, Baruch became mortified by the whole episode. He used his influence with the press to downplay the espionage angle and paint the blackballing of Craufurd-Stuart as being all about Edith's inability to forget a slight.[32]

Regardless, Edward Grey did not want to get rid of Craufurd-Stuart. He depended on his aide to navigate Washington for him. Plus, Craufurd-Stuart was about to marry an American woman. Sending him home in disgrace would end his career and his engagement. Grey transferred him from the embassy staff to his personal staff. It wasn't enough; the White House wanted him gone. Finally Grey withdrew his name from the diplomatic rolls and sailed back to England himself. He never did meet with the president or anyone else in the White House. Did Edith and Baruch's petty grudge have international historical repercussions? Had he been able to do his job, would Grey have convinced Woodrow to compromise on the treaty to ensure U.S. involvement in the League of Nations? The columnists at *Town Topics* thought so. "Had Woodrow Wilson consented to see Lord Grey, for a few minutes," the paper speculated, then corrected, "or rather, had Admiral Grayson, Private Secretary Joe Tumulty, and Mrs. Wilson, the triumvirate controlling all access to our Chief Magistrate" allowed Grey access, "the deadlock in the Senate . . . would have ended weeks and weeks ago."[33] After he returned to England, Grey published a letter to the editor of the London *Times*. He reaffirmed that he thought U.S. participation in the league was essential, and that Britain, for one, was open to American ratification of the treaty with the Lodge reservations. This undermined a major reason Woodrow gave for rejecting Lodge—he insisted that the other signatories to the treaty would never accept changes made after the fact.

More so than any legislative action Edith took during Woodrow's illness, her decision to keep him in total isolation had the most impact on his presidency. He never heard bad news, never met with advisers who contradicted his opinions. He completely lost touch with the mood of the voters. On the other hand, even before his stroke Woodrow was given to self-righteous confidence in his own moral superiority. He loved playing the martyr. In all likelihood, a frank conversation with Grey would have made little difference to the president. He had dug his heels in deep over the notion of no reservations. When Edith read Grey's London *Times* letter to him, he was absolutely incensed. At Woodrow's urging, Edith dashed off a furious note insisting that "had Lord Grey ventured upon any such an utterance while he was still at Washington as ambassador . . . his government would have been promptly asked to withdraw him."[34]

AS 1920 BEGAN, Woodrow's physical strength improved a little. He was able to leave his bed and sit up in the Atlantic City rolling chair for a few hours every day. Usher Ike Hoover, who had once been responsible for making sure the president had time for several impossible tasks before breakfast, described his new routine with pity. He was "taken from his bed about ten o'clock, placed in the chair, and rolled to the south grounds; or, in bad weather, to the porch or to some other room. The last year of his stay saw him in the East Room every day at twelve o'clock to look at a motion picture. We scoured the country that he might have a different picture each day. He would return to his bedroom at one o'clock, have his lunch, and be placed back in bed, where he would remain until the next morning."[35] His stamina slowly improved, but those around him felt his moods deteriorated. "His temper was the worse for the defeat he had suffered and the illness he was undergoing," said Agent Starling. "Frequently he was irascible, and we had trouble evading his unreasonable orders without embarrassment."[36] Woodrow had now been isolated for over three months. Any disturbing news or critical opinions had been scrupulously kept from him. Add a short temper and constant self-involvement, and you have a man who is almost delusional in his worldview. He remained convinced that the American people were desperate for a League of Nations and were just waiting for the chance to contradict their shortsighted senators. He went so far as to ask his advisers to compile a list of the men who opposed the treaty. Then he worked with Joe to draft a remarkable statement: "I challenge the following named gentlemen, members of the Senate of the United States, to resign their seats in that body and take immediate steps to seek re-election to it on the basis of their several records with regards to the ratification of the treaty. For myself, I promise and engage if all of them or a majority of them are re-elected, I will resign the Presidency."[37] It was an irrational, even self-destructive plan. If it had been made public, surely new rumors about the president's mental fitness would have been the immediate and understandable result. Edith and Joe had to work to convince him not to release it to the public.

But they were unable to completely contain his grandiose instincts for the presidential statement to the annual Jackson Day dinner. They managed to keep the idea of an actual referendum out of the final draft. But the president could not resist a chance to reiterate the importance of ratifying the treaty with no amendments. He also suggested

188 ✦ UNTOLD POWER

the 1920 election should take "the form of a great and solemn referendum by the voters of the country in this great matter."[38] He did not, would
not, recognize that if the election were a referendum on the league, he
would lose. Alice Longworth spoke for many Republicans when she
claimed, "We welcomed the League in the campaign as a fighting issue, and a winning one."[39]

The treaty and the league seemed to be the only issues that held the
president's attention, but they certainly weren't the only ones facing the
nation. Cabinet secretaries started to resign. Treasury Secretary McAdoo
had returned to the private sector after the armistice was signed and was
replaced by Carter Glass. Now Glass wanted to leave to take over a vacant senate seat in Virginia. Edith summoned Secretary of Agriculture
David Houston to tea and asked him to move to Treasury. Loyal Houston answered, "I am in the harness until March 4, 1921, if he wishes it,
and as long as I am with him, I will dig stumps, or act as Secretary of the
Treasury, or assume any other task he assigns me."[40] That left the Department of Agriculture open. A week later, after basically no vetting or
interest from the White House, the post was filled by a forgettable publisher named Edwin Meredith. Then Franklin Lane at Interior began
letting his restlessness show. He had been hoping to resign for months
but waited to see how Woodrow's illness would play out. Lamenting that
"the President is broken in body, and obstinate in spirit,"[41] Lane resigned
in February. He was replaced by Judge John Payne.

And Robert Lansing was still secretary of state. He was miserable.
He, more than any other member of the cabinet, was appalled at the
silence from the White House and the conspiracy to pretend that
Woodrow was a fully functioning president. For months, he kept a
draft of his resignation letter handy, ready for the first excuse to call it
quits. "Mr. Lansing should have retired long before," Edith believed.

"In Paris he had been a hindrance rather than a help. The same situation continued after we reached home and my husband was expending the last ounces of his strength for the Treaty. As soon as the President became ill, Mr. Lansing started agitation to put his Chief out of office."[42] Lansing made no secret of the fact that he thought Woodrow should step down. But when it became clear that would never happen, Lansing convened other cabinet members somewhat regularly, in an attempt to meet at least the basic requirements of the executive branch. In early February 1920, the president abruptly asked for that long-cherished resignation letter. His excuse was that no one but the president has the right to call cabinet meetings. Lansing pointed out that since the secretaries were denied access to the president for months, waiting for his participation would have crippled their departments. Wilson's return letter included the circular logic that "no action could be taken without me by the Cabinet" and therefore there should be no problem "awaiting action with regard to matters concerning which action could not have been taken without me."[43] Lansing gleefully tendered his resignation and called himself lucky. Edith pushed her husband to issue a statement explaining all the many reasons Lansing had to go. She was worried if the press discussed only who had the right to hold the recent cabinet meetings, Woodrow would come off as a petty tyrant. She was right. The *Los Angeles Times* called Lansing's firing "Wilson's last mad act."[44] *The New York Times* pointed out the obvious flaw in the president's position: "If Congress had accepted the theory which Mr. Wilson now propounds, that the cabinet could do nothing without his presence, and consequently that Government business was at a standstill,"[45] the paper explained, then Congress should have invoked Article II, section 1, and determined whether he was able to discharge the powers and duties of the office. Bainbridge

Colby, a lawyer with no diplomatic experience but unquestioned loyalty to the president, became the new secretary of state. No one was more surprised than he was at his own nomination.[46]

There was one cabinet member who didn't want to leave. He was enjoying the power he wielded with little presidential oversight. At the beginning of 1920, Mitchell Palmer had been attorney general for less than a year, but he was already considering a presidential run. He figured he had a winning issue in national security.[47] Taking advantage of wartime sedition laws, Palmer investigated anyone remotely associated with anarchy, communism, socialism, labor unions, or anything that could be even slightly construed as anti-American and unpatriotic. Enlisting the help of a very young J. Edgar Hoover, Palmer organized a series of raids on the homes and meeting places of suspected subversives. The largest of these, encompassing over forty cities nationwide, began on January 2, 1920. Hundreds were arrested without warrants and deported without hearings. Not only were many Americans' civil rights trampled that night, but the (largely fictional) red scare Palmer ginned up empowered months of anti-immigrant vigilantism. There is no evidence the president had prior knowledge of this massive abuse of power within his own cabinet.[48]

Almost six months had passed since the president had been seen in public. Everyone in Washington knew that all official business was going through Edith. Now the rest of the world was beginning to grasp the scope of her influence. After Lansing's very public resignation, London's *Daily Mail* reported, "Nothing more startling has been disclosed in this week of endless sensations at Washington than the fact that the wife of President Wilson has for months been acting President of the United States."[49] In Canton, Ohio, the *Daily News* disclosed, "One of the foremost statesmen in Washington is a woman—Mrs.

Woodrow Wilson, wife of the President of the United States."[50] Reports like these were echoed in many other papers. Not all of them were critical of Edith's power. In fact, some were downright admiring. The Baltimore *Star* claimed she deserved "nothing but the greatest deference and admiration as 'Mrs. Wilson, the acting President.'" Of course, it was Edith's modesty and self-effacement the paper admired; they certainly weren't advocating for ambitious political women to take charge. "The idea of a President Jane Addams or a President Carrie Chapman Catt is as annoying as it is ridiculous," the article sniffed.[51] But other journalists were starting to lose their patience. "The limit of our endurance has been reached," declared *Town Topics*. "The position in which we are placed by Woodrow Wilson is too costly, too embarrassing, too humiliating to last any longer. Either his convalescence is stationary or retrogressive, and in either of these contingencies he should delegate his duties and his authority to Vice President Marshall or else resign. . . . If Woodrow Wilson is no longer ill enough to incapacitate him from work, then let him show himself."[52]

Edith had not for one second relaxed her control of access to her husband. But now it became clear that he had to be seen outside of the confines of his bedroom. The only way the public and the press would accept this "Madam President" insinuation was if it was seen as distinctly temporary. Warmer spring weather coincided with some improvement in the president's mobility. By April he could even walk a few steps with a cane. On nice days his rolling chair was set on the South Lawn, where the flock of sheep still grazed. His favorite companion was two-year-old Gordon Grayson, Cary and Altrude's son, who would perch himself on the chair's footrest and chatter away about anything but the League of Nations. Eventually, Edith decided it was time to try an automobile ride, which Woodrow had always enjoyed before the stroke. They found a cape-style coat that would not require him to thread his useless left arm through a sleeve. The Secret Service built a platform that allowed the chair to roll up to the same level as the car door. "Then the President would stand," explained Agent Starling, "and we would lift him into the car and place him in the right hand corner, arranging his cape and adjusting his cap, so that when he appeared on the streets there was no indication that anything was wrong with him."[53] They resumed driving the same old routes, passing the same landmarks and waving to the same people. But Woodrow fixated on odd things. "He got the idea that no automobiles should pass us while we were driving," explained a bewildered Starling, "despite the fact that we proceeded at a very moderate rate of speed, frequently going at fifteen or twenty miles an hour so he could enjoy the scenery. Whenever a car passed us he would order the Secret Service to pursue it and bring back the driver for questioning."[54] The agents would always claim that the offending car was speeding too fast to be overtaken. The last time he had been out in public, the president had been greeted by thousands of cheering Americans. Now, pathetically, the Secret Service gathered whoever was on hand to stand at the gate as the presidential car returned. "The White House staff would go out and cheer him when he would return from his ride," remembered seamstress Lillian Rogers Parks, daughter of the White House housekeeper. "Mama would come home and cry about that. The First Lady would cry a little too when he would say to her, 'You see, I'm not too unpopular.'"[55]

Not only did Woodrow continue to believe he had the hearts of the American people, but he did not seem to think his illness had hindered his ability to govern. Edith constantly told him how wise and brave he was. Since all bad news was kept from him, he did not see the nation's growing displeasure with Wilsonian democracy. When setbacks could not be reasonably hidden, as with the defeat of the treaty, the president would always fault others. There had been a final, last-ditch vote on the treaty March 19. It failed again—the final nail in the monthslong coffin. Woodrow blamed the Senate. "They have shamed us in the eyes of the world," he told Joe.[56]

The only person in his inner circle who described Woodrow as having even a moment of self-doubt was Cary Grayson. In mid-April, Cary recalled, the president confided in his doctor and friend. "I am seriously thinking what is my duty to the country on account of my physical condition," Woodrow told him. "My personal pride must not be allowed to stand in the way of my duty to the country. If I am only half efficient I should turn the office over to the Vice-President. If it is going to take much time for me to recover my health and strength, the country cannot afford to wait for me."[57] Instead of telling his patient that his recovery might still take months, if it ever came at all, Cary suggested a cabinet meeting. "I said, "If you will call a Cabinet meeting and come in contact with your advisors in a body . . . you can then determine just what your leadership represents. If you will do this I am confident that you will find that you are accomplishing more than you realize; and it will reassure you of your ability to continue to handle the situation."[58] Edith agreed. If they could stage it right and limit the duration, a cabinet meeting might be just the thing to improve the president's outlook.

The meeting was called for April 14. The president had not attended a cabinet meeting since August.[59] They met in a White House study, not the cabinet room. The president, freshly shaved and dressed, was already propped up in a chair when his secretaries entered the room. The new members of the cabinet, who didn't know their boss very well, thought the president looked in decent form. But the veteran members noticed the changes. The president did not ever rise from his chair. Usher Ike Hoover loudly announced each of their names as they entered, something that had never happened before. Josephus Daniels worried this meant the president was now completely blind. David Houston looked on his friend with pity. "One of his arms was useless. In repose, his face looked very much as usual, but, when he tried to speak, there were marked evidences of his trouble. His jaw tended to drop on one side, or seemed to do so. His voice was very weak and strained."[60] Several secretaries worried the president was having trouble following the discussion. It was clear it was his first time hearing about some of the issues discussed. But when Cary poked his head into the room an hour later to check on his patient, Woodrow shook him off, unwilling to adjourn. Cary tried again fifteen minutes later. The president dismissed him again. Finally Cary returned with backup, in the form of Edith. With a hint of reprimand she said, "This is an experiment, you know."[61] The meeting was adjourned.

This effort to invigorate Woodrow and convince him of his relevance might have been somewhat too successful, for, astonishingly, the president now began to talk about running for a third term. In early June, the Republicans nominated Ohio senator Warren Harding. The Democratic convention was set for late June in San Francisco, and the field of candidates was taking shape. There was Mitchell Palmer, milking his red-menace agenda. William McAdoo, long considered the president's heir apparent, believed his moment had finally come. And Ohio governor James Cox, a mild-mannered progressive, built support as a safe alternative to the more controversial candidates. Each of these men asked the president to endorse him, or at least to announce he wasn't running himself.

Woodrow didn't want to do either of those things. Joe, who did not want to see his beloved chief humiliated, sent Edith a letter suggesting it was time for the president to make a conclusive statement that he wasn't running. His message could be gracious and statesmanlike, and he could devote the rest of his career to seeking world peace without any political gain of his own. Edith showed the letter to her husband. He brought the matter up with Cary. He didn't want to withdraw. At first he tried to make it a question of manners. "I feel it would be presumptuous and in bad taste for me to decline something that has not been offered to me," he told Cary. But that was not the whole truth. It turned out the president harbored a secret fantasy that the convention would be hopeless and he could ride in as the great savior of the party. "The Convention may come to a deadlock as to candidates, and there may be practically a universal demand for the election of someone to lead them out of the wilderness," Woodrow imagined. "The members of the Convention may feel that I am the logical one to lead—perhaps the only one to champion this cause. In such circumstances I would feel obliged to accept the nomination even if I thought it would cost me my life."[62] The president so treasured this image of himself as the great martyr, Cary didn't have the heart to burst his bubble. "For medical reasons, I preferred not to volunteer any advice. I did not want to tell him that it would be impossible for him to take part in such a campaign, as I was fearful that it might have a depressing effect upon him."[63]

Edith, too, indulged this delusion. In mid-June, Edith agreed to let the president be interviewed for the New York *World*. The reporter was Louis Seibold, a friendly journalist who had covered the disastrous train trip and promised a flattering report. Joe worked out some questions with Seibold in advance, including some that would draw the president into saying unequivocally he was not running for a third term. Edith quickly vetoed that plan. There would be no questions about the election, she insisted in a note to Joe. He conceded, but when he filed Edith's note away, he first wrote across it that in his opinion she could go straight to hell.[64]

No one wanted to tell the president that a third term was impossible. The topic would occasionally come up in cabinet meetings, and no one had the guts to shoot it down. Ike Hoover watched this play out with disgust. "There was not a member of that cabinet present who did not know that it would be an impossibility, physically, mentally, and morally, even to harbor such a thought, and yet there were some who did encourage it. Whether they did it for sentiment, charity, or really expected to put such a thing over on the Convention, only they can answer. It was really sad how they deceived him."[65] Inevitably, Woodrow began to believe he was the true choice of the people. No one told him otherwise. Cary now became seriously worried that his patient would actually start campaigning. Still unwilling to challenge Woodrow's ambition to his face, the doctor sought a back channel with Robert Woolley, the publicist who had helped stage the "smelling committee" drama. "He just must not be nominated," the doctor insisted to Woolley. "No matter what others may tell you, no matter what you may read about the President being on the road to recovery, I tell you that he is permanently ill physically, is gradually weakening mentally and can't recover. He couldn't possibly survive the campaign."[66] Woolley assured him the convention would never nominate the president. But Cary wasn't convinced. He and Joe sought the confidence of Carter Glass, who was about to catch a train to San Francisco. "If anything comes up," they begged him, "save the life and fame of this great man from the juggling of false friends."[67]

Joe, in particular, knew this was not a hypothetical fear. Bainbridge Colby, the new and very eager secretary of state, planned to place

Woodrow's name in nomination if the convention deadlocked. Joe hoped with all his strength matters would not come to that point. But they did. Day after day of balloting failed to produce a nominee. Colby wired the White House a coded message: "I propose, unless otherwise definitely instructed, to take advantage of the first moment to move suspension of rules and place your name in nomination."[68] Edith wired back that the president agreed. He would be nominated for a third term. She would not be the one to stop it.

Finally, the president's allies stepped in. Carter Glass, Albert Burleson, Newton Baker, Josephus Daniels, Vance McCormick, Senator Joseph Robinson, Congressman Cordell Hull, and Homer Cummings, chair of the Democratic National Committee, summoned Colby to a hotel room and let him have it. He had no right to send that message to the White House, they insisted. He was digging the president's grave. If the president were to be nominated, he would die campaigning. If he lost, he would die humiliated. Furthermore, if any of the men in that room for one second believed Woodrow Wilson to be an appropriate candidate for the 1920 election, they would not have needed a rookie like Colby to engineer the nomination. Colby was cowed. "I felt like a criminal," he admitted.[69] He sent a sheepish second telegram to the White House. Humbly he apologized for his overeagerness. He had been wrong to think there was sufficient support at the convention for a third Wilson term. The president's name would be withdrawn. On the forty-fourth ballot, the convention nominated James Cox. He chose Assistant Navy Secretary Franklin Roosevelt as his running mate.

Woodrow was despondent. His treaty was dead, the league was convening without him, and now his Democratic Party had moved on. Cox and Roosevelt made a brief visit to the White House to pay their respects. Cox assured the president that he would continue to fight for the ratification of the League of Nations. Still cocooned in his echo chamber, Woodrow was confident this agenda would ensure a Cox victory in November. He was the only one. "I doubt any intelligent citizen from Maine to California had a doubt as to the result," wrote Dolly Gann in her diary.[70] Warren Harding won in a landslide, carrying thirty-seven states and 61 percent of the popular vote. Republicans posted big majorities in the House and Senate. After years of war and sacrifice, Americans wanted what Harding promised: a "Return to Normalcy."

Edith craved a return to something like normalcy herself. She had done it—she had pulled off an astonishing conspiracy for over a year. And it looked like she would get away with it. The president was now the lamest of lame ducks. No one would expect much of anything from either of them in the four months until Harding's inauguration. Her grueling time as her husband's proxy had taken its toll, and she was ready to leave the spotlight. She had her portrait painted one more time, this time by Seymour Stone. She wears a black velvet gown with a daringly sheer neckline. The Lalique peace brooch adorns her waist. She looks content.* She had spent years imagining their life after the White House. In none of those daydreams had Woodrow been an invalid. But she knew she would figure out what came next. She always did.

---

* Edith actually disliked this flattering portrait, believing it made her look "too young, too thin, and too authoritative." She much preferred the very feminine official portrait painted in 1916. The original Stone portrait hangs in the Woodrow Wilson House in Washington. A copy of the Müller-Ury portrait hangs there too.

Chapter Nine

AFTER THE WHITE HOUSE

1921–1924

dith and Woodrow had nowhere to live. Edith had sold her Dupont Circle house in 1915. Woodrow hadn't owned a house since he left Princeton for the New Jersey governor's mansion in 1910. As they planned for the life they would begin on March 4, 1921, they realized they were free to move anywhere they liked. Together they sat down and made a chart of their favorite cities: Baltimore, Washington, Richmond, Boston, and New York. They scored each city across six categories: climate, friends, opportunities, freedom, amusements, and libraries. Libraries made the list because Woodrow planned to spend his retirement writing the definitive work on systems of government. Washington scored lowest of all (the zero in the "freedom" category brought the total way down), but they decided to settle there nonetheless. Edith knew more about Woodrow's health than he did—and she continued to tell him how healthy and strong he was.

But in her heart, she knew he would not live long, and she would be a widow for much longer than she would be married. In fact, even though "libraries" appears as a category on their city chart, she never actually factored them into each total. She knew Woodrow's book would never be finished. As it happened, he wrote only one page: the dedication, a glowing tribute to Edith.

And Washington was Edith's home. It had been before she became First Lady and would be for many years after. So after the election, she set about finding the perfect Washington house. They considered building one from scratch but decided it was too expensive. Money was an issue. Edith still owned Galt's, and Wilson had some savings. But they had no regular source of income. At the time, ex-presidents did not receive a pension. Edith knew her husband's future earning potential was not as high as he believed it to be. But then in December 1920, they got some good news: Woodrow was being awarded the 1919 Nobel Peace Prize for his work on the League of Nations. The Nobel Committee had considered his nomination in 1919. But when the treaty failed in the Senate, they deadlocked on whether Woodrow's contribution merited a prize and chose to reserve the 1919 award until the following year. In 1920, a majority of the committee decided to recognize his work, and the prize, along with a nice sum of money, was awarded[1] retroactively. The windfall allowed the Wilsons to consider some pretty tony neighborhoods. Edith enlisted her brother Wilmer, who had become a successful builder, to help find the perfect home.

It wasn't easy. The houses they could afford were often unsuitable in other ways. Some weren't private enough, which was an absolute deal breaker. Even after the presidency, Edith knew she and Woodrow would be a subject of speculation and gossip. They had to be able to protect themselves from prying eyes. Some houses were only sold furnished. With Woodrow's specific medical needs, that would never do. One house Edith loved sat on twenty-six acres across from the Bureau of Standards near Connecticut Avenue and Van Ness Street NW. It checked all her boxes. But with the stubborn fastidiousness he showed at often-inconvenient times, the president refused to buy it. He was convinced the bureau would eventually need to expand, and it would be awkward for the government to negotiate with a former president for the necessary land.[2] Edith was disappointed but knew better than to try to change his mind. The search continued.

One day in December 1920, Edith went to look at two houses on S Street NW in Kalorama, a gracious, wealthy neighborhood about a mile and a half northwest of the White House. Neither property was right for them. But just as Edith was about to leave discouraged, the owner of a house across the street emerged to say he was interested in selling. Sure of another disappointment, Edith reluctantly crossed S Street to make a polite visit. The house was perfect. Well, it was almost perfect. It needed a garage, and a few doorways rearranged. It also needed an elevator, but it had a hand-crank trunk lift, a sort of giant dumbwaiter, that could probably be converted without too much effort.[3] Edith was certain this was the right house.

She went back to the White House and gushed about the S Street house. Designed in the Georgian Revival style by society architect Waddy Butler Wood, it was only five years old and "fitted to the needs of a gentleman's home."[4] She wouldn't quite let herself fall all the way in love with it. She worried the owner had offered to sell on a whim and might rescind his offer just as spontaneously.[5] But Woodrow could tell this was the house Edith really wanted. So without her knowledge, he called Wilmer and asked him to contact the agent, determine the price, and search the house's title. Then he insisted that Edith attend a concert by the New York Philharmonic. Edith was suspicious of her husband's adamance, but she hadn't heard music performed in far too long and consented to attend. When she got back, he handed her the deed to the S Street house. He had purchased it outright while she was out. But he had never seen it, and now Edith panicked that she had overlooked some fatal flaw. They went together to see the house the next day. On the doorstep, Woodrow presented Edith with the key and a small piece of sod, which he claimed was an old Scotch custom.[6]

The house cost $150,000, an astonishing sum in 1920. Woodrow's savings and Nobel Prize money only went so far. It turned out Cary had rallied ten of the president's friends to contribute $10,000 each.[7] Bernard Baruch even bought the lot next door to ensure greater privacy.[8] They would take possession a month before the Hardings turned them out of the White House.

The short deadline made Edith nervous. There was so much to do to make the house ready for an invalid—not to mention finding a place for Woodrow's eight thousand books and the massive Gobelins tapestry. Since he spent so much time in it, the president had become accustomed to the huge Lincoln bed, which measures over eight feet long. This historic artifact remained with the White House, so Edith ordered a duplicate and had it sent to S Street.[9] She arranged to have her own furniture from the old Dupont Circle house retrieved from storage. Some Wilson family pieces were unearthed from a warehouse in Princeton, where they had sat unused for ten years. Edith had a huge to-do list, and the clock was ticking on her time to get it all accomplished.

Meanwhile, she continued to present a serene air to her husband, although it cost her. "Not the least difficult of my responsibilities during these days of stress," she wrote later, was having to "maintain about

my husband the atmosphere of calm essential to his physical condition."[10] She got in the habit of staying with him until he fell asleep,
then heading to the S Street house after ten, moving furniture and
directing servants until two or three in the morning.[11] With just two
days left before the inauguration, she had to admit the house just
wouldn't be ready. There were no rugs on the floors, no pictures on the
walls, and the installation of the elevator had left dust and construction debris everywhere. She decided to concentrate on making the
bedrooms as comfortable as possible. She planned to take a few of
Woodrow's personal items over to the new house so they would be all
set up for him from the first day. But usher Ike Hoover stepped in with
a suggestion: the president could keep his White House bedroom just
as he liked it until Inauguration Day. Then, while the Wilsons were at
the Capitol watching Warren Harding take the oath of office, Hoover
would rush all of Woodrow's things over to Kalorama and set them up
exactly the same way. The Hardings would never know. Edith was
touched by the offer and accepted, knowing that "in this way my husband would at once feel at home and would not be inconvenienced on
his last night in the White House by the deprivation of the small things
that make for the comfort of an invalid."[12] She knew he would never
get better. She must have known it for some time. The best she could
hope for was to keep him as happy as possible for as long as she could.
That would be her only goal until the day he died. After seventeen
months of trying to accomplish that goal while also keeping the federal government running, it sounded like a vacation.

Finally March 4 arrived. Edith and Woodrow woke early and
dressed carefully. They bade the White House staff goodbye, then
went to the Blue Room to greet the president-elect. Edith found Warren and Florence Harding vulgar. He swung his leg over the arm of a

chair when he sat. She was "highly rouged" and "so voluble" that Edith
could "hardly stem the torrent of words."[13] Everyone was eager to skip
the pleasantries and get to the business of the day. The men climbed in
a car to drive to the Capitol. Their wives followed in another car. As
Florence Harding "called out in hearty tones"[14] to the crowds lining
the streets, Edith sat silent, hiding her expression behind a fur stole.
This was her last official public duty, and she would just have to grit
her teeth until it was over.

Traditionally, the outgoing and incoming presidents climb the Capitol steps together. But this feat was absolutely impossible for one of
them. When the cars slowed at the bottom of the steps, only Warren
Harding alighted and bounded up the stairs to his future. Woodrow,
now alone in the back seat, was driven to a hidden lower entrance
where he could take an elevator to the chamber. One car behind, Edith
watched this scene play out in silent fury. When the women's car
stopped, "Mrs. Harding fairly raced up the steps. How I longed to follow the lonely figure just making his painful way through the lower
entrance! But I knew he would want me to play the game. With a heart
hot within me, I followed Mrs. Harding."[15] Once inside, Edith found
Woodrow performing his final act as president, signing last-minute
legislation. Traditionally, the chairman of the Senate Foreign Relations
Committee then informs the outgoing president that Congress is ready
to adjourn. So in one final humiliation, the very last person to speak
to Woodrow Wilson as president was Henry Cabot Lodge. It was almost more than Edith could bear. But bear it she must. And then it
was done.

Edith and Woodrow, along with the ever-present Cary and Joe,
drove straight to S Street to begin their new chapter. Edith spent the
whole drive fuming about the indignities of the morning. Her husband

just laughed. "Where I was bitter, he was tolerant; where I resented, he was amused; and by the time we reached the corner of Massachusetts Avenue where we turned into S Street we were both happy and felt a great burden had been lifted from our shoulders and that we could return to our own affairs in a home of peace and serenity."[16]

At least, Edith aspired to peaceful and serene. She wasn't at all sure what state the house would actually be in. But they opened the door to a miracle: Edith's brother Wilmer, with help from their brother Randolph, Margaret Wilson, and the new household staff, had stayed up all night to make the house perfect. Not a book or rug was out of place. Curtains hung from every window and pictures from every wall. The rooms were filled with fresh flowers. And lunch was ready in the dining room. Edith could finally exhale.

Freed from the requirements of the White House, Edith built an inner circle at S Street that served her needs and those of her invalid husband. Her brother Randolph signed on as personal secretary. He ruled a ground-floor office from which he parsed the daily mail, answered what needed answering, and carefully filed the rest away. For the couple's personal needs, Edith hired Isaac and Mary Scott, who had worked for Norman Galt's father.[17] The couple, whom Edith described as "the best of the old-time colored Virginia stock,"[18] initially lived at S Street, although they moved to their own home after Woodrow's death. There was also a driver, a nurse, a cook, and initially, a guard. No president had retired in Washington before, and Edith wasn't sure what level of security they would need. But before long, the guard was dismissed. It was clear their quiet life on S Street would suffer few interruptions.

Edith again surrounded herself with family. There was Randolph, of course, right there in the house. Gertrude and Hunter Galt still lived in Washington. Brother Wilmer and his wife, Eleanor, lived nearby with their four young children. Bertha still lived with Mrs. Bolling at the Powhatan Hotel. Youngest brother Julian still worked at Galt's. And though they were all grown and needed her less acutely, Edith enjoyed being back in the Bolling family circle. Meanwhile, the Wilsons were scattering. Washington was never their home. Nell and William McAdoo and their two little girls moved to California, from where Mac hoped to launch a 1924 presidential bid. Margaret lived mainly in New York, where she continued to pursue a singing career. And Jessie and Frank Sayre, with their three children, moved halfway around the world. Frank accepted a post in Bangkok to serve as an adviser on international law. Even loyal Helen Bones fled the capital for Manhattan, taking a job in publishing.

But Cary Grayson was still in town. President Harding graciously arranged to have Cary's naval assignment transferred from the White House to the U.S. Naval Dispensary so he could stay in Washington and continue to tend to Woodrow. Cary and Altrude had two more sons in quick succession after little Gordon. In 1920 they bought the Highlands, a grand house on Wisconsin Avenue (now the administration building of the Sidwell Friends School). Cary came to S Street almost every day and remained both physician and confidant to his ailing mentor.

But Cary's visits were the exception. Not many people saw Woodrow Wilson most days. This man who maintained a lifelong suspicion of anything novel quickly developed a rigid daily routine at S Street. The couple would eat breakfast together and read the papers. Then Woodrow would go through the mail with Randolph and take his doctor-prescribed walk back and forth across the hall. Isaac Scott would help give him his shave (this was a slow process with Woodrow's

Edith Bolling, age three, in
Wytheville, Virginia. *(Edith Bolling
Wilson Birthplace Museum)*

WILLIAM HOLCOMBE BOLLING, 1839-1899
Father of Mrs. Woodrow Wilson. From a daguerreotype.

SALLIE WHITE BOLLING, 1843-1925
Mother of Mrs. Woodrow Wilson. From a daguerreotype.

Edith's father, William Bolling, was a respected judge and
popular speaker. Her mother, Sallie Bolling, was timid and deferential.
(University of Virginia Special Collections)

Edith described her
Grandmother Bolling
as "a tiny lady who sat
enthroned on a dog-skin."
*(Edith Bolling Wilson
Birthplace Museum)*

The Bolling family lived in a series of cramped rooms above three storefronts on Wytheville's
Main Street, in the foothills of the Appalachian Mountains. *(photograph by the author)*

Edith at fifteen, with the hated canaries on the back
porch in Wytheville. *(Library of Congress)*

Edith at nineteen,
embarking on a new
life in Washington, DC.
(Library of Congress)

Edith was known for tooling around town in her electric car. She claimed to be the first woman in Washington, DC, to get a driver's license in 1904. *(Library of Congress)*

After the death of her first husband, Norman Galt, Edith inherited his venerable family jewelry store, Galt & Bro. *(Library of Congress)*

Edith as a young widow of
means in Washington, DC,
1913. (*Library of Congress*)

The Wilson family in 1911, before Woodrow entered politics. From left: Margaret, Ellen,
Eleanor (Nell), Jessie, and Woodrow. (*National Portrait Gallery, Smithsonian Institution*)

FOR PRESIDENT FOR VICE-PRESIDENT

WOODROW WILSON THOMAS R. MARSHALL

A 1912 campaign poster for the Democratic ticket of Wilson and Marshall. The two men had never met before becoming running mates. *(Library of Congress)*

Alice Gertrude ("Altrude") Gordon Grayson was Edith's closest friend in Washington. *(Library of Congress)*

Cary Grayson was Edith's friend and Woodrow's physician when he engineered their meeting in 1915. *(Library of Congress)*

The president's cousin Helen Bones, physician Cary Grayson, and daughter Nell Wilson enjoy a horse show in 1913. Helen befriended Edith before introducing her to Woodrow. *(Library of Congress)*

When Woodrow was courting Edith, his secret service agents waited for hours outside her narrow home (the left half of this duplex) on Twentieth Street. The couple married in the house in 1915. *(Library of Congress)*

PHOTO COPYRIGHT, 1915, BY AMERICAN PRESS ASSOCIATION...

When the president announced his engagement to Edith Galt in 1915, the American Press Association created this collage of the sweethearts. *(Library of Congress)*

Edith Bolling Galt's official
engagement photo, 1915.
(Library of Congress)

Edith was ambivalent about Woodrow's decision to seek reelection in 1916, but enthusiastically accompanied him on the campaign trail. *(National Portrait Gallery, Smithsonian Institution. Gift of Aileen Conkey)*

A 1916 portrait of first lady Edith Wilson, age forty-three. This was her favorite of her official portraits. *(Portrait by Adolfo Müller-Ury. White House Historical Association)*

When the president sailed to France to negotiate the peace in 1918, Edith accompanied him everywhere. *(Library of Congress)*

Edith and Woodrow were showered with flowers when
they arrived in Europe in 1918. *(Library of Congress)*

Joseph Tumulty was
the president's secretary,
functioning as his chief of
staff. He was instrumental
in helping Edith keep
the truth of Woodrow's
incapacity secret.
(Library of Congress)

Robert Lansing learned quickly that the president preferred to serve as his own secretary of state. Woodrow fired him in 1920 for holding cabinet meetings in his absence. *(Library of Congress)*

By the spring of 1920, Woodrow was deemed well enough to resume his much-loved car rides. Edith and Cary Grayson kept close watch. *(Library of Congress)*

This photograph accompanied the first newspaper profile of President Wilson after his stroke. Edith had to hold the page steady for his signature. *(Library of Congress)*

A 1920 portrait of first lady Edith Wilson, wearing the Lalique peace dove brooch. Edith thought this painting made her look too young, too thin, and too authoritative. *(Portrait by Seymour Stone. Bruce White for the White House Historical Association/Collection of Woodrow Wilson House)*

Edith and Woodrow were rarely seen in public after leaving the White House.
They greeted crowds from their car on Armistice Day, 1922. *(Library of Congress)*

A 1924 portrait of
Edith, age fifty-one,
recently widowed
for the second time.
(Portrait by Emile Alexay.
National Portrait Gallery,
Smithsonian Institution.
Gift of Dr. Alan Urdang)

When President John F. Kennedy authorized the Woodrow Wilson Memorial Commission in 1961, he gave Edith one of the ceremonial pens. *(Abbie Rowe. White House Photographs. John F. Kennedy Presidential Library and Museum, Boston)*

slack facial muscles and paralyzed arm); then came lunch and a nap. If there were any visitors, they could find the ex-president in his library till late afternoon, when he and Edith went for their daily drive. They traveled the same well-worn roads they always had and returned in time for Woodrow's early dinner, which he ate on a tray in the library. Edith would then read to him until he was sleepy. Isaac Scott got him ready for bed while Edith and Randolph had their own dinner. If they had guests, Edith would always excuse herself to say good night to her husband, then rejoin the dinner party for drinks and billiards. On Saturday nights they went to Keith's theater.[19] The manager there took to setting aside two seats that were easily accessible from a side door so Woodrow would not have to walk very far. It was sometimes the only moment all week when either of them left the house for more than a drive.

But even with their limited expenditures, money was tight. Edith was eager to find a project for her husband. She wanted to see his mind engaged with something, but she wanted it also, she admitted, "for a more material reason, as our expenses were running higher than I had calculated, and there were some unpaid bills."[20] In stepped ex–secretary of state Bainbridge Colby. Since his ill-conceived plan to nominate Woodrow in 1920 was summarily thwarted, eager Colby had been looking for a way to honor his chief. Almost idly, he suggested they build a law practice together. Woodrow had not practiced law since 1883, and he had hated it then. But now the idea of the firm of Wilson and Colby took hold. Edith was all for it. The DC bar duly admitted the former president to its ranks. Two lavish offices were established— one in New York for Colby and one in Washington. Woodrow never expected to be there much but thought he could handle an hour or two a day. Colby didn't care how often his illustrious partner worked. He knew clients would be eager to hire them to negotiate lucrative deals with the federal government.

And they were eager. Case after potential case came through the doors, some offering staggeringly large retainers. Colby was delighted. But Woodrow turned them all down. It was inappropriate, he said, to trade on their former positions to try to influence government contracts and favors. Colby was heartbroken. "Day after day I sit in my office," he told Edith, "and see a procession walk through—thousands and thousands of dollars—and not one to put in our pockets."[21] Woodrow would take only cases that had nothing to do with trading on his reputation. But of course, that was the only reason anyone wanted to hire him. Finally, Edith realized her husband's scruples were preventing Colby from earning a living. At her urging, Woodrow dissolved the partnership and closed the office. He had visited it only once.[22] He earned one $5,000 retainer, which he used to buy Edith a new electric car of her own.

So passed 1921 and 1922. They played endless games of cards, mainly a form of solitaire called Canfield. Sometimes they watched movies in the evening. Edith read detective stories out loud until they made her too jumpy, then switched to Dickens and Walter Scott.[23] They developed a taste for popular magazines, especially ones with rich photography, which Woodrow could peruse even as his eyesight deteriorated. Old friends occasionally came by to visit.

In the spring of 1922, Joe Tumulty, who was still deeply involved in Democratic politics, headed to New York for the National Democratic Club's Jefferson dinner. On the way out of town, he stopped at S Street and asked his old boss to compose a message he could read at the banquet. Woodrow declined, saying he didn't want to break his long public silence with something frivolous, and he wasn't up to writing a more serious message. Joe, disappointed, asked Edith to try to change his mind. She also refused, saying, "You know him well enough to know that when he has thought a thing out and decided it, there is no use to continue argument; and besides, I thoroughly agree with him."[24] Joe went to the dinner without a message from the last Democratic president. But, either caught up in his own importance or unthinking of the consequences, Joe decided to deliver the message he thought Woodrow should have given. The press coverage enraged the scrupulous former president. Not only had he given no message, but the one Tumulty distributed was interpreted as an endorsement of James Cox, the 1920 loser Woodrow would never support again. He wrote to the editor of *The New York Times,* insisting he "did not send any message whatever to that dinner, nor authorize anyone to convey a message."[25] Joe, mortified, tried to smooth the whole thing over with his own letter to the editor. It was just a misunderstanding, he insisted, a casual conversation that was taken as an official endorsement. But Woodrow would not allow Joe to save face this way. He made it clear Joe had gone rogue. Edith, who had never warmed to Joe, would not soften the blow. After ten years of devoted service, Joe became another former friend. He would not see his chief again. After Woodrow's death, William Allen White published one of the first Wilson biographies. Joe Tumulty retold the whole Jefferson dinner affair from his own point of view and even gave White copies of the letters he and Woodrow and Edith exchanged at the time, which White reproduced in full. White was clearly on Joe's side, calling his message "irrelevant and innocuous" and blaming the ailing ex-president for giving "such a bitter, cruel lashing, by public letter, to Tumulty that all Wilson's friends were ashamed beyond words."[26] This version, in turn, incensed Edith. In her memoir fourteen years later, she devoted six full pages to this incident, even citing the page numbers of White's book that contained the most objectionable statements.

So the Wilsons stayed out of politics, at least publicly. The Democrats did well in the 1922 midterm elections, picking up seats in both the Senate and the House, but did not win back the majority in either chamber. Woodrow's old political allies assured him this was just the beginning of a resurgence of support for him and his ideals.

The Wilsons' money problems remained unsolved. Edith decided not to tell her husband how she and Randolph sweated their expenses. She worried he would offer to sacrifice himself, by firing the nurse or some similar martyr's bargain.[27] So when Woodrow began to talk about writing again, Edith was encouraging. First they had to work out the logistics. His grip was too unsteady for longhand. They tried his old typewriter, but the going was just too slow with one useless arm. Dictation was the only solution. He would call out for Edith or Randolph, and they would dutifully record a sentence or two that was rattling around his mind. Edith began to worry that her patient's sleep was suffering—sometimes he would ring his bell for her in the middle of the night to capture a thought he didn't want to lose.[28]

The result, finally, was "The Road Away from Revolution," a simplistic essay that cautioned leaders and capitalists to be more Christlike in their actions in order to avoid angering the masses enough to rebel. Edith sent it to George Creel, who had worked in propaganda during the war and had recently offered to act as Woodrow's agent. Creel was shocked at this shallow attempt from a man who had once been known as a deep thinker. He wrote Edith a tortured letter. The essay was inadequate, he said. Under other circumstances, he would caution strongly against publication. The reaction, he feared, might be ugly. But Creel also understood that rejecting the work outright might crush

Woodrow's fragile spirits. He suggested publishing the essay in *Collier's* magazine, where the editor was sympathetic to the delicate circumstances and had offered $2,000. "Surely you can understand how painful it is for me to have to write this letter," Creel lamented. "It leaves me sick at heart. . . . This letter is for your own eyes, to be torn up instantly, and I enclose herewith another letter for you to show Mr. Wilson."[29] That second letter contained no criticism at all, just the offer from *Collier's*[30] and an endorsement of this modest publication. Edith was worried Woodrow would be insulted by the offer, so she gently tried to explain to him that friends worried the piece was not up to his previous standards. Predictably, he lashed out. He hadn't wanted to write it anyway, he was tired of people bothering him, and he wasn't going to do any more. Then he took to his room in a pout.[31] Edith, exhausted, experienced a very rare moment of public despair. Stockton Axson found her sobbing in the hallway. An English professor himself, Axson took the essay in hand, edited it down to a clear one thousand words, and urged Woodrow to consider publishing it as a challenge to the reader, rather than a lengthy analysis. Woodrow agreed, and they sent it to *The Atlantic Monthly*, which paid $200.[32]

This is yet another history that Edith revised for the purposes of her memoir. In her version, Creel begged for the chance to act as agent and promised to sell the essay to the highest bidder. When the offer came in, which "ran to the thousands," it was with a (unnamed) publication that Woodrow found beneath him. Unwilling to let his name be associated with this inferior outlet, Woodrow refused the offer and asked Creel to return the manuscript. He then sent it to *The Atlantic Monthly*, a magazine "with which he had long and pleasant relations," and happily accepted the more modest fee.[33] Edith even praised the essay itself: "It is remarkable now as an evidence of Mr. Wilson's powers of premonition."[34] This section of her book describes her husband's declining physical state with unflinching detail. But even in an episode as minor as this one, she would not admit Woodrow's mental faculties were not what they once were. The fiction that he was as sharp as ever must still be maintained, even years after his death. But this was the last attempt he made at writing.

Meanwhile, the 1920s were roaring right outside the Wilsons' windows. Washington was still booming, adding 100,000 new residents between 1910 and 1920; 50,000 more would arrive by 1930. Prohibition was now the law of the land, and Washington was meant to be a model dry city. But over three thousand speakeasies flourished in the capital, and congressmen even employed their own bootleggers. In the West End neighborhood, a young piano player named Duke Ellington was making a name for himself, playing a syncopated ragtime of his own composition. Even fancy DC society women cut their hair and raised their hemlines. But most of these trends passed the Wilsons by. Edith traded some of her huge picture hats for the new, close-fitting cloches. She was known to serve alcohol sometimes, but only on the upper, private floors of the house. But she certainly never went to speakeasies or jazz clubs. In 1922, when the Lincoln Memorial was dedicated in front of a prominent crowd, the two seats reserved for Edith and Woodrow remained empty. Neither was able to attend— Woodrow was far too weak, and Edith would not leave him.

One 1920s innovation that did intrigue Edith was the radio. She hoped Woodrow would be captivated by it too. By the summer of 1922, radio was a genuine craze, and its popularity exploded from there.[35] In 1923, the first home radios with loudspeakers were produced, allowing families to all listen together instead of on individual headsets. With her husband's eyesight failing, Edith hoped the radio might provide an alternative to reading. Woodrow, never a fan of novelty, refused to have one installed until April of 1923. That was when the newly formed Woodrow Wilson Foundation bestowed its first award on British diplomat Lord Robert Cecil for his advocacy for the League of Nations. There was no question of Woodrow attending the New York ceremony in person. Edith went as his representative but knew the evening would be full of laudatory speeches that would gratify her pitiful husband, "sitting alone, like a wounded eagle chained to a rock."[36] He consented to have a radio installed at S Street so he could listen to the proceedings from the comfort of his library. Perhaps the broadcast would change his mind about the new technology, Edith thought. She "hoped it would open a new interest in his life, now so circumscribed."[37] Alas, the batteries of the machine failed just as the honoree began his speech. Woodrow never did come around to the pleasures of that "infernal thing."[38]

So it was not the radio but the cries of newspaper boys that brought the shocking news, in August 1923, of the sudden death of President Harding. Rumors swirled about the cause of death, but the truth was no more exotic than a heart attack. Vice President Calvin Coolidge was sworn in to the top job in the middle of the night at his parents' home in rural Vermont and quickly returned to Washington to preside over the funeral.

It was a typical sweltering August day in Washington, but Edith and Woodrow rallied to dress and drive to the White House in an open car. Woodrow could not physically get out of the car, walk into his former home, and participate in the funeral service, so they parked near the North Portico[39] and waited. When the ceremony was over, they watched the funeral procession gather, and when it did, they fell in line. Slowly the line of cars traveled down Pennsylvania Avenue to the Capitol, where Harding's body would lie in state. It was the same route the two men had traveled together just two and a half years earlier. Anyone who bet in 1920 that Woodrow Wilson would outlive his successor would have made a lot of money.

But after the long, hot summer of 1923, it was not Woodrow's health but Edith's that caused alarm among their friends. Edith was only fifty that August, though she suddenly looked much older. Her characteristic vivacity was dulled and gray. She seemed exhausted all the time. Cary worried she would completely break down. Even she admitted that "I felt my splendid health deserting me, and I could hardly drag myself around."[40] Since his collapse in 1919, she had been away from her husband only for the one night she went to New York that April. She had not left his side in four years. She desperately needed a vacation.

Cary and Randolph assured Edith they would watch over Woodrow in her absence. Cary even offered to move in while she was gone. Randolph promised daily updates. So in late August, Edith accepted an invitation from friends to visit them at their home in Mattapoisett, a seaside Massachusetts town across Buzzards Bay from Cape Cod. It was just what she needed: rest, easy company, and time to walk and read. She loved her hosts, the Hamlin family, and "the serenity of their home, 'way off from every city sound, with life-giving air blowing in from Buzzard's Bay, made me a new being."[41] She stayed ten days. Every day she wrote Woodrow a chatty and affectionate letter, enthusiastically describing everyone she met and everything she did. He wrote back telling her how much he missed her and detailing his daily discomforts. The correspondence was a pale echo of the summer of 1915, when they exchanged constant letters of love and news. Then he had been the president, ardently courting a beautiful widow. Now he was a housebound invalid, and she was enjoying a well-deserved break from his daily care.

She returned to S Street in early September, refreshed and ready to resume her caregiving. But ten days away had given her a perspective daily contact with Woodrow had prevented. Seeing her husband with fresh eyes, she had to face the truth: he was dying. "Since my return from the Hamlins," she wrote, "I saw that, unmistakably, a decline had set in. I gathered my resources to arrest it if I could, and if not to accept the issue with such a fortitude as my womanhood would allow."[42] After the previous four years, the notion that Edith's fortitude was weakened by her womanhood was almost laughable. But she consistently maintained the daintily feminine image of the devoted wife of a superior man, even as she detailed her constant strength and self-control.

The fall of 1923 was pretty bleak. One bright spot came in the form of Belle Baruch, Bernard's daughter. With her friend Evangeline Johnson, heir to the Johnson & Johnson fortune, Belle traveled the world promoting the League of Nations through a group called the Nonpartisan League. Belle was also a devotee of radio, having served in the U.S. Signal Corps in the war. Now she and Johnson came to Edith and Woodrow with a proposal. On November 10, the eve of the fifth anniversary of the armistice, they wanted Woodrow to deliver a live radio address. "This meant a tremendous effort and a brand new experience," Edith explained, "for radio was then a strange instrument in the hands of ordinary mortals."[43] Woodrow had never learned to enjoy the technology. But the two young women, with their charming optimism and beauty, made it all sound possible. "Who could have resisted those two gorgeous girls and their sweeping enthusiasm for the League?" Not Edith, and not Woodrow. "My husband granted their request."[44]

But once the women had secured a promise and swept away to start planning the logistics, Edith and Woodrow were left to face the reality of what they had just agreed to. They had two weeks to figure out what he was going to say. Once, that would have been plenty of time. Woodrow had always prided himself on writing his own speeches, sometimes with very little notice. As Edith well knew, that was no longer true. "Now, alas, failing vitality and eyesight made the creation of every sentence a problem."[45] She still would not admit to any mental decline on the part of her husband. For the next two weeks she stood by, ready with pen and paper, to write down whatever he needed at any hour. She worried the speech was preoccupying him in an unhealthy way, making him nervous and sleepless. At one point she even suggested he back out. He wouldn't hear of it.

Inevitably, to Edith's relief, the day arrived. The speech was planned for eight thirty in the evening. The radio broadcast van arrived at S Street first thing in the morning, and technicians took most of the day to run wires into the house, set up a microphone in the library, and deputize Randolph to do a voice check. Everything was ready on time. But the star of the show was still in bed, blinded by one of his periodic headaches. At the last minute, he rose up, put on his dressing gown, and hobbled to the library. His headache still raged. He could barely see. But as the announcer intoned, "Mr. Woodrow Wilson will now say a few words,"[46] he leaned on his cane and stepped up to the unfamiliar microphone. Edith stood just behind him, with her own copy of the speech. He started weakly, almost inaudibly, but steadied himself as he went on. The speech went out across the nation's airwaves. It was the largest single audience yet reached by one human voice.[47] New York station WOR had the clearest signal. Those listening closely could hear a quiet female voice prompting the next words whenever the speaker faltered.[48] But most Americans heard just their former president, broadcast on loudspeakers in auditoriums and town squares across the country. Had he been able to wield this power of mass communication in 1919, he might never have had to embark on that fateful train trip.*

The next day the Armistice Day crowds converged on Kalorama. Folks came to pay their respects every November 11, but this crowd was extra large and extra enthusiastic. Perhaps the daily revelations of Harding administration scandals made them nostalgic for a president with scruples. Perhaps they sensed this Armistice Day would be their hero's last. Some twenty thousand people traveled to S Street—so many the trolley lines had to add extra cars.[49] As they converged around the front door of the Wilsons' house, ex–service members were encouraged to move to the front.[50] Joe Tumulty, still exiled, quietly arranged for a band to play. At two thirty, Woodrow emerged on the arm of Senator Carter Glass and the band quieted. Edith stood just behind. Glass gave some introductory remarks. And then Woodrow spoke, for only two minutes, but he was interrupted three times by deafening applause.[51] Tears filled his eyes. On previous occasions he had apologized for his tendency to weep, embarrassed that his lifelong rigid emotional control seemed to have fled with his illness. But today he let the tears speak for themselves. His speech was simple and heartfelt. Before leaving, he turned back to the crowd for one last thought. He was certain the principles he fought for would triumph, he said. "That we shall prevail is as sure as that God reigns."[52] It was the last speech he ever gave.

Christmas passed quietly, followed by Woodrow's sixty-seventh birthday. A group of old friends gave him a snazzy Rolls-Royce limousine, customized to make it as easy as possible for him to climb in and

---

* You can hear a somewhat fuzzy recording of this four-minute speech at c-span.org, which claims it is the earliest known recording of a radio broadcast: c-span.org/video/?418067-1/woodrow-wilson-1923-radio-address.

out. It had a removable roof and a Princeton-inspired orange stripe down its shiny black exterior and a *WW* monogram on the door. The whole household and the press knew it was coming, but the gift was a complete surprise to the birthday boy. Edith worried the surprise was a little too complete: "for it was almost a shock, which was something I always tried to avoid. He was overwhelmed by such a princely remembrance, and his poor nerves set so on edge that he could not restrain his emotion."[53]

The Wilson family rang in 1924 with little fanfare. For the residents of S Street, it was just another page on the calendar. But for the Democratic Party, it was the dawn of an election year and a chance to build on the gains of the 1922 midterms. Woodrow had not announced support for any of the potential candidates, not even his son-in-law. Incredibly, he seems to have held out a fantasy of becoming the nominee himself. He even made notes for a third inaugural address.[54] On January 16, 1924, the entire Democratic National Committee, some 125 men and women, trooped to S Street to shake the old man's hand. Edith stood by, polite and solicitous, watching as her husband greeted every pilgrim with a kind remark. He still failed to make an endorsement. In California, William McAdoo quietly fumed.

In late January, Woodrow finalized one important piece of business. He confirmed he wished Ray Stannard Baker to serve as his official biographer and assured he would have exclusive access to correspondence. It was such an enormous task that Baker would later have moments of regretting his acceptance. Edith persuaded him by sharing a letter Woodrow had drafted to Baker on January 25, celebrating their agreement. It was among the very last letters he dictated to anyone.[55] Baker took it as a deathbed request.

But Woodrow wasn't quite on his deathbed yet. By late January, it was Cary Grayson who looked terrible and clearly needed a break. Confident that his patient was stable, Cary accepted an invitation from Bernard Baruch to enjoy a week of low-country horses and hunting at Hobcaw Barony, his estate on the South Carolina coast. Woodrow felt abandoned. He told Edith, "Somehow I hate to have Grayson leave." She offered to call him back immediately, but Woodrow wouldn't let her. Within days, his health plummeted. By January 30, Edith was alarmed enough to cable for Cary, who cut his trip short and rushed back to DC. The next day, she sent for Margaret and Nell, telling them to hurry home if they wanted a chance to say goodbye to their father. Margaret caught the next train down from New York. Nell and William McAdoo arranged for train tickets the next day, but the journey from California would be a slow one. Jessie was still in Bangkok.

By the first of February, it was clear the end was imminent. Randolph alerted the media, and friends and strangers alike flocked to the S Street house to leave flowers and messages. Cary emerged at intervals to give the crowd updates, but there was not much to say. On Saturday the patient regained consciousness long enough to utter one word: *Edith*.

Woodrow Wilson died on Sunday, February 3, 1924. Edith, Cary, and Margaret were by his side. Edith's own memoir ends with that moment. The final line is "The peace which passeth all understanding had come to Woodrow Wilson."[56]

It may have been the end of Edith's book, but it was not the end of her story. She was only fifty-one—she would live another thirty-seven years. But of course she could not know that then. For the moment, she just had to get through the challenges of the next few days, starting with planning her husband's funeral. This was not an easy task—to begin with, there wasn't an obvious place to bury him. The Coolidge administration dutifully offered to have Woodrow's body lie in state at the Capitol and be interred at Arlington National Cemetery.[57] Edith declined. Her husband hadn't wanted a big public funeral, and he disapproved of Arlington, believing the land had been illegally taken from Robert E. Lee.[58] Nor was Princeton Cemetery, the final resting place of most Princeton University presidents, the appropriate place. Woodrow had not called Princeton home for many years, and it held no associations for Edith. No family was buried at his birthplace in Staunton, Virginia. Ellen was buried in the Axson family plot in Rome, Georgia. There was a Wilson family plot in Columbia, South Carolina, where Woodrow's parents were interred, but Woodrow's sister Annie had taken the last available space when she died in 1916.[59]

Finally, the Episcopal bishop of Washington, James Edward Freeman, stepped forward with an idea. Washington National Cathedral, just up Massachusetts Avenue from Kalorama, was only seventeen years into its eighty-three years of construction and nowhere near finished. But Freeman hoped it would one day become a new-world Westminster Abbey, with great Americans interred under its flagstones. Woodrow Wilson could be buried in the crypt beneath the Bethlehem Chapel.* Edith approved of this idea. There could be a funeral service at S Street, then a procession up the hill for the burial. He would remain forever in Washington, where he had done his greatest work and he had chosen to make his last home.[60] Or maybe not forever—one reason Edith chose the cathedral was that, in case she later should find it "wise to make a change, removal would be simple as it would be necessary only to open the crypt."[61]

---

* Wilson's remains were moved to the cathedral nave in 1956, the centenary of his birth. See cathedral.org/what-to-see/exterior/wilson-bay.

The newspapers announced the private funeral would take place on Wednesday February 6. The tightly controlled guest list included President and Mrs. Coolidge, members of the Wilson cabinet, representatives from the Axson, Bolling, and Galt families, Princeton friends, Cary and Altrude Grayson, Helen Bones, Ike Hoover, Edmund Starling, Bernard Baruch, and, after personal intervention from McAdoo and Cary, Joe Tumulty. Colonel House was not included. Neither was Mary Hulbert Peck. The Senate would send an official delegation.

When Edith read of this last addition, she was horrified to discover Henry Cabot Lodge's name among the delegates. "I felt to let that man come to my house would be a betrayal of the dead,"[62] she insisted. She fired off a letter. "My dear Sir," she wrote, "I note in the papers that you have been designated by the Senate of the U.S. as one of those to attend Mr. Wilson's funeral. As the funeral is private and not official and realizing that your presence would be embarrassing to you and unwelcome to me I write to request that you do *not* attend. Yours truly, Edith Bolling Wilson."[63] Lodge wrote back immediately, promising the new widow he would stay away. "You may rest assured that nothing could be more distasteful to me than to do anything which by any possibility could be embarrassing to you."[64]

As the day of the funeral approached, Nell and her family arrived from California. Nell was brokenhearted over the loss of her father. But her emotions were further strained by the news that her husband, who thought he might finally win the 1924 Democratic nomination, had received huge fees from one of the Teapot Dome coconspirators.[65] His ambitions looked like they would be thwarted once again, this time for good. When he arrived at S Street, McAdoo promptly took over the library to strategize with his campaign advisers. Edith was disgusted and no longer had the patience or emotional reserves to keep her distaste from showing.[66] She accused Nell of caring more about her husband's political prospects than her father's death. It was a beginning of a rift between Edith and Woodrow's daughters that would never really heal.

February 6 dawned appropriately cold and gray. Two hundred mourners arrived at S Street for the family service. Edith, behind a heavy veil, let herself weep as she never had while her husband lived. She no longer had to keep up the pretense of serenity for him. When the ceremony was over, Randolph escorted her to a waiting car. McAdoo came next, with Nell on one arm and Margaret on the other. The pallbearers, friends and colleagues, carried the casket to the waiting hearse. A long line of cars sedately traveled the mile and a half to the cathedral, where another service followed, this one for three hundred guests. Thousands more stood outside, huddled under umbrellas in the stinging winter rain.[67] Finally, finally, her husband's casket was lowered into the vault, and the slab placed atop it. Then Edith went home to S Street to begin the rest of her life.

Chapter Ten

WOMAN OF WASHINGTON REPRISE

1924–1961

E dith gritted her teeth and hoped her horror didn't show. She had perfected her public facade of serenity over the years and counted on it now to mask her true reaction. But it took every ounce of her considerable self-control. This ceremony was shaping up to be a disaster. In the seven years since her husband's death, Edith had attended endless dedications and honors and tributes to him. Some were grand and some were homely. Some statues and paintings were more attractive than others. This particular tribute should have been wonderful—it was sponsored by Ignacy Paderewski, the internationally famous Polish musician and statesman. He wanted to build a heroic monument to Woodrow in the Polish town of Poznań, in gratitude for his efforts to secure Polish independence. Paderewski, who had given up his brief tenure in politics to return to his life as a composer and pianist, knew good art when he saw it. After much consideration, he chose

American sculptor Gutzon Borglum. Borglum agreed to take a break from blasting the busts of presidents out of the face of a South Dakota mountain to accept this commission.[1] The sculptor asked Edith if he could borrow an academic gown that had belonged to her husband. He wanted to depict Woodrow stepping out of the gown as he symbolically abandoned academia for public service.[2] Edith was a little dubious about this metaphor but happily complied with the request.

Now she sat in the front row at the ceremonial unveiling. She was the official guest of the Polish government, traveling first to Warsaw and then to Poznań. Edith had chosen as her companion her niece Lucy Moeling, who had never been abroad.[3] They had been wined and feted in "real medieval splendor"[4] for over a week, Lucy wide-eyed and delighted with everything. The day of the ceremony was bright and sunny (it had been symbolically scheduled for July 4, 1931), and although the ill health of Paderewski's wife prevented his attendance, many important dignitaries and crowds of Polish citizens packed the Poznań park. A makeshift curtain, composed of American and Polish flags, hung from a cable in front of the statue. Hymns were sung. Finally the moment came. As one witness described it, "The flags of the two nations parted, revealing to the sun's rays the bronze statue of President Wilson. The sight caused tears of joy to flow from many eyes."[5]

Joy was not Edith's reaction. The statue was beyond ugly. As she wrote to her brother Randolph, "the monument as a portrait is the worst thing I have ever seen. It is all out of drawing and there is no resemblance."[6] Lucy agreed. "I almost shrieked when I saw it," she wrote to her husband, "it's so terrible."[7] The statue was destroyed by drunken Nazi storm troopers in 1940,[8] but photos show their opinion was not wrong. Woodrow's head was huge and bald, balanced on an oddly narrow neck. The discarded academic gown looked like a bathrobe. It was not Borglum's best work.* Happily for Edith, hundreds of carrier pigeons were released to circle the monument, giving her a moment to compose herself in the din of their flapping.

But worse was still to come. The American ambassador rose to deliver a brief message from President Herbert Hoover. Hoover's first political appointment had been head of the Food Administration in Wilson's wartime cabinet, but when he ran for president for the first time in 1920, he announced he was a Republican. Edith found his terse, eight-sentence message insulting. "There was not one tribute to Mr. Wilson . . . nothing to even hint at the knowledge that it was sent to represent America's head of Government at a ceremony in a foreign country where they were honoring his fellow countryman, his predecessor in the great office of The Presidency, the man to whom he owed his opportunity for the high official position he then occupied!"⁹ Edith took it as a personal insult on her late husband's behalf but consoled herself that "the omission was so marked that it was spoken by everyone and belittled the author far more than the one he tried to slight."¹⁰

Managing how people felt about Woodrow had become Edith's full-time job. The memoirs and biographies were coming in thick and fast. Joe Tumulty published *Woodrow Wilson as I Know Him* in 1921; it was followed quickly by Colonel House's volume *What Really Happened at Paris*. William Allen White had the first biography off the presses, publishing *Woodrow Wilson* just months after Woodrow's death. Robert Lansing and Henry Cabot Lodge both published their accounts of the treaty fight. Edith found fault with them all. The books, as well as several articles, quoted letters from the ex-president,

---

* There is a small-scale model of this work on display in the parlor at the house on S Street. It is much better looking in miniature.

often, in Edith's view, out of context. She was particularly outraged by a series of magazine articles written by James Kerney, editor of the Trenton *Times*. "After reading the first one of these, in which he stated absolute falsehoods, I asked my lawyer's advice regarding such publications." Her lawyer advised her that she could legally claim "that the paper on which a letter was written was the property of the person to whom it was inscribed, but the context vested in the author or his or her heirs or assigns; in other words, the tangible paper and ink I could not demand, but I could prohibit the publication of the text."[11] So began Edith's campaign to control all of her husband's correspondence and forbid anyone from publishing even their own private letters without her permission. Her actions did not go unnoticed by the newspapers. Under the headline WIDOW FORBIDS PUBLICATION OF WILSON LETTERS, *The New York Times* reported, "It is Mrs. Wilson's intention, as executrix of the war president's estate, either to have his letters and manuscripts assembled and published by someone who will act on her authority, or to gather them into a collection of Wilsonia."[12]

The only person Edith gave permission to publish was Woodrow's handpicked biographer, Ray Stannard Baker. By the spring of 1925, Baker's neighbors in Amherst, Massachusetts, had become accustomed to seeing moving trucks full of documents unload into his fireproof basement vault. Gathered from the White House, the S Street house, and various storage facilities, the collection ultimately contained hundreds of thousands of documents and weighed over eleven tons.[13] Missing, however, was the bulk of Woodrow's correspondence with Colonel House, vital documents for a biographer. House's papers were held at Yale, under the control of Charles Seymour, who was editing *The Intimate Papers of Colonel House* for publication. Seymour proposed a mutually beneficial exchange: he would give Baker copies of all of Woodrow's letters to House, if permission would be granted to publish at least some of them in his upcoming book. Edith refused. Somehow, she got all of House's papers without allowing Seymour to publish anything written by the president. The final version of *The Intimate Papers of Colonel House* resorts to paraphrasing Woodrow's side of the correspondence.[14]

Meanwhile, Edith began to make notes for her own book, believing ultimately that only she could represent her husband accurately. She would work on the manuscript off and on for the next ten years. During that time various friends and colleagues read early drafts, written entirely in longhand, and made suggestions. Some thought she should tone down the harsh, personal nature of her criticism. Some enjoyed her colloquial and idiomatic tone, while others edited it out. At some point, the decision was made to end the book with Woodrow's death.* The final version was published as *My Memoir* by Bobbs-Merrill in 1939. To maximize readership, some of it was also serialized in *The Saturday Evening Post,* accompanied by lavish illustrations. For someone who had never sought the spotlight for herself, the resulting attention must have been overwhelming. After all, this was the first memoir written by a former First Lady—yet another precedent set by Edith. One paper claimed, "In Washington one must read it to participate in the discussion that is carried on in every circle, from the taxicab driver in the street, to the drawing room of the elite."[15] The reviews were predictably mixed. Some claimed it did "service to Woodrow Wilson because it humanizes him without detracting from his dignity and celebrates him without recourse to eulogy."[16] The *Fort Worth Star-Telegram* went so far

---

* The chapters covering the fifteen years from 1924 to 1939 remained only in Edith's scrawling longhand until 2021. Then some dedicated volunteers at the Edith Bolling Wilson Birthplace Museum undertook the daunting task of transcribing them, after which they generously provided this author with copies. This is the first biography of Edith to make use of that material.

as to claim, "*My Memoir* is one of the most important historical books of the decade. All Americans should read it."[17] Others dismissed it as "at once acid and saccharine" and sniffed that Edith harbored "hates so sharp . . . that they instill in the reader doubts about the author."[18] Some seem to have read an entirely different book. "It is a book of value," patronized the *New York Daily News*, "despite its utter, utter sweetness."[19] Sweetness is not the most obvious quality of the book, but even today, it remains extremely readable. Edith's conversational style and willingness to dish personal details contrast attractively with the staid autobiographies of men who never relaxed their own self-importance. But her witty observations and occasionally unflattering details, sometimes directed at herself, are never aimed at her husband. He is, in all circumstances, heroic.

Although she always insisted she wasn't political, her husband's death did not end Edith's interest in politics. In 1924 she was unable to attend the Democratic convention in person. (While visiting a friend, she bent over to pick up what she thought was a glove. It turned out to be a chimney swallow, which flew up in her face, startling her into tripping down a couple of stairs, breaking her shoulder and arm. In the cast she "felt like a traffic cop with my arm held for four weeks above my head in order that the union of the shoulder bone be made possible."[20] She certainly wasn't going all the way to New York City like that.) Instead, she and her brother Randolph gathered around the radio every night, listening until the delegates adjourned in the wee hours. The convention still holds the record for being the longest continually running convention in American history. The delegates, unable to choose between front-runners William McAdoo and Al Smith, took 103 ballots to finally settle on dark horse John Davis. Edith admired Davis but was put off by the civil war of the convention. "It was a sorry exhibition of disorganization, and the whole democracy felt disheartened. Mr. Davis made a great sacrifice of himself to the Party but with no avail and Mr. Coolidge was returned to office by the November vote."[21]

When Coolidge declined to run again in 1928, Edith renewed her keen interest in the Democratic Party nomination fight. There was even a small movement to draft Edith as the vice presidential nominee. The *Associated Press* reported that the Democratic Iowa women endorsed her, saying, "Mrs. Wilson will grace the office and would fill it capably."[22] Nor were they the only ones. The *New York Herald Tribune* quoted Hugh Wallace, who had been ambassador to France in the Wilson administration, saying that an Al Smith/Edith Wilson ticket "would be invincible." "I am sure that at least ten percent of Republican women voters would be glad of the opportunity to elect a woman vice president," Wallace told the paper. "Especially one as well versed in statecraft as Mrs. Wilson."[23] One (female) editorial writer pointed out, "To link Mrs. Wilson's name with that of Al Smith, is, well, to most women, having the ballot, much more of a credit to Smith than to Mrs. Wilson—a literal case of the tail flying the kite."[24] Edith's reaction to these attempted drafts was not recorded, although she did save the newspaper clippings in her scrapbooks. Neither major political party would nominate a female vice presidential candidate until 1984, nor elect one until 2020.

In the summer of 1928, the Democratic convention was held in Houston, and Edith was invited to travel with both Bernard Baruch and Cary Grayson. But she chose to join the private railcar of Hugh Wallace and his wife, so presumably she did not hold his promotion of her candidacy against him. She did, however, have reason to regret her choice when their train broke down five hours outside of their destination. After a sweaty hour of waiting, their car was attached to another train heading the same place. Aboard the new train were both Baruch and Cary, who teased Edith that she should have traveled with them all along. But their gloating didn't last—this second train broke down too. Finally a third engine succeeded in getting them all to Houston—late, hot, and somewhat worse for wear. The convention chair, lumber tycoon Jesse Jones, rushed Edith up onto the stage, where she hoped she could take her usual role of waving royally (and silently) to the crowd. But Jones went rogue. "After a benediction, and a welcome from the Mayor of Houston, Mr. Jones made a brief speech expressing his regret at the unfortunate delay and then, to my horror, introduced me to the audience, saying I would say 'just a word of greeting.' I, who never made a speech, and felt I could not marshal an idea!"[25] This is one of the very few speeches Edith ever gave anywhere. What she said, exactly, is lost to history. According to her, "it was noblesse oblige, and I went forward and said something as briefly as possible."[26]

Edith downplayed her role in Houston as ceremonial, but the newspapers gave her much greater power. The *San Francisco Chronicle* called her "Democracy's Joan of Arc" and predicted she might have to step in as peacemaker if the convention grew contentious. "Having received the greatest popular acclaim of any incoming notable, Mrs. Wilson apparently was in position to wield great power over contending forces."[27] Could this have been true? It's interesting to speculate. Would Edith have ever acted overtly political in public? Would she have embraced the role of kingmaker as the widow of the last Democratic president? She much preferred her acts of power to remain behind the scenes, but she also took her husband's legacy as a sacred trust. We'll never know. As it happened, her arbitration skills were not needed— New York governor Al Smith was nominated on the first ballot,[28] with Arkansas senator Joe T. Robinson as his running mate.

Edith supported Smith. When he lost in a landslide to Herbert Hoover in November, she regretted that his opposition to Prohibition and his Catholicism had lost him votes. "Personally I liked and admired the man, and felt he would have made a fine executive; and that the religious prejudice against his faith was unworthy and distressing."[29] Edith's own knee-jerk prejudices seemed to mellow as she aged.

Backing a loser did not dissuade Edith from Democratic politics. In 1932 she was back at the convention, this time in Chicago, cheering on Franklin Roosevelt. She was so enthusiastic about his candidacy she actually campaigned for him. After his inauguration in 1933, he and First Lady Eleanor Roosevelt invited her often to the White House. Edith was happy to accept. Years later, President Roosevelt displayed his genius for political stagecraft when he invited Edith to sit next to his wife as he asked Congress for a declaration of war. The next day, December 9, 1941, Eleanor Roosevelt wrote in her column, "I had a curious sense of repetition for I remembered very vividly the description of the same gallery, when Mrs. Woodrow Wilson listened to President Wilson speak to the assembled members of Congress. Today she sat beside me, as the president spoke the words which branded a nation as having departed from the code of civilized people."[30]

Freed from the burdens of caring for an invalid husband, Edith renewed friendships with many characters from her past. In 1929, she spent some quality time in Richmond with her cousin Rudolf Teusler, the son of her Aunt Jeff and the romantic wounded German Confederate. Rudolf and his wife, May, had moved to Tokyo in 1900, where he founded St. Luke's International Hospital, which still operates. Rudolf was an internationally respected doctor, but to Edith, he was the same adventuresome boy of their youth. "The more remote or impossible a thing seemed the more eager he was to tackle it,"[31] Edith said admiringly. The impossible thing he proposed to Edith was this: a trip together around the world. Edith thought it was a wonderfully reckless idea.

It was the adventure of a lifetime. She set off in June of 1929 for the now-familiar Atlantic crossing to Paris. Then on to Marseilles, Pompeii, Cairo. Elephants in Kandy and minarets in Singapore. They rode terrifying trains through China and Rudolf's chauffeur-driven Cadillac through Japan. Finally the unfamiliar Pacific crossing from Yokohama to Vancouver, and trains across America to be home in time for Christmas. She was gone almost six months. Edith clearly treasured this trip for the rest of her life, calling it "a voyage of discovery that will always make my memories rich."[32] Several souvenirs from that adventure still decorate the house on S Street.

But while friends and family continued to occupy Edith's time, the big project of her post–White House years was ensuring Woodrow's legacy. She traveled every year to Geneva to attend the opening ceremonies of the League of Nations. She sat through portrait unveilings and building dedications and train station naming ceremonies around the world. Increasingly, she felt the urgency of a permanent memorial to Woodrow in the U.S. In 1938, the Woodrow Wilson Birthplace Foundation was created to preserve the home where Woodrow was born in Staunton, Virginia. Woodrow's father had been the minister at the First Presbyterian Church in town, and this hilltop house was the "manse"— the minister's official residence. The Wilsons left Staunton for a church in Augusta, Georgia, before the future president turned two, so nothing in the house had personal significance. Still it was as good a place as any to create an enduring and dignified memorial, and Edith jumped in with characteristic dedication. She had opinions on everything from paint colors to invited guests to the wording of the visitors' guide.

What she didn't have was the money to ensure the foundation was financially secure. That changed when Hollywood came calling. When the eighth and final volume of Baker's official biography and Edith's own memoir were both published in 1939, Twentieth Century Fox proposed a cinematic tribute to add to the laudatory record. The film languished in development until 1943, when studio mogul Darryl Zanuck returned from serving the U.S. War Department in London and North Africa. Zanuck made the film his personal crusade; he thought a world consumed by a new global conflict needed to be reminded of the American president who dreamed of lasting international peace.[33] Both Edith and Baker served as consultants. Baker was more involved, traveling to Hollywood to watch the production, the studio's most expensive to date.[34] He wrote to Edith regularly, updating her on the film's progress and keeping her apprised of any changes. A relatively unknown actor named Alexander Knox was chosen to play Woodrow. Edith was disappointed Fox hadn't gone with a star like Alfred Lunt but approved of the choice of Knox when she was assured he had a particularly fine voice.[35] After testing twenty-five different actresses, Zanuck's pick to play Edith was Geraldine Fitzgerald, best known for portraying Isabella Linton in William Wyler's *Wuthering Heights*. Fitzgerald looked nothing like Edith and didn't attempt to imitate her voice or manner. Instead she said, "My only concession to authenticity took into account Mrs. Wilson's light hearted, laughing nature. I kept every scene buoyant, even the serious ones."[36]

The movie *Wilson* was released in 1944 and was nominated for ten Academy Awards, winning five. But because it was so expensive, it was considered a box office flop. It is a gorgeous film to look at, filled with saturated Technicolor and spectacular costumes and sets. But the plot is two and a half hours of earnest propaganda, unbroken by humor or nuance. Edith approved and sent Fitzgerald a note thanking her for the "quiet dignity in which she had clothed the part."[37] Edith took the

money the studio offered her and sent it to Staunton to start an endow-
ment for the Woodrow Wilson Birthplace Foundation.[38] Today, the
campus in Staunton includes not only the manse but also a museum, a
gift shop, gardens, and the Woodrow Wilson Presidential Library and
Research Center.

As the 1940s rolled inevitably into the 1950s, Edith did not update
the S Street house, preferring to keep it much as it had been when her
husband was alive. The kitchen appliances got an upgrade, but most of
the house was kept as a time capsule from her husband's years there. She
did not participate in local charities or causes, although she did allow
the Women's National Democratic Club to elect her honorary president. She liked to entertain a few guests at home for luncheon, often
enticing them to stick around for a hand or two of cards. Happily, much
of her family remained in Washington, including five of her eight siblings and many of their children and grandchildren. She would invite
these relatives over regularly, preferring to host just one or two at a time
rather than large gatherings of Bollings. Wilmer's grandson Cary Fuller
remembers visiting after church on Sundays. After lunch his great-aunt
would inevitably suggest a hand of cards, which Cary's mother had instructed him to lose. Fortunately, Edith's game was canasta, which
Cary claimed was easy to lose on purpose, since he could quietly hold
on to high-value cards until his opponent collected her own.[39]

A hectic flurry of Wilson memorial activity occurred in 1956,
the hundredth anniversary of Woodrow's birth. A federal celebration
commission gathered information on countless tributes. There was a
commemorative stamp, a hall of fame induction, and a plan to build a
new bridge over the Potomac River in his honor. Plaques and portraits
and buildings were unveiled around the world. There was a learned
panel in Geneva, a church service in Carlisle, and a military concert in

Paris.[40] Edith, eighty-four and increasingly frail, attended as many of them as she could, photographed over and over in her signature hat and orchid corsage.

But the ceremony that meant the most to her was right up the street at the National Cathedral. In 1951, Woodrow's grandson Francis Sayre (older son of Jessie Wilson Sayre) had become dean of the cathedral and reenergized the languishing construction schedule. So by 1956, enough of the nave was finished to be able to move Woodrow's grave out of the crypt and up into the main part of the church. A marble sarcophagus, adorned with a Crusader's cross and Scottish thistles, was placed in a bay on the south side of the nave, and Woodrow's remains were reinterred there. Today the "Wilson Bay" also includes four of his quotations etched in the stone and small carvings of the Staunton manse and Nassau Hall at Princeton. The stone below the tomb features the seals of Princeton University, the state of New Jersey, and the United States. Above the sarcophagus a triptych stained-glass window depicts war and peace through the lens of Christianity.* The new grave site was dedicated on Armistice Day, November 11, 1956. Edith herself did not speak at the event, although Eleanor Roosevelt did read a passage from *The Pilgrim's Progress*.[41]

There were some final events to mark Woodrow's actual birthday on December 28, and then it was 1957. Edith was exhausted. "I have been to so many things in honor of Woodrow that I am glad the Centennial year is over," she wrote to a friend.[42] But it was vitally important to her to attend these milestones. A few years later, she told a young

---

* Cathedral guide Andy Bittner prefers to call this the "peace and war" window, since peace is on the left if you are looking at it from inside the church. He also finds the depiction of war to be one of the most moving images in the whole cathedral. Instead of soldiers or weaponry, it shows a mother desperately beating back the flames of war to protect her children.

visitor she hoped to live at least until Woodrow's 105th birthday, when the planned Potomac River bridge was set to be dedicated.[43]

ONE BY ONE, Edith began to outlive her siblings. In 1951 she lost all three of her younger brothers, Julian in July, followed by Wilmer in October and Randolph in November. Randolph's death was particularly hard, as he had lived with Edith at S Street since the day they moved in thirty years earlier. Edith's oldest sister, Gertrude Galt, also a widow, moved into S Street for the final decade of their lives. Also present at the house was Margaret Cherrix Brown, known to all as Cherie, who served as secretary and companion. If Edith's social prejudices mellowed with age, her personal grudges did not. One Washington journalist brought his teenage son, a huge Woodrow Wilson fan, to visit at S Street. When Edith was showing him some presidential correspondence, a letter slipped from the file to the floor unnoticed by Edith, who stepped on it. The boy timidly pointed out she was standing on a letter from Secretary of State Lansing. Edith glanced down, saw Lansing's hated signature under her heel, and declared, "Leave him there! It's where he belongs."[44] On another occasion Cary Fuller drove over to the house in his own car, which sported a NIXON/LODGE bumper sticker. Richard Nixon's running mate in the 1960 election was Henry Cabot Lodge's grandson, and the sticker was sure to annoy Edith, but Fuller hoped it would go unnoticed. It was Cherie who spotted it and tattled. "Cherie didn't have to say anything," Fuller says, "but she did. Aunt Edith demanded I remove either the sticker or the car immediately. I sheepishly moved the car down the street."[45]

Edith was invested in the 1960 election not just because of the hated name of Henry Cabot Lodge but also because she thoroughly approved of the Kennedys. Senator Kennedy reached out to Edith before his nomination and won her over completely. Edith also admired Jacqueline Kennedy and thought her style and manners would serve the White House well.[46] Jessie Wilson Sayre's grandson Thomas Sayre remembers one night in January 1961. His mother was driving him and his siblings home from downtown when snow started coming down hard and icy. (Washington's perennial poor preparation for snow is an inevitability that cuts across the city's history, but this turned out to be a historic blizzard.)[47] Mrs. Sayre, nervously piloting the family wagon, was worried they wouldn't make it up the last steep mile of Massachusetts Avenue to the cathedral. As they passed Kalorama, she decided they would drop in on "Granny Edith" to wait out the worst of the weather in her parlor. This was highly unusual: the Sayre kids visited Granny Edith only by invitation for very formal teas and lunches. But the storm was getting dangerous. So they pulled over to the S Street house and rang the bell. Miss Edith was not home, the butler told them. She was dancing the night away at the Kennedys' inaugural ball.[48] The next day Edith attended the swearing-in, warming flasks of bourbon discreetly tucked in her pockets.[49]

Edith's support of First Ladies was not confined to Democrats. She knew better than anybody else what an impossible job First Lady is, and how unprepared even the most savvy political spouse was for the job. So she invited every incoming First Lady to lunch at S Street, to let them know they had a friend in town who understood.[50] She served them on ornate asparagus plates she had brought back from her round-the-world tour.* If the new presidential wives felt they were being summoned to

---

* Several of these lovely plates survive, and if you are lucky enough to get an invitation from Cary Fuller, he will serve chocolates on one. Another can be found in the collection at the Edith Bolling Wilson Birthplace Museum in Wytheville.

pay homage to the grande dame, that is really not what Edith was going for. She did not host extravagant dinners with dozens of courses. This was a friendly lunch at her home. And although the house was formal, it was not intimidating. Edith filled it with personal touches, such as the cushions on the dining room chairs. They had all been personally needlepointed by Edith and her friends and signed with their initials. The pattern, a dark rose-leaf design on a burgundy background, was chosen to hide stains and wear.[51] Those chair cushions were like Edith: lovely, invested with care and thought, but eminently practical.

Gertrude's death in May of 1961 was a blow, although she had just celebrated her ninety-eighth birthday. Edith was now the last of her generation. She had no one left to care for. Caregiving had always been such a vital part of her character, from those childhood nights spent tending terrifying Grandmother Bolling on through Norman, Woodrow, her mother, and most of her siblings. She took a special interest in certain nieces and nephews, but they just didn't need her in quite the same way.

Her time tending the Wilson flame had also largely been brought to a close with the tributes of his centennial year. The Woodrow Wilson Birthplace in Staunton was secure. The Woodrow Wilson School of Public and International Affairs was thriving at Princeton. She planned to leave the S Street house to the National Trust for Historic Preservation for use as a museum. Pilgrims came by the thousands to his grave at the cathedral. Still, Edith hoped there might be some official federal memorial in Washington, as there were for other historically significant presidents. The Wilson Centennial Commission had recommended one, but the authorizing legislation had never made it out of committee.[52]

Finally, in October 1961, President Kennedy invited Edith to the

White House for a bill signing. He was authorizing the creation of the Woodrow Wilson Memorial Commission. The commission was charged with deciding between two options: "One which would be a monument similar to those which honor Presidents Washington, Jefferson, and Lincoln; or one which will serve as a building of a functional nature, or, as it is often called, a "living* memorial."[53] Kennedy signed the bill with Edith sitting next to him, using three ceremonial pens. He gave one each to eleven-year-old Thomas Sayre and his twelve-year-old sister, Jessie. And although the newspapers reported that "Kennedy had Mrs. Wilson's smiling approval as he bypassed her in presenting the first two of the pens,"[54] she was honored to receive the third. "I didn't dare ask you for it," she admitted.[55] Everyone in the room chuckled—the notion that there was something Edith didn't dare was laughable.

Edith didn't make it to that bridge dedication on Woodrow's 105th birthday. As it happened, that was the day she died, December 28, 1961. She was eighty-nine, the longest-lived First Lady ever to that date.† She had been out of the White House for over forty years. That apparently was not enough time for her obituary writers to decide how to characterize her time as First Lady.

The New York Times described the ambivalence: "The woman who was the wife of the twenty-eighth President of the United States was regarded in almost as many lights as there were shades of contemporary political opinion. Some went so far as to characterize her as the first woman president of the United States. Others thought her the best of all possible wives. Milder critics suggested that she carried her fierce

---

* The "living memorial" was the commission's ultimate choice. Today it is the Wilson Center, a nonpartisan think tank in Washington, established in 1968.
† Her longevity has since been surpassed by Bess Truman (ninety-seven), Nancy Reagan and Lady Bird Johnson (ninety-four), Betty Ford (ninety-three), and Barbara Bush (ninety-two). As of this writing, Rosalynn Carter is still alive at ninety-four.

partisanship of Woodrow Wilson and his opinion too far." In a final understatement, the paper concluded, "There was no lack of opinion."[56]

Other papers took it upon themselves to downplay her power, or rationalize it. The *Richmond Times-Dispatch* claimed the extent of Edith's role was that "she protected the partially paralyzed president from unwanted callers."[57] The Raleigh *News & Observer*, owned by the family of Josephus Daniels, defended Edith in an editorial: "Damned as The Regent, she died as a lady who in the critical period of Woodrow Wilson's illness did her best to serve both her husband and her country."[58]

A widely printed eulogy from the Associated Press was edited to varying lengths in different papers, but almost all versions included this paragraph: "She retained into old age the charm and erect carriage of a grand lady. It was said of her that when she made a public appearance, the orchid was always in place, the picture hat tilted at the correct, slight angle, and the dress, which she may have sewn herself, always in the best style."[59] Some versions of that obituary added this hedge at the end, with no details: "At one time critics raised a cry that she herself took too much of a hand in making history."[60]

In the sixty-plus years since Edith's death, we have somewhat relaxed our gatekeeping of who gets to take a hand in making history. We are better at acknowledging the contributions of people who are not highly educated white men. But we still cling to a hall-of-fame model of historical biography. No one elected Edith. Her actions after Woodrow's stroke were clearly unconstitutional. Her official role as First Lady did not include the duties she took upon herself in 1919 and 1920. But serving as a duly elected executive is not the only history worth making. Edith's story, with all its complications, requires rethinking not only who gets to make history but also exactly what "making history" is.

EPILOGUE

Time has not stood still in the century since the Wilsons left the White House. Today it would be unthinkable for a president to disappear from public view for five months, while assuring the public he was just fine. To be fair, it was pretty shocking in 1919. But the intervening hundred years have seen a total revolution in the media, and the press corps would never stand for a stonewall on that scale now.

The control Edith maintained over access to Wilson's papers after his death is impossible today. Presidential papers and effects are no longer the private property of the family. Since Herbert Hoover (thirty-first president, 1929–1933), the records of every presidency are now conserved and made available through presidential libraries, managed by the National Archives. Wilson's papers are scattered around. The bulk of them reside at the Library of Congress—Edith agreed to have all originals shipped there as Ray Stannard Baker finished with them. The Library of Congress collection also includes papers Edith found later at the S Street house, and Edith and Woodrow's love letters. The Woodrow Wilson Birthplace museum in Staunton, Virginia, includes a library and research center, but since it predates the Presidential

Library Acts, it is not part of the National Archives' presidential library system. The collection there includes, among other items, the papers of Cary and Altrude Grayson, Ellen Wilson, and two of Wilson's three daughters. The Seeley G. Mudd Manuscript Library at Princeton University also collects Wilson material, largely but not exclusively predating his presidency. Edith's papers, to the extent they were preserved, are at the Library of Congress.

IN 1965, IN THE WAKE of the Kennedy assassination, Congress passed the Twenty-fifth Amendment to the Constitution. It was ratified and became law in 1967. The first two sections clarify that the vice president becomes president (as opposed to acting president) if the president dies, resigns, or is removed from office and establish procedures for filling a vacancy in the vice presidency. Section 3 allows a president to notify Congress that he or she is temporarily "unable to discharge the powers and duties of the office" and transmits those powers to the vice president until they are rescinded in writing. Several presidents have exercised this section when undergoing medical procedures that require general anesthesia.

SECTION 4, the most controversial, is most relevant to Edith:

> Whenever the Vice President and a majority of either the principal officers of the executive departments or of such other body as Congress may by law provide, transmit to the President pro tempore of the Senate and the Speaker of the House of Representatives

their written declaration that the President is unable to discharge the powers and duties of his office, the Vice President shall immediately assume the powers and duties of the office as Acting President.

IF THE PRESIDENT OBJECTS to the notion that he or she is "unable" to do the job, Congress must decide the issue by a two-thirds vote. To date, this is the only section of the amendment that has never been invoked. During the 1965 debate over section 4, senators referenced both Woodrow Wilson and James Garfield. Both Wilson and Garfield had vice presidents with no appetite for the top job, unwilling to take the responsibility and be seen as a usurper. Section 4 attempts to legitimize the vice president's role: serving only as "Acting President" with the written support of others in the administration. If the Twenty-fifth Amendment had been law in 1919, perhaps things would have played out very differently. It's not hard to imagine Albert Fall or Robert Lansing writing a searing declaration of Wilson's inability or lobbying relentlessly for its support. It is equally easy to imagine Edith fighting that movement with everything she had.

IN ADDITION TO all her siblings, Edith outlived almost all of the other major players in her life story. Cary Grayson retired from the navy after Woodrow's death and became chairman of the American Red Cross. He died in 1938 and is buried at Arlington National Cemetery. In 1940 Altrude Gordon Grayson married insurance executive George Leslie Harrison. As her three sons grew up and left home, she enjoyed traveling the world, as she and Edith had done throughout their friendship. Altrude died unexpectedly in 1961 while on one of her trips. She and Edith had been friends for fifty years.

Joe Tumulty left public life after the Wilson administration but stayed in Washington and practiced law. After the controversy over the Jefferson dinner statement and his almost-exclusion from Woodrow's funeral, he never reconciled with Edith. He also never said an unkind word about either Wilson in public. He and his wife raised five children. Joe died in 1954 at age seventy-three.

Helen Bones, who was so instrumental in introducing Edith to Woodrow, moved out of the White House in 1919 and resumed her career in publishing. She retired to her hometown of Rome, Georgia, where she died in 1951 at the age of seventy-eight.

White House usher Ike Hoover stayed in his role to serve presidents Harding, Coolidge, Hoover, and Roosevelt. He was still head usher when he died in 1933. His memoir, *Forty-Two Years in the White House*, was published posthumously the next year.

One of the few contemporaries who did outlive Edith was Bernard Baruch, who continued to play the role of presidential adviser up through the Truman administration. In the 1950s, he sold his South Carolina hunting retreat, Hobcaw Barony, to his daughter Belle, who in turn bequeathed it to the Belle W. Baruch Foundation. Today it is a center for ecology research but still gives tours to the public by request. Bernard Baruch died in 1965 at the age of ninety-five. He left his personal papers to Princeton, as a tribute to Woodrow's legacy there.

None of Woodrow's daughters followed him into public life. Margaret Wilson's singing career never really took off, and she spent her post–White House years searching for personal meaning. In 1938 she moved to an ashram in India, where she worked to translate the work of Hindu mystics. She died on the ashram in 1944 at the age of fifty-seven.

Jessie Wilson Sayre and her family moved back from Bangkok in the 1920s and settled for a time in Cambridge, Massachusetts. Jessie was active in Democratic politics and became secretary of the Massachusetts Democratic State Committee but demurred when her name was floated as a potential candidate. She died in 1933 at the age of forty-five from complications from abdominal surgery. She did not live to see her son Francis become dean of the Washington National Cathedral.

Eleanor (Nell) Wilson McAdoo divorced William McAdoo in 1935 and stayed in California with their two children. Two years later, she published a biography of her parents called *The Woodrow Wilsons.* As the last living Wilson daughter, she was very present in the centennial celebrations of 1956, often pictured alongside Edith at various unveilings and commemorations. Their relationship was strained. Nell could match Edith in grudges held and hurts nursed. Nell died at seventy-seven in 1967.

Edith and Woodrow are no longer the only presidential couple to have stayed in Washington after leaving the White House. In 2017, Michelle and Barack Obama bought a house in Kalorama, just a few blocks from S Street. The S Street house opened to the public in 1963 and continues to operate as a museum. Since he was, by law, able to keep gifts from foreign dignitaries, Woodrow displayed many artifacts from his eight years in office in his private home. Today, foreign gifts over a certain value are considered the property of the American people, and a president who wants to keep them after retirement must pay the (often prohibitive) fair market value.

Although three other presidents are buried in the nearby Virginia suburbs (Kennedy and Taft at Arlington, Washington at Mount Vernon), Woodrow Wilson remains the only U.S. president buried in the city of Washington, DC. Edith also rests at the cathedral, although she is not up in the nave with her husband. Carved in the wall to the left of his sarcophagus is this inscription:

IN LOVING MEMORY

OF

EDITH BOLLING WILSON

1872 1961

BURIED IN THE VAULT

BENEATH THIS BAY

EVERY YEAR ON DECEMBER 28, Woodrow's birthday, members of the U.S. military place a wreath at his grave. A second floral tribute, generally including orchids, is included for Edith. This is mainly because she had the excellent political timing to die on her late husband's birthday. But for visitors ignorant of that coincidence, it looks like she is being honored as part of his presidency. As it should.

The only place you can find a tribute to Edith that does not include her husband is in her hometown of Wytheville, Virginia. The building where Edith was born still stands and in 1989 was purchased by local business owners Bill and Farron Smith. The three street-level storefronts have housed many different tenants, although Skeeter's World Famous Hot Dogs has anchored the corner unit since 1943. Farron Smith worked for years to get the building listed on the National Register of Historic Places and collect enough images and artifacts to open a small museum to Edith in one of the other storefronts. The Edith Bolling Wilson Birthplace Museum opened in 2008.

The upstairs residential area, where Edith and her brothers and sisters grew up, is still in need of restoration. But members of the public can tour the narrow rooms where young Edith learned bad French, resented canaries, and tortured boring teenage boys. Gazing at the Blue Ridge Mountains, you can imagine one grandmother scolding her to be feminine and submissive and another prodding her to be outspoken and fearless. And you can picture Edith, tall and proud, embodying the traits of the latter lessons while cloaking them in the guise of the former. She would go on to become the most powerful woman in the nation. She would go on further to pretend she was nothing of the kind.

ACKNOWLEDGMENTS

My first and most heartfelt thanks must go to Heath Hardage Lee. Heath and I met in 2019 when I asked her to speak at the Smithsonian about her excellent book *The League of Wives*. Meanwhile, I was promoting one book on the suffrage movement and finishing another, and at every talk I gave, someone would inevitably ask me about Edith Wilson. I read up on Edith to answer those questions more effectively. But the more I learned about this fascinating woman, the more I wanted to write about her. As I dug into the topic in earnest, I heard that Heath was also working on an Edith biography. Rumors of my research must have reached Heath, because she called me and told me she had shelved her Edith research indefinitely while she worked on a biography of First Lady Pat Nixon and was delighted I was taking up the project. Then she sent me all her notes, introduced me to everyone she had already interviewed, and recommended me whenever someone asked her to participate in a program about Edith. I stand in awe of Heath's generosity and collegiality. Plus she's really funny and has a dog named Dolly Parton. I can't wait to read her Pat Nixon book.

Heath introduced me to Farron Smith, keeper of Edith's flame in

Wytheville, Virginia. Farron and her husband own Edith's childhood home, and she has been tireless in her efforts to preserve and promote the Edith Bolling Wilson Birthplace Museum. My time in Wytheville with Farron, Betsy Ely, and Morgan Herbert was crucial in understanding the Bolling family. Farron trusted me with the unpublished chapters of Edith's memoir, for which I am more grateful than I can say.

Farron and Heath introduced me to Cary Fuller, Edith's great-nephew, who turned out to live just a few blocks from me in Washington, DC. Cary has been incredibly generous with his time and stories of Aunt Edith, and I look forward to seeing him around the neighborhood.

At the Woodrow Wilson House in Washington, DC, Elizabeth Karcher welcomed this project from the beginning. Her knowledge of every nook and cranny of the S Street house made it much easier to imagine Edith's long life there.

At the Woodrow Wilson Presidential Library and Museum in Staunton, Virginia, archivist Rosalind Calhoun pulled dozens of boxes of research, set me up in a (possibly haunted) room, and left me alone for the day, only breaking to take me to lunch with executive director Robin von Seldeneck. I think all researchers will agree that is a truly perfect day.

Rachel Faulkner tackled the newspaper archives. She even managed to convince the New York Public Library to give her access to the treasure trove of *Town Topics* archives during a pandemic.

Testing the limits of how many Rebeccas can fit at one café table, Becca Grawl and Rebecca Fachner met me for tea and cookies and a gossip session about Edith. With Canden Arciniega, they are the geniuses behind the podcast *Tour Guide Tell All*, and their wit and insight helped me shape this narrative.

I am lucky to have friends who are excellent editors and allow me to pay them in cocktails. Kristin Jensen Cohen read many early chapters and gave invaluable feedback. Garrett Peck read through the World War I chapters to double-check my timeline and characterizations. All errors are, of course, my own.

I also recommend, if you can arrange it, having a family full of writers and editors who are generous with their time and talent. My brother, Lee Roberts, was the first person to read this manuscript in its entirety, and apparently stopped everything else in his busy life to turn around thoughtful, thorough comments inside of a week. My father, Steve Roberts, and sister-in-law, Liza Roberts, both of whom published their own books while I was working on this one, formed a mini support group when we all faced deadlines, word counts, and imposter syndrome. Liza also introduced me to Thomas Sayre, Woodrow Wilson's great-grandson, who shared his stories of Granny Edith.

My agent, Anna Sproul-Latimer, was Team Edith before she was even my agent. Not only is Anna really good at her job, she is the kind of person who nerds out on metal detecting, enjoys hanging out in cemeteries, and develops devastating crushes on chestnut trees. So you can see why I love her. COVID has prevented me from actually meeting my editor, Emily Wunderlich, in person, but she is also *really* good at her job. Plus, she is totally down with the cemeteries and trees, so you know she's good people. Graveyard picnic soon, okay? And we must invite Paloma Ruiz, who ably shepherded this manuscript through the publishing process.

Finally, eternal thanks to my family. My hilarious sons Jack, Cal, and Roland Hartman only made mild fun of me when I gushed about Edith, which they aptly dubbed "Edithing." Jack even found me an Edith Bolling Galt Wilson coffee mug, which I'm certain has wrecked his Amazon algorithms for all time. And to my husband, Dan, my best cheerleader, most trusted sounding board, and rock-solid partner. I write this the week we celebrate our twenty-fifth wedding anniversary, and marrying you remains the smartest decision I ever made.

NOTES

The following abbreviations are used for some of the more frequently cited persons and institutions.

AGG   Alice Gertrude ("Altrude") Gordon

BB   Bertha Bolling

CTG   Cary Travers Grayson

EBG   Edith Bolling Galt

EBW   Edith Bolling Wilson

JWS   Jessie Wilson Sayre

LoC   Library of Congress

MWW   Margaret Woodrow Wilson

NG   Norman Galt

NYPL   New York Public Library

SB   Sallie Bolling

WW   Woodrow Wilson

WWPL   Woodrow Wilson Presidential Library

INTRODUCTION

1. Molly Meijer Wertheimer, ed., *Inventing a Voice: The Rhetoric of American First Ladies of the Twentieth Century* (Lanham, MD: Rowman & Littlefield, 2004), 103.

2. Wertheimer, *Inventing a Voice*, 3.

3. Wertheimer, *Inventing a Voice*, 3.

4. "President to Wed Mrs. Norman Galt," *Evening Star* (Washington, DC), October 7, 1915.

5. Woodrow Wilson Papers, Series 9: Scrapbooks, 1864–1944, Clippings, Peace Conference, 1918–1919, image 40, LoC, Washington, DC.

6. John Milton Cooper, *Woodrow Wilson: A Biography* (New York: Knopf, 2009), chapter 23.

7. "Mrs. Woodrow Wilson, 89, Dies on the Birthday of Her Husband; Center of Controversy During President's Illness, When She Was Intermediary," *New York Times*, December 29, 1961.

8. Alden Hatch, *Edith Bolling Wilson: First Lady Extraordinary* (New York: Dodd, Mead, 1961), 272.

9. Edith Bolling Wilson, *My Memoir* (Indianapolis: Bobbs-Merrill, 1939), foreword, page 2.

PROLOGUE

1. Edith Bolling Wilson, *My Memoir* (Indianapolis: Bobbs-Merrill, 1939), 296.

2. Wilson, *My Memoir*, 297.

3. A. Scott Berg, *Wilson* (New York: G.P. Putnam's Sons, 2013), 420.

4. Berg, *Wilson*, 628.

5. Gene Smith, *When the Cheering Stopped: The Last Years of Woodrow Wilson* (New York: Open Road, 2016), 135.

6. Smith, *When the Cheering Stopped*, 135.

7. Berg, *Wilson*, 660.

8. Smith, *When the Cheering Stopped*, 135.

9. Phyllis Lee Levin, *Edith and Woodrow: The Wilson White House* (New York: Scribner, 2001), 389.

10. Smith, *When the Cheering Stopped*, 136.

11. Smith, *When the Cheering Stopped*, 136.

12. Irwin (Ike) Hood Hoover, *Forty-Two Years in the White House* (Boston: Houghton Mifflin, 1934), 104.

13. Levin, *Edith and Woodrow*, 389.

14. William Hazelgrove, *Madam President: The Secret Presidency of Edith Wilson* (Washington, DC: Regnery History, 2016), 167.

15. Cary T. Grayson, *Woodrow Wilson: An Intimate Memoir* (Washington, DC: Potomac Books, 1960), 109.

16. "Senators See President," *New York Times*, December 6, 1919.

17. Smith, *When the Cheering Stopped*, 137.
18. Levin, *Edith and Woodrow*, 390.
19. Wilson, *My Memoir*, 299.
20. "Senators See President."
21. "Senators See President."
22. "Senators See President."
23. Wilson, *My Memoir*, 299.

CHAPTER ONE: A VIRGINIA CHILDHOOD
1872–1891

1. Edith Bolling Wilson, *My Memoir* (Indianapolis: Bobbs-Merrill, 1939), 9.
2. Carl Anthony, "A First Lady's Princess Complex: Royalty, Racism & Edith Wilson's Pocahontas Blood," firstladies.org, September 18, 2012.
3. Wilson, *My Memoir*, 1.
4. Wilson, *My Memoir*, 1.
5. Phyllis Lee Levin, *Edith and Woodrow: The Wilson White House* (New York: Scribner, 2001), 60.
6. Wilson, *My Memoir*, 3.
7. Wilson, *My Memoir*, 3.
8. Alden Hatch, *Edith Bolling Wilson: First Lady Extraordinary* (New York: Dodd, Mead, 1961), 47.
9. Wilson, *My Memoir*, 21.
10. Wilson, *My Memoir*, 1.
11. Anthony, "A First Lady's Princess Complex."
12. Mark Twain, *Pudd'nhead Wilson* (1894; repr., New York: W.W. Norton, 2004), 60.
13. Kevin N. Maillard, "The Pocahontas Exception: The Exemption of American Indian Ancestry from Racial Purity Law," *Michigan Journal of Race & Law* 12, no. 351 (2007).
14. Wilson, *My Memoir*, 2.
15. Catherine A. Jones, *Intimate Reconstructions: Children in Postemancipation Virginia* (Charlottesville: University of Virginia Press, 2015), 77.
16. Wilson, *My Memoir*, 2.
17. Wilson, *My Memoir*, 5.
18. Wilson, *My Memoir*, 10
19. Wilson, *My Memoir*, 6.
20. Wilson, *My Memoir*, 6.
21. Wilson, *My Memoir*, 5.
22. Wilson, *My Memoir*, 7.

23. Barbara Welter, "The Cult of True Womanhood: 1820–1860," *American Quarterly* 18, no. 2, part 1 (Summer 1966): 151–74.

24. Wilson, *My Memoir*, 20.

25. Wilson, *My Memoir*, 12.

26. Hatch, *Edith Bolling Wilson*, 44.

27. Wilson, *My Memoir*, 13.

28. Wilson, *My Memoir*, 13.

29. Wilson, *My Memoir*, 15.

30. Advertisement in *Virginia Seminary Magazine,* 1892.

31. Wilson, *My Memoir*, 15.

CHAPTER TWO: WOMAN OF WASHINGTON 1891–1908

1. Campbell Gibson, "Population of the 100 Largest Cities and Other Urban Places in the United States: 1790 to 1990" (U.S. Census Bureau working paper no. POP-WP207, June 1998).

2. John P. Richardson, *Alexander Robey Shepherd: The Man Who Built the Nation's Capital* (Athens: Ohio University Press, 2016), 124.

3. Richardson, *Alexander Robey Shepherd*, 27.

4. Scott W. Berg, *Grand Avenues: The Story of Pierre Charles L'Enfant, the French Visionary Who Designed Washington* (New York: Vintage, 2007), 248–49.

5. Kathryn Allamong Jacob, *Capital Elites* (Washington, DC: Smithsonian Institution Press, 1995), 189.

6. Tom Lewis, *Washington: A History of Our National City* (New York: Basic, 2015), 209.

7. Jacob, *Capital Elites*, 238.

8. Edith Wharton, *The Age of Innocence* (New York: W.W. Norton, 2002), 110.

9. Jacob, *Capital Elites*, 201.

10. Jacob, *Capital Elites*, 224.

11. Jacob, *Capital Elites*, 169.

12. Mark N. Ozer, *Massachusetts Avenue in the Gilded Age: Palaces & Privilege* (Mount Pleasant, SC: Arcadia, 2010).

13. Ishbel Ross, *Power with Grace: The Life Story of Mrs. Woodrow Wilson* (New York: G.P. Putnam's Sons, 1975), 13.

14. Alden Hatch, *Edith Bolling Wilson: First Lady Extraordinary* (New York: Dodd, Mead, 1961), 12.

15. Phyllis Lee Levin, *Edith and Woodrow: The Wilson White House* (New York: Scribner, 2001), 51.

16. Ross, *Power with Grace*, 13.

17. Lewis, *Washington*, 231.

18. Edith Bolling to BB, October 10, 1893, Edith Bolling Galt Wilson Papers, Box 1: Family Correspondence, 1833–1946, LoC, Washington, DC.

19. Edith Benham Helm, *The Captains and the Kings* (New York: G.P. Putnam's Sons, 1954), 37.

20. Dolly Gann, *Dolly Gann's Book* (New York: Doubleday, 1933), 39.

21. Edith Bolling Wilson, *My Memoir* (Indianapolis: Bobbs-Merrill, 1939), 16–17.

22. Hatch, *Edith Bolling Wilson*, 50.

23. Liz Halloran, "A Glittering History," *Hartford Courant*, July 27, 2001.

24. "Norman Galt Dead," *Washington Herald*, January 28, 1908.

25. Hatch, *Edith Bolling Wilson*, 50.

26. Wilson, *My Memoir*, 17.

27. "Deaths at Wytheville," *News* (Lynchburg, VA), March 9, 1898.

28. Wilson, *My Memoir*, 18.

29. Wilson, *My Memoir*, 18.

30. Wilson, *My Memoir*, 18.

31. Wilson, My Memoir, 18.

32. Wilson, *My Memoir*, 20.

33. BB to EBG, September 23, 1903, Edith Bolling Galt Wilson Papers, Box 1.

34. Wilmer Bolling to EBG, September 24, 1903, Edith Bolling Galt Wilson Papers, Box 1.

35. Annie Bolling to EBG, September 25, 1903, Edith Bolling Galt Wilson Papers, Box 1.

36. SB to EBG and NG, September 23, 1903, Edith Bolling Galt Wilson Papers, Box 1.

37. BB to EBG and NG, September 27, 1903, Edith Bolling Galt Wilson Papers, Box 1.

38. Annie and Rolfe Bolling to EBG and NG, September 23, 1903, Edith Bolling Galt Wilson Papers, Box 1.

39. SB to EBG, September 30, 1903, Edith Bolling Galt Wilson Papers, Box 1.

40. SB to EBG, October 14, 1903, Edith Bolling Galt Wilson Papers, Box 1.

41. Levin, *Edith and Woodrow*, 69.

42. Wilson, *My Memoir*, 21.

43. The original license is in the collection at the Edith Bolling Wilson Birthplace Museum, Wytheville, VA, https://www.edithbollingwilson.org/permit.html.

44. Helm, *Captains and the Kings*, 39.

45. Ellen Maury Slayden, *Washington Wife* (New York: Harper, 1962), 7.

46. Wilson, *My Memoir*, 38.

47. Virginia Scharff, "Femininity and the Electric Car," Automobile in American Life and Society, no date, autolife.umd.umich.edu/Gender/Scharff/G_casestudy.htm.

48. Wilson, *My Memoir*, 38.

49. Gann, *Dolly Gann's Book*, 181.

50. Lewis, *Washington*, 255.

51. Slayden, *Washington Wife*, 7.

52. Henry Adams, *The Education of Henry Adams* (Overland Park, KS: Neeland Media, 2004), loc. 232 of 8036, Kindle.

53. Slayden, *Washington Wife*, 104.

54. Stacy A. Cordery, *Alice: Alice Roosevelt Longworth, from White House Princess to Washington Power Broker* (New York: Penguin, 2008), 194.

55. Cordery, *Alice*, 86.

56. Lewis, *Washington*, 256.

57. Lewis, *Washington*, 252.

58. Lewis, *Washington*, 259.

59. Gann, *Dolly Gann's Book*, 38.

60. Lewis, *Washington*, 259.

61. EBG to Gertrude and Hunter Galt, August 22, 1907, Edith Bolling Galt Wilson Papers, Box 1.

62. Tom Shachtman, *Edith and Woodrow: A Presidential Romance* (New York: G.P. Putnam's Sons, 1981), 71.

63. Hatch, *Edith Bolling Wilson*, 53.

64. "Norman Galt's Death Shocks Business Friends; Prominent in Trade Bodies," *Washington Times*, January 28, 1908.

65. "Galt Funeral Tomorrow," *Washington Post*, January 29, 1908.

66. Wilson, *My Memoir*, 22.

CHAPTER THREE: MERRY WIDOW 1908-1914

1. Joan Hoff, *Law, Gender & Injustice* (New York: New York University Press, 1991), 188.

2. Edith Bolling Wilson, *My Memoir* (Indianapolis: Bobbs-Merrill, 1939), 22.

3. Wilson, *My Memoir*, 22.

4. Wilson, *My Memoir*, 23.

5. Warren Van Slyke to EBG, July 25, 1911, Edith Bolling Galt Wilson Papers, Box 1.

6. Herbert Biggs to BB, July 27, 1911, Edith Bolling Galt Wilson Papers, Box 1.

7. Herbert Biggs to BB, July 6, 1911, Edith Bolling Galt Wilson Papers, Box 1.

8. Lillian Rogers Parks, *My Thirty Years Backstairs at the White House* (New York: Fleet, 1961), 128.

9. Alice Roosevelt Longworth, *Crowded Hours* (New York: Scribner's, 1933), 168.

10. Wilson, *My Memoir*, 29.

11. Alden Hatch, *Edith Bolling Wilson: First Lady Extraordinary* (New York: Dodd, Mead, 1961), 54.

12. Hatch, *Edith Bolling Wilson*, 55.

13. Wilson, *My Memoir*, 29.

14. Wilson, *My Memoir*, 31.

15. Wilson, *My Memoir*, 32.

16. Wilson, *My Memoir*, 31–32.

17. Wilson, *My Memoir*, 33.

18. Ellen Maury Slayden, *Washington Wife* (New York: Harper, 1962), 176.

19. Slayden, *Washington Wife*, 177.

20. John Morton Blum, *Joe Tumulty and the Wilson Era* (Cambridge, MA: Riverside Press, 1951), 44.

21. Longworth, *Crowded Hours*, 206.

22. Blum, *Joe Tumulty*, 44.

23. Blum, *Joe Tumulty*, 45.

24. Kristie Miller, *Ellen and Edith: Woodrow Wilson's First Ladies* (Lawrence: University Press of Kansas, 2010), 61.

25. David J. Bennett, *He Almost Changed the World: The Life and Times of Thomas Riley Marshall* (Bloomington, IN: AuthorHouse, 2007), 136.

26. Bennett, *He Almost Changed the World*, 139.

27. William Allen White, *Woodrow Wilson* (Boston: Houghton Mifflin, 1929), 269.

28. Slayden, *Washington Wife*, 182–83.

29. Wilson, *My Memoir*, 33.

30. Wilson, *My Memoir*, 48.

31. Miller, *Ellen and Edith*, iii-iv.

32. Slayden, *Washington Wife*, 199–200.

33. Ellen Wilson McAdoo, *The Woodrow Wilsons* (New York: Macmillan, 1937), 197.

34. McAdoo, *Woodrow Wilsons*, 228.

35. McAdoo, *Woodrow Wilsons*, 198.

36. Dolly Gann, *Dolly Gann's Book* (New York: Doubleday, 1933), 43.

37. Slayden, *Washington Wife*, 180.

38. Slayden, *Washington Wife*, 202.

39. Slayden, *Washington Wife*, 202.

40. McAdoo, *Woodrow Wilsons*, 191.

41. Rebecca Boggs Roberts, *Suffragists in Washington, D.C.: The 1913 Parade and the Fight for the Vote* (Mount Pleasant SC: History Press, 2017), 21.
42. McAdoo, *Woodrow Wilsons*, 205.
43. Wilson, *My Memoir*, 36.
44. Wilson, *My Memoir*, 39.
45. McAdoo, *Woodrow Wilsons*, 210–11.
46. Ishbel Ross, *Power with Grace: The Life Story of Mrs. Woodrow Wilson* (New York: G.P. Putnam's Sons, 1975), 31.
47. AGG to CTG, January 15, 1913, Cary T. Grayson Papers, Box 26: Grayson, Alice Gertrude Gordon to Cary T. Grayson 1913 to 1916-04-09, WWPL, Staunton, VA.
48. Wilson, *My Memoir*, 42.
49. EBG to BB, August 6, 1913, Edith Bolling Galt Wilson Papers, Box 1: Family Correspondence, 1833–1946, LoC, Washington, DC.
50. Wilson, *My Memoir*, 43.
51. McAdoo, *Woodrow Wilsons*, 246.
52. John Milton Cooper, *Woodrow Wilson: A Biography* (New York: Knopf, 2009), loc. 5009 of 15641, Kindle.
53. Wilson, *My Memoir*, 40.
54. Wilson, *My Memoir*, 40.
55. Cooper, *Woodrow Wilson*, chapter 12.
56. Cooper, *Woodrow Wilson*, chapter 12.
57. Marie Smith and Louise Durbin, *White House Brides* (Washington, DC: Acropolis Books, 1966), 139.
58. Cary T. Grayson, *Woodrow Wilson: An Intimate Memoir* (Washington, DC: Potomac Books, 1960), 2.
59. Edmund W. Starling, *Starling of the White House* (Chicago: Peoples Book Club, 1941), 39.
60. Starling, *Starling of the White House*, 34.
61. Cooper, *Woodrow Wilson*, loc. 5414 of 15641, Kindle.
62. Wilson, *My Memoir*, 51.
63. Wilson, *My Memoir*, 51.
64. AGG to CTG, August 24, 1914, Cary T. Grayson Papers, Box 26.
65. Miller, *Ellen and Edith*, 89.
66. Miller, *Ellen and Edith*, 91.
67. Irwin (Ike) Hood Hoover, *Forty-Two Years in the White House* (Boston: Houghton Mifflin, 1934), 60.
68. Florence Jaffrey Hurst Harriman, *From Pinafores to Politics* (New York: Henry Holt, 1923), 214.

69. Phyllis Lee Levin, *Edith and Woodrow: The Wilson White House* (New York: Scribner, 2001), 49.
70. Miller, *Ellen and Edith*, 97.

CHAPTER FOUR: ROMANCED BY THE PRESIDENT 1915

1. Edith Bolling Wilson, *My Memoir* (Indianapolis: Bobbs-Merrill, 1939), 53.
2. MWW to JWS, September 1, 1914, Jessie Wilson Sayre Collection, Box 1: Correspondence to Jessie Wilson (Sayre), Seeley G. Mudd Manuscript Library, Princeton, NJ.
3. *Town Topics*, October 21, 1915, NYPL.
4. Wilson, *My Memoir*, 53.
5. Wilson, *My Memoir*, 53–54.
6. Wilson, *My Memoir*, 54.
7. Wilson, *My Memoir*, 54.
8. A. Scott Berg, *Wilson* (New York: G.P. Putnam's Sons, 2013), 361.
9. Wilson, *My Memoir*, 54.
10. Cary T. Grayson, *Woodrow Wilson: An Intimate Memoir* (Washington, DC: Potomac Books, 1960), 48.
11. Berg, *Wilson*, 339.
12. WW to JWS, October 15, 1914, Jessie Wilson Sayre Collection, Box 1.
13. Berg, *Wilson*, 337.
14. Woodrow Wilson, "Address to Congress," August 19, 1914, Miller Center, University of Virginia, transcript, millercenter.org/the-presidency/presidential-speeches/august-19-1914-message-neutrality.
15. Berg, *Wilson*, 337.
16. Edith Gittings Reid, *Woodrow Wilson: The Caricature, the Myth and the Man* (New York: Oxford University Press, 1934), 173–74.
17. Kerri K. Greenidge, *Black Radical: The Life and Times of William Monroe Trotter* (New York: Liveright, 2019), 198.
18. Berg, *Wilson*, 346.
19. Berg, *Wilson*, 346.
20. Berg, *Wilson*, 349.
21. Irwin (Ike) Hood Hoover, *Forty-Two Years in the White House* (Boston: Houghton Mifflin, 1934), 61.
22. Grayson, *Woodrow Wilson*, 46.
23. Hoover, *Forty-Two Years in the White House*, 61.
24. Grayson, *Woodrow Wilson*, 50.

25. Ellen Maury Slayden, *Washington Wife* (New York: Harper, 1962), 247.

26. Phyllis Lee Levin, *Edith and Woodrow: The Wilson White House* (New York: Scribner, 2001), 137.

27. *Town Topics*, February 11, 1915, NYPL.

28. Wilson, *My Memoir*, 56.

29. Wilson, *My Memoir*, 56.

30. Wilson, *My Memoir*, 56.

31. Margaret Axson Elliott, *My Aunt Louisa and Woodrow Wilson* (Chapel Hill: University of North Carolina Press, 1944), 273.

32. Hoover, *Forty-Two Years in the White House*, 61.

33. Edmund W. Starling, *Starling of the White House* (Chicago: Peoples Book Club, 1941), 44.

34. Starling, *Starling of the White House*, 41.

35. WW to EBG, April 28, 1915, Woodrow Wilson Papers, Series 20: Additions, 1881–1957; 1978–1980 Addition; Edith Bolling Galt Wilson file, 1915–1931, LoC, Washington, DC.

36. EBG to WW, April 28, 1915, Woodrow Wilson Papers, Series 20.

37. Hoover, *Forty-Two Years in the White House*, 63.

38. Wilson, *My Memoir*, 60.

39. Wilson, *My Memoir*, 61.

40. WW to EBG, May 5, 1915 Woodrow Wilson Papers, Series 20.

41. Hoover, *Forty-Two Years in the White House*, 66.

42. EBG to WW, May 11, 1915, Woodrow Wilson Papers, Series 20.

43. EBG to WW, August 3, 1915, Woodrow Wilson Papers, Series 20.

44. EBG to WW, May 4, 1915, Woodrow Wilson Papers, Series 20.

45. EBG to WW, June 9, 1915, Woodrow Wilson Papers, Series 20.

46. EBG to WW, May 10, 1915, Woodrow Wilson Papers, Series 20.

47. WW to EBG, May 5, 1915, Woodrow Wilson Papers, Series 20.

48. WW to EBG, May 31, 1915, Woodrow Wilson Papers, Series 20.

49. WW to EBG, May 27, 1915, Woodrow Wilson Papers, Series 20.

50. WW to EBG, May 31, 1915, Woodrow Wilson Papers, Series 20.

51. WW to EBG, June 19, 1915, Woodrow Wilson Papers, Series 20.

52. Hoover, *Forty-Two Years in the White House*, 64.

53. WW to EBG, June 1, 1915, Woodrow Wilson Papers, Series 20.

54. WW to EBG, July 21, 1915, Woodrow Wilson Papers, Series 20.

55. WW to EBG, July 23, 1915, Woodrow Wilson Papers, Series 20.

56. EBG to WW, June 21, 1915, Woodrow Wilson Papers, Series 20.

57. Ellen Wilson McAdoo, *The Woodrow Wilsons* (New York: Macmillan, 1937), 271.

58. EBG to WW, May 5–6, 1915, Woodrow Wilson Papers, Series 20.

59. Berg, *Wilson*, 363.

60. WW to EBG, May 9, 1915, Woodrow Wilson Papers, Series 20.

61. WW to EBG, May 11, 1915, Woodrow Wilson Papers, Series 20.

62. Erik Larson, *Dead Wake: The Last Crossing of the Lusitania* (New York: Penguin Random House, 2015), 331.

63. Wilson, *My Memoir*, 63.

64. Starling, *Starling of the White House*, 48.

65. EBG to WW, May 20, 1915, Woodrow Wilson Papers, Series 20: Additions, 1881–1957; 1978–1980 Addition; Edith Bolling Galt Wilson file, 1915–1931, LoC, Washington, DC.

66. Wilson, *My Memoir*, 66.

67. EBG to WW, May 28, 1915, Woodrow Wilson Papers, Series 20.

68. WW to EBG, May 28, 1915, Woodrow Wilson Papers, Series 20.

69. WW to EBG, May 29, 1915, Woodrow Wilson Papers, Series 20.

70. WW to EBG, May 29, 1915, Woodrow Wilson Papers, Series 20.

71. Larson, *Dead Wake*, 182.

72. WW to EBG, June 1, 1915, Woodrow Wilson Papers, Series 20.

73. EBG to WW, June 3, 1915, Woodrow Wilson Papers, Series 20.

74. EBG to WW, June 3, 1915, Woodrow Wilson Papers, Series 20.

75. WW to EBG, June 5, 1915, Woodrow Wilson Papers, Series 20.

76. WW to EBG June 8, 1915, Woodrow Wilson Papers, Series 20.

77. EBG to WW, June 9, 1915, Woodrow Wilson Papers, Series 2.

78. EBG to WW, May 4, 1915, Woodrow Wilson Papers, Series 20.

79. Levin, *Edith and Woodrow*, 75.

80. WW to EBG, June 18, 1915, Woodrow Wilson Papers, Series 20.

81. WW to EBG, June 18, 1915, Woodrow Wilson Papers, Series 20.

82. EBG to WW, August 5, 1915, Woodrow Wilson Papers, Series 20.

83. "Chum of Wilson's Cousin," *Davey (NE) Mirror*, August 19, 1915.

84. *Town Topics*, August 5, 1915, Woodrow Wilson Papers, Series 20.

85. "President to Wed Once More? Ask Gossips," *Stockton (CA) Evening Mail*, July 29, 1915.

86. WW to EBG, August 9, 1915, Woodrow Wilson Papers, Series 20.

87. Wilson, *My Memoir*, 71.

88. Wilson, *My Memoir*, 71.

89. Starling, *Starling of the White House*, 49.

90. Wilson, *My Memoir*, 73.

91. JWS to MWW, January 23, 1927, Jessie Wilson Sayre Correspondence, WWPL, Staunton, VA.

92. Eleanor Wilson McAdoo to JWS, December 4, 1915, Jessie Wilson Sayre Correspondence.

93. Wilson, *My Memoir*, 75.

94. WW to EBG, August 6, 1915, Woodrow Wilson Papers, Series 20.

95. WW to EBG, August 15, 1915, Woodrow Wilson Papers, Series 20, Washington, DC.

96. WW to EBG, August 15, 1915, Woodrow Wilson Papers, Series 20.

97. EBG to WW, August 7, 1915, Woodrow Wilson Papers, Series 20.

98. WW to EBG, August 9, 1915, Woodrow Wilson Papers, Series 20.

99. WW to EBG, August 16, 1915, Woodrow Wilson Papers, Series 20.

100. WW to EBG, August 19, 1915, Woodrow Wilson Papers, Series 20.

101. EBG to WW, August 26, 1915, Woodrow Wilson Papers, Series 20.

102. John Morton Blum, *Joe Tumulty and the Wilson Era* (Cambridge, MA: Riverside Press, 1951), 88.

103. WW to EBG, August 28, 1915, Woodrow Wilson Papers, Series 20.

104. WW to EBG, August 28, 1915, Woodrow Wilson Papers, Series 20.

105. Hoover, *Forty-Two Years in the White House*, 65.

106. Lillian Rogers Parks, *My Thirty Years Backstairs at the White House* (New York: Fleet, 1961), 140.

107. WW to EBG August 13, 1915, Woodrow Wilson Papers, Series 20.

108. Edwin Tribble, ed., *President in Love: The Courtship Letters of Woodrow Wilson and Edith Bolling Galt* (Boston: Houghton Mifflin, 1981), 30.

109. Hoover, *Forty-Two Years in the White House*, 66.

110. WW to EBG, September 13, 1915, Woodrow Wilson Papers, Series 20: Additions, 1881–1957; 1978–1980 Addition; Edith Bolling Galt Wilson file, 1915–1931, LoC, Washington, DC.

111. Starling, *Starling of the White House*, 55–56.

112. *Town Topics*, September 9, 1915, NYPL.

113. WW to EBG, August 26, 1915, Woodrow Wilson Papers, Series 20.

114. WW to EBG, September 3, 1915, Woodrow Wilson Papers, Series 20.

115. Hoover, *Forty-Two Years in the White House*, 68.

116. Tom Shachtman, *Edith and Woodrow: A Presidential Romance* (New York: G.P. Putnam's Sons, 1981), 108.

117. WW to EBG, September 19, 1915, Woodrow Wilson Papers, Series 20.

118. EBG to WW, September 19, 1915, Woodrow Wilson Papers, Series 20.

119. Wilson, *My Memoir*, 76.

120. Wilson, *My Memoir*, 77.

121. Wilson, *My Memoir*, 77.

122. Wilson, *My Memoir*, 78.

123. Levin, *Edith and Woodrow*, 137.

124. Wilson, *My Memoir*, 79.

125. "White House Fiance Wears Happy Smile; to Buy Ring Today," *Atlanta Constitution*, October 8, 1915.
126. Patrick W. Flournoy to AGG, October 16, 1915, Cary T. Grayson Papers, Box 26: Grayson, Alice Gertrude Gordon to Cary T. Grayson 1913 to 1916-04-09, WWPL, Staunton, VA.
127. *Town Topics*, November 11, 1915, NYPL.
128. "White House Fiance Wears Happy Smile."
129. *Town Topics*, November 25, 1915, NYPL.
130. CTG to AGG, October 19, 1915, Cary T. Grayson Papers, Box 44: Grayson, Alice Gertrude Gordon to Cary T. Grayson 1913 to 1916-04-09, WWPL, Staunton, VA..
131. AGG to CTG, November 2, 1915, Cary T. Grayson Papers, Box 26.
132. Wilson, *My Memoir*, 82.
133. Hoover, *Forty-Two Years in the White House*, 69.
134. Wilson, *My Memoir*, 84.
135. Wilson, *My Memoir*, 85.
136. Starling, *Starling of the White House*, 61.
137. Starling, *Starling of the White House*, 62.
138. Wilson, *My Memoir*, 87.
139. Starling, *Starling of the White House*, 64.
140. Levin, *Edith and Woodrow*, 153.

CHAPTER FIVE: THE FIRST LADY IN WAR
1916–1918

1. Edith Bolling Wilson, *My Memoir* (Indianapolis: Bobbs-Merrill, 1939), 128.
2. Edith Benham Helm, *The Captains and the Kings* (New York: G.P. Putnam's Sons, 1954), 48.
3. Wilson, *My Memoir*, 127.
4. Lillian Rogers Parks, *My Thirty Years Backstairs at the White House* (New York: Fleet, 1961), 149.
5. "President to Wed at Bride's Home, Not White House," *Brooklyn Daily Eagle*, October 7, 1915.
6. "President to Wed at Bride's Home."
7. *Town Topics*, November 14, 1915, NYPL.
8. Helm, *Captains and the Kings*, 47.
9. Helm, *Captains and the Kings*, 49.
10. Wilson, *My Memoir*, 91.
11. Wilson, *My Memoir*, 100.

12. Wilson, *My Memoir*, 104.

13. Kristie Miller, *Ellen and Edith: Woodrow Wilson's First Ladies* (Lawrence: University Press of Kansas, 2010), 134.

14. *Town Topics*, July 6, 1916, NYPL.

15. Joseph P. Tumulty, *Woodrow Wilson as I Know Him* (New York: Doubleday, 1921), 167.

16. Tom Shachtman, *Edith and Woodrow: A Presidential Romance* (New York: G.P. Putnam's Sons, 1981), 135.

17. "Mrs. Wilson's Birthday," *New York Times*, October 16, 1916.

18. Wilson, *My Memoir*, 113.

19. John Milton Cooper, *Woodrow Wilson: A Biography* (New York: Knopf, 2009), chapter 16.

20. A. Scott Berg, *Wilson* (New York: G.P. Putnam's Sons, 2013), 412–13.

21. Wilson, *My Memoir*, 113.

22. Twenty-third Amendment to the Constitution, ratified March 29, 1961.

23. Wilson, *My Memoir*, 114.

24. Wilson, *My Memoir*, 114.

25. Wilson, *My Memoir*, 115.

26. Edmund W. Starling, *Starling of the White House* (Chicago: Peoples Book Club, 1941), 77.

27. Wilson, *My Memoir*, 118–19.

28. Wilson, *My Memoir*, 116.

29. Wilson, *My Memoir*, 118.

30. Wilson, *My Memoir*, 119.

31. Berg, *Wilson*, 416.

32. Ishbel Ross, *Power with Grace: The Life Story of Mrs. Woodrow Wilson* (New York: G.P. Putnam's Sons, 1975), 315.

33. Molly Meijer Wertheimer, ed., *Inventing a Voice: The Rhetoric of American First Ladies of the Twentieth Century* (Lanham, MD: Rowman & Littlefield, 2004), 109.

34. CTG to AGG, October 19, 1915, Cary T. Grayson Papers, Box 44: Grayson, Alice Gertrude Gordon to Cary T. Grayson 1913 to 1916-04-09, WWPL, Staunton, VA.

35. Phyllis Lee Levin, *Edith and Woodrow: The Wilson White House* (New York: Scribner, 2001), 181.

36. Ross, *Power with Grace*, 309.

37. "Gives Joy to Suffragists," *New York Times*, October 1, 1918.

38. Leslie King, "The Devils in the Workhouses: Edith Bolling Wilson, Woman Suffrage, and Equity," *Wythe County Historical Review*, Summer 2011.

39. Ross, *Power with Grace*, 317.

40. *Town Topics*, December 16, 1915, NYPL.
41. Elizabeth Gillespie McRae, "Caretakers of Southern Civilization: Georgia Women and the Anti-suffrage Campaign, 1914–1920," *Georgia Historical Quarterly* 82, no. 4 (1998): 801–28, jstor.org/stable/40583906.
42. Ross, *Power with Grace*, 321.
43. McRae, "Caretakers of Southern Civilization."
44. Berg, *Wilson*, 418.
45. Michael Beschloss, *Presidents of War* (New York: Crown, 2018), 308.
46. Berg, *Wilson*, 420.
47. Berg, *Wilson*, 421.
48. Wilson, *My Memoir*, 127.
49. Berg, *Wilson*, 422.
50. Alice Roosevelt Longworth, *Crowded Hours* (New York: Scribner's, 1933), 237.
51. Longworth, *Crowded Hours*, 242.
52. Beschloss, *Presidents of War*, 309.
53. 64th Congress, 2nd session, quoted in Cooper, *Woodrow Wilson*, loc. 7931 of 15641, Kindle.
54. Beschloss, *Presidents of War*, 296.
55. Berg, *Wilson*, 428.
56. Levin, *Edith and Woodrow*, 165.
57. Starling, *Starling of the White House*, 85.
58. Berg, *Wilson*, 430.
59. Levin, *Edith and Woodrow*, 536.
60. Beschloss, *Presidents of War*, 314.
61. Berg, *Wilson*, 432.
62. Levin, *Edith and Woodrow*, 177.
63. Florence Jaffray Hurst Harriman, *From Pinafores to Politics* (New York: Henry Holt, 1923), 214.
64. Wilson, *My Memoir*, 132–33.
65. Starling, *Starling of the White House*, 89.
66. Parks, *My Thirty Years Backstairs*, 152.
67. Wilson, *My Memoir*, 135.
68. *Town Topics*, July 26, 1917, NYPL.
69. Ellen Maury Slayden, *Washington Wife* (New York: Harper, 1962), 290.
70. "Mrs. Wilson's Food Pledge," *New York Times*, July 1, 1917.
71. "Mrs. Wilson Posts Pledge," *New York Times*, July 7, 1917.
72. "Mrs. Wilson Joins Lower Meat Drive," *New York Times*, March 26, 1920.
73. "Mrs. Wilson and Society Leaders to Economize as Example to the Country," *Washington Post*, April 13, 1917.

74. Starling, *Starling of the White House*, 113.

75. *Town Topics*, February 26, 1920, NYPL.

76. Helm, *Captains and the Kings*, 52.

77. Wilson, *My Memoir*, 159.

78. "More White House Sheep," *Washington Post*, March 3, 1918.

79. Parks, *My Thirty Years Backstairs*, 152.

80. "Ike, Famous Tobacco Chewing White House Sheep, Is Dead," *Spartanburg (SC) Herald*, August 14, 1927.

81. "Wilson's Sheep Scared by Autos," *Washington Post*, May 12, 1918.

82. "Pershing's 'Jeff' Will Lead Parade," *Washington Post*, April 12, 1920.

83. William Woodward to CTG, April 29, 1918 Cary T. Grayson Papers, Box 85, WWPL, Staunton, VA.

84. Starling, *Starling of the White House*, 110.

85. Wilson, *My Memoir*, 161.

86. Wilson, *My Memoir*, 140.

87. Wilson, *My Memoir*, 140–41.

88. Ross, *Power with Grace*, 103.

89. "Launch First Ship at Hog Island," *New York Times*, August 6, 1918.

90. Wilson, *My Memoir*, 134.

91. Wilson, *My Memoir*, 146.

92. Starling, *Starling of the White House*, 89.

93. Wilson, *My Memoir*, 135.

94. Starling, *Starling of the White House*, 90.

95. Dolly Gann, *Dolly Gann's Book* (New York: Doubleday, 1933), 47.

96. Gann, *Dolly Gann's Book*, 48.

97. Slayden, *Washington Wife*, 330.

98. Berg, *Wilson*, 445.

99. Wilson, *My Memoir*, 155.

100. Woodrow Wilson, "Address to a Joint Session of Congress on the Conditions of Peace," January 8, 1918.

101. Wilson, *My Memoir*, 157.

102. Wilson, *My Memoir*, 158.

103. Marie Smith and Louise Durbin, *White House Brides* (Washington, DC: Acropolis Books, 1966), 157.

104. Wilson, *My Memoir*, 167.

105. Wilson, *My Memoir*, 167.

106. Berg, *Wilson*, 493.

107. John Morton Blum, *Joe Tumulty and the Wilson Era* (Cambridge, MA: Riverside Press, 1951), 164–65.

108. Levin, *Edith and Woodrow*, 217.

109. Tumulty, *Woodrow Wilson as I Know Him*, 299.

110. Longworth, *Crowded Hours*, 274.

CHAPTER SIX: THE FIRST LADY IN PEACE
1918–1919

1. Edmund W. Starling, *Starling of the White House* (Chicago: Peoples Book Club, 1941), 116.

2. Edith Bolling Wilson, *My Memoir* (Indianapolis: Bobbs-Merrill, 1939), 171.

3. Travels Abroad of the President, Office of the Historian of the Department of State, https://history.state.gov/departmenthistory/travels/president.

4. Phyllis Lee Levin, *Edith and Woodrow: The Wilson White House* (New York: Scribner, 2001), 229.

5. A. Scott Berg, *Wilson* (New York: G.P. Putnam's Sons, 2013), 515.

6. Berg, *Wilson*, 517.

7. Levin, *Edith and Woodrow*, 227.

8. James Srodes, *On Dupont Circle: Franklin and Eleanor Roosevelt and the Progressives Who Shaped Our World* (Berkeley, CA: Counterpoint, 2012), 77.

9. Srodes, *On Dupont Circle*, 68.

10. Wilson, *My Memoir*, 174.

11. Wilson, *My Memoir*, 176.

12. Wilson, *My Memoir*, 177–78.

13. Wilson, *My Memoir*, 180.

14. Wilson, *My Memoir*, 182.

15. Cary T. Grayson, *Woodrow Wilson: An Intimate Memoir* (Washington, DC: Potomac Books, 1960), 67.

16. Jane Ridley, *George V: Never a Dull Moment* (New York: HarperCollins, 2022), 275.

17. Wilson, *My Memoir*, 195.

18. Edith Benham Helm, *The Captains and the Kings* (New York: G.P. Putnam's Sons, 1954), 76.

19. Helm, *Captains and the Kings*, 79.

20. Helm, *Captains and the Kings*, 88.

21. "England Make Precedent by Welcoming Mrs. Wilson," *Washington Post*, December 26, 1918.

22. Wilson, *My Memoir*, 212.

23. Wilson, *My Memoir*, 220.

24. Wilson, *My Memoir*, 221.

25. Wilson, *My Memoir*, 228–29.
26. Helm, *Captains and the Kings*, 93.
27. Wilson, *My Memoir*, 226.
28. Wilson, *My Memoir*, 226.
29. Wilson, *My Memoir*, 227.
30. Helm, *Captains and the Kings*, 92.
31. Wilson, *My Memoir*, 239.
32. Starling, *Starling of the White House*, 135.
33. Wilson, *My Memoir*, 245–46.
34. Starling, *Starling of the White House*, 137.
35. Irwin (Ike) Hood Hoover, *Forty-Two Years in the White House* (Boston: Houghton Mifflin, 1934), 92.
36. Wilson, *My Memoir*, 245.
37. CTG to Joseph P. Tumulty, April 10, 1919, Cary T. Grayson Papers, Box 83: Grayson, Alice Gertrude Gordon to Cary T. Grayson 1913 to 1916-04-09, WWPL, Staunton, VA.
38. Wilson, *My Memoir*, 250.
39. John Milton Cooper, *Woodrow Wilson: A Biography* (New York: Knopf, 2009), chapter 21.
40. Helm, *Captains and the Kings*, 108.
41. Berg, *Wilson*, 568.
42. Levin, *Edith and Woodrow*, 294.
43. Hoover, *Forty-Two Years in the White House*, 95.
44. Starling, *Starling of the White House*, 138.
45. Joseph P. Tumulty, *Woodrow Wilson as I Know Him* (New York: Doubleday, 1921), 318.
46. Hoover, *Forty-Two Years in the White House*, 98.
47. Levin, *Edith and Woodrow*, 296.
48. Helm, *Captains and the Kings*, 107–8.
49. Wilson, *My Memoir*, 262.

CHAPTER SEVEN: THE STROKE 1919

1. Joseph P. Tumulty, *Woodrow Wilson as I Know Him* (New York: Doubleday, 1921), 416.
2. Edith Bolling Wilson, *My Memoir* (Indianapolis: Bobbs-Merrill, 1939), 273.
3. Wilson, *My Memoir*, 274.
4. Alice Roosevelt Longworth, *Crowded Hours* (New York: Scribner's, 1933), 285.
5. A. Scott Berg, *Wilson* (New York: G.P. Putnam's Sons, 2013), 606–7.

6. Berg, *Wilson*, 609.
7. Berg, *Wilson*, 612.
8. Berg, *Wilson*, 613.
9. Berg, *Wilson*, 620.
10. Cary T. Grayson, *Woodrow Wilson: An Intimate Memoir* (Washington, DC: Potomac Books, 1960), 96.
11. "Wilson on Long Trip," *Washington Post*, September 4, 1919.
12. "Shows Fighting Temper," *Evening Star* (Washington, DC), September 5, 1919.
13. "Progress to Omaha Made After President Rests on Sunday at Des Moines," *Evening Star* (Washington, DC), September 8, 1919.
14. Wilson, *My Memoir*, 276.
15. Robert T. Small, "Street Crowded Calm Greeting President," *Washington Post*, September 9, 1919.
16. "Shows Fighting Temper."
17. Grayson, *Woodrow Wilson*, 97.
18. Louis Seibold, "President Now in Foe's State," *Baltimore Sun*, September 17, 1919.
19. Wilson, *My Memoir*, 281.
20. Wilson, *My Memoir*, 281.
21. Wilson, *My Memoir*, 281.
22. Mary Allen Hulbert, *The Story of Mrs. Peck* (New York: Minton, Balch, 1933), 272.
23. Edmund W. Starling, *Starling of the White House* (Chicago: Peoples Book Club, 1941), 150.
24. Hulbert, *Story of Mrs. Peck*, 272–73.
25. Wilson, *My Memoir*, 281.
26. Wilson, *My Memoir*, 282.
27. Starling, *Starling of the White House*, 150.
28. Starling, *Starling of the White House*, 152.
29. Grayson, *Woodrow Wilson*, 98.
30. Starling, *Starling of the White House*, 152.
31. Wilson, *My Memoir*, 284.
32. Tumulty, *Woodrow Wilson as I Know Him*, 427.
33. Starling, *Starling of the White House*, 153.
34. Tumulty, *Woodrow Wilson as I Know Him*, 427.
35. Wilson, *My Memoir*, 285.
36. Grayson, *Woodrow Wilson*, 100.
37. "Wilson Ill: Cancels Tour," *Capital Times* (Madison, WI), September 26, 1919.
38. "Wilson Ill: Cancels Tour."

39. "President Suffers Collapse; Cancels Dates," *Belvidere (IL) Daily Republican*, September 26, 1919.

40. Wilson, *My Memoir*, 286.

41. Irwin (Ike) Hood Hoover, *Forty-Two Years in the White House* (Boston: Houghton Mifflin, 1934), 101.

42. Wilson, *My Memoir*, 286.

43. Hoover, *Forty-Two Years in the White House*, 102.

44. Wilson, *My Memoir*, 288.

45. Wilson, *My Memoir*, 288.

46. Grayson, *Woodrow Wilson*, 101.

47. Hoover, *Forty-Two Years in the White House*, 103.

48. Tumulty, *Woodrow Wilson as I Know Him*, 434.

49. Hoover, *Forty-Two Years in the White House*, 100.

CHAPTER EIGHT: "STEWARDSHIP" 1919–1921

1. Edith Bolling Wilson, *My Memoir* (Indianapolis: Bobbs-Merrill, 1939), 289.

2. Wilson, *My Memoir*, 289.

3. Wilson, *My Memoir*, 289.

4. Wilson, *My Memoir*, 290.

5. U.S. Constitution, Article II, § 1, cl. 6.

6. Candice Millard, *Destiny of the Republic* (New York: Anchor, 2011), 219.

7. Joseph P. Tumulty, *Woodrow Wilson as I Know Him* (New York: Doubleday, 1921), 424.

8. Thomas R. Marshall, *Recollections of Thomas R. Marshall: A Hoosier Salad* (Indianapolis: Bobbs-Merrill, 1925), 368.

9. Irwin (Ike) Hood Hoover, *Forty-Two Years in the White House* (Boston: Houghton Mifflin, 1934), 102–3.

10. Alice Roosevelt Longworth, *Crowded Hours* (New York: Scribner's, 1933), 288.

11. Albert Fox, "'Very Sick Man' Says Grayson of President in Late Night Bulletin," *Washington Post*, October 3, 1919.

12. A. Scott Berg, *Wilson* (New York: G.P. Putnam's Sons, 2013), 645.

13. Marshall, *Recollections*, 368.

14. Wilson, *My Memoir*, 292.

15. Wilson, *My Memoir*, 292.

16. Wilson, *My Memoir*, 295.

17. John Milton Cooper, *Breaking the Heart of the World: Woodrow Wilson and the Fight for the League of Nations* (Cambridge: Cambridge University Press, 2001), 254.

18. Cooper, *Breaking the Heart*, 260.

19. Wilson, *My Memoir*, 297.

20. Wilson, *My Memoir*, 297.

21. Wilson, *My Memoir*, 297.

22. Cooper, *Breaking the Heart*, 266.

23. Longworth, *Crowded Hours*, 292.

24. Wilson, *My Memoir*, 297.

25. Phyllis Lee Levin, *Edith and Woodrow: The Wilson White House* (New York: Scribner, 2001), 357.

26. Tumulty, *Woodrow Wilson as I Know Him*, 391.

27. John Milton Cooper, *Woodrow Wilson: A Biography* (New York: Knopf, 2009), chapter 23.

28. Tom Shachtman, *Edith and Woodrow: A Presidential Romance* (New York: G.P. Putnam's Sons, 1981), 221.

29. Kristie Miller, *Ellen and Edith: Woodrow Wilson's First Ladies* (Lawrence: University Press of Kansas, 2010), 194.

30. Gene Smith, *When the Cheering Stopped: The Last Years of Woodrow Wilson* (New York: Open Road, 2016), 121.

31. Levin, *Edith and Woodrow*, 405.

32. Levin, *Edith and Woodrow*, 410.

33. *Town Topics*, February 15, 1920, NYPL.

34. Levin, *Edith and Woodrow*, 412.

35. Hoover, *Forty-Two Years in the White House*, 107–8.

36. Edmund W. Starling, *Starling of the White House* (Chicago: Peoples Book Club, 1941), 157.

37. Smith, *When the Cheering Stopped*, 146.

38. Cooper, *Woodrow Wilson*, chapter 23.

39. Longworth, *Crowded Hours*, 295.

40. Berg, *Wilson*, 663.

41. Franklin K. Lane to Elizabeth Ellis, January 19, 1920, published in Franklin K. Lane, *Letters of Franklin Lane* (Boston: Houghton Mifflin, 1922), 391.

42. Wilson, *My Memoir*, 300.

43. Levin, *Edith and Woodrow*, 422.

44. "Wilson's Last Mad Act," *Los Angeles Times*, February 15, 1920.

45. Levin, *Edith and Woodrow,* 424.

46. Smith, *When the Cheering Stopped*, 151.

47. Berg, *Wilson*, 669.

48. Berg, *Wilson*, 671.

49. Woodrow Wilson Papers, Series 9: Scrapbooks, 1864–1944, Vol. 5, 1920, image 5, LoC, Washington, DC.

50. Woodrow Wilson Papers, Series 9: Scrapbooks, 1864–1944, Vol. 5, 1920, image 18, LoC, Washington, DC.

51. Levin, *Edith and Woodrow*, 429.

52. *Town Topics*, February 5, 1920, NYPL.

53. Starling, *Starling of the White House*, 156.

54. Starling, *Starling of the White House*, 157.

55. Lillian Rogers Parks, *My Thirty Years Backstairs at the White House* (New York: Fleet, 1961), 157.

56. Berg, *Wilson*, 677.

57. Cary T. Grayson, *Woodrow Wilson: An Intimate Memoir* (Washington, DC: Potomac Books, 1960), 112.

58. Grayson, *Woodrow Wilson*, 112.

59. Smith, *When the Cheering Stopped*, 157.

60. Berg, *Wilson*, 680.

61. Berg, *Wilson*, 682.

62. Grayson, *Woodrow Wilson*, 116–17.

63. Grayson, *Woodrow Wilson*, 117.

64. Smith, *When the Cheering Stopped*, 163–64.

65. Hoover, *Forty-Two Years in the White House*, 106.

66. Smith, *When the Cheering Stopped*, 165.

67. Berg, *Wilson*, 688.

68. Smith, *When the Cheering Stopped*, 166.

69. David Pietrusza, *1920: The Year of the Six Presidents* (New York: Basic, 2009), 253.

70. Dolly Gann, *Dolly Gann's Book* (New York: Doubleday, 1933), 53.

CHAPTER NINE: AFTER THE WHITE HOUSE 1921–1924

1. "Woodrow Wilson: Facts," NobelPrize.org, last modified December 5, 2021, nobelprize.org/prizes/peace/1919/wilson/facts.

2. Edith Bolling Wilson, *My Memoir* (Indianapolis: Bobbs-Merrill, 1939), 311.

3. Elizabeth Karcher, interview with the author, January 2022.

4. Wilson, *My Memoir*, 312.

5. Wilson, *My Memoir*, 312.

6. Wilson, *My Memoir*, 313.

7. A. Scott Berg, *Wilson* (New York: G.P. Putnam's Sons, 2013), 697.

8. Gene Smith, *When the Cheering Stopped: The Last Years of Woodrow Wilson* (New York: Open Road, 2016), 178n.

9. Wilson, *My Memoir*, 321.
10. Wilson, *My Memoir*, 314.
11. Wilson, *My Memoir*, 317.
12. Wilson, *My Memoir*, 317.
13. Wilson, *My Memoir*, 316.
14. Wilson, *My Memoir*, 318.
15. Wilson, *My Memoir*, 318.
16. Wilson, *My Memoir*, 319.
17. Berg, *Wilson*, 704.
18. Wilson, *My Memoir*, 322.
19. Wilson, *My Memoir*, 324–25.
20. Wilson, *My Memoir*, 328.
21. Wilson, *My Memoir*, 328.
22. Phyllis Lee Levin, *Edith and Woodrow: The Wilson White House* (New York: Scribner, 2001), 470.
23. Wilson, *My Memoir*, 346.
24. Wilson, *My Memoir*, 333.
25. "Ex-President Wilson's Repudiation of Message Attributed to Him at Democratic Dinner," *New York Times*, April 14, 1922.
26. William Allen White, *Woodrow Wilson* (Boston: Houghton Mifflin, 1929), 472.
27. Wilson, *My Memoir*, 348.
28. Wilson, *My Memoir*, 347–48.
29. Smith, *When the Cheering Stopped*, 224.
30. Levin, *Edith and Woodrow*, 484–85.
31. Berg, *Wilson*, 727.
32. Levin, *Edith and Woodrow*, 486.
33. Wilson, *My Memoir*, 348.
34. Wilson, *My Memoir*, 348.
35. Frederick Lewis Allen, *Only Yesterday: An Informal History of the 1920s* (New York: Open Road Media, 2015), 142.
36. Wilson, *My Memoir*, 345.
37. Wilson, *My Memoir*, 346.
38. Wilson, *My Memoir*, 346.
39. Smith, *When the Cheering Stopped*, 226.
40. Wilson, *My Memoir*, 351.
41. Wilson, *My Memoir*, 351.
42. Wilson, *My Memoir*, 353.
43. Wilson, *My Memoir*, 353.
44. Wilson, *My Memoir*, 353.

45. Wilson, *My Memoir*, 354.

46. Smith, *When the Cheering Stopped*, 230.

47. Wilson, *My Memoir*, 355.

48. Smith, *When the Cheering Stopped*, 230.

49. Smith, *When the Cheering Stopped*, 231.

50. White, *Woodrow Wilson*, 467.

51. Berg, *Wilson*, 732.

52. Smith, *When the Cheering Stopped*, 234.

53. Wilson, *My Memoir*, 357.

54. John Milton Cooper, *Woodrow Wilson: A Biography* (New York: Knopf, 2009), chapter 25.

55. Wilson, *My Memoir*, unpublished 1924–1939 chapters, transcribed for the author by the Edith Bolling Wilson Birthplace Museum.

56. Wilson, *My Memoir*, 360.

57. Berg, *Wilson*, 738.

58. Wilson, *My Memoir*, unpublished 1924–1939 chapters.

59. Cary T. Grayson, *Woodrow Wilson: An Intimate Memoir* (Washington, DC: Potomac Books, 1960), 140.

60. Grayson, *Woodrow Wilson*, 140.

61. Wilson, *My Memoir*, unpublished 1924–1939 chapters.

62. Wilson, *My Memoir*, unpublished 1924–1939 chapters.

63. Smith, *When the Cheering Stopped*, 251.

64. Smith, *When the Cheering Stopped*, 252.

65. Berg, *Wilson*, 740.

66. Wilson, *My Memoir*, unpublished 1924–1939 chapters.

67. Ishbel Ross, *Power with Grace: The Life Story of Mrs. Woodrow Wilson* (New York: G.P. Putnam's Sons, 1975), 260.

CHAPTER TEN: WOMAN OF WASHINGTON REPRISE 1924-1961

1. Bronislas A. Jezierski, "The Wilson Monument in Poland," *Polish American Studies* 12, no. 1/2 (1955): 21, jstor.org/stable/20147379.

2. Ishbel Ross, *Power with Grace: The Life Story of Mrs. Woodrow Wilson* (New York: G.P. Putnam's Sons, 1975), 275.

3. Edith Bolling Wilson, *My Memoir*, unpublished 1924–1939 chapters, transcribed for the author by the Edith Bolling Wilson Birthplace Museum.

4. Wilson, *My Memoir*, unpublished 1924–1939 chapters.

5. Jezierski, "Wilson Monument in Poland," 28.

6. Alden Hatch, *Edith Bolling Wilson: First Lady Extraordinary* (New York: Dodd, Mead, 1961), 269.

7. Ross, *Power with Grace*, 286.

8. "Wilson Statue Dynamited by Nazis," Jewish Telegraphic Agency, February 7, 1940.

9. Wilson, *My Memoir*, unpublished 1924–1939 chapters.

10. Wilson, *My Memoir*, unpublished 1924–1939 chapters.

11. Wilson, *My Memoir*, unpublished 1924–1939 chapters.

12. "Widow Forbids Publication of Wilson Letters," *New York Times*, March 12, 1924.

13. Phyllis Lee Levin, *Edith and Woodrow: The Wilson White House* (New York: Scribner, 2001), 503.

14. Edward Mandell House, *The Intimate Papers of Colonel House* (Cambridge, MA: Riverside Press, 1926), 10–11.

15. Everett C. Watkins, "Mrs. Woodrow Wilson's Story Sets Tongues Wagging," *Indianapolis Star*, March 12, 1939.

16. Ross, *Power with Grace*, 292.

17. "Wilson: Crescendo and Diminuendo," *Fort Worth Star-Telegram*, March 12, 1939.

18. Levin, *Edith and Woodrow*, 507.

19. "The Book of the Week," *New York Daily News*, March 12, 1939.

20. Wilson, *My Memoir*, unpublished 1924–1939 chapters.

21. Wilson, *My Memoir*, unpublished 1924–1939 chapters.

22. Woodrow Wilson Papers, Series 9: Scrapbooks, 1864–1944, Vol. 11, 1924–1929, image 252, LoC, Washington, DC.

23. Woodrow Wilson Papers, Series 9: Scrapbooks, 1864–1944, Vol. 11, 1924–1929, image 253, LoC, Washington, DC.

24. Woodrow Wilson Papers, Series 9: Scrapbooks, 1864–1944, Vol. 11, 1924–1929, image 257, LoC, Washington, DC.

25. Wilson, *My Memoir*, unpublished 1924–1939 chapters.

26. Wilson, *My Memoir*, unpublished 1924–1939 chapters.

27. "Wife of Late Pres. Wilson Favors Smith," *San Francisco Chronicle*, June 26, 1928.

28. "Governor Smith," *New York Times*, June 29, 1928.

29. Wilson, *My Memoir*, unpublished 1924–1939 chapters.

30. Eleanor Roosevelt, My Day, December 9, 1941.

31. Wilson, *My Memoir*, unpublished 1924–1939 chapters.

32. Wilson, *My Memoir*, unpublished 1924–1939 chapters.

33. Mark Wheeler, "Darryl F. Zanuck's *Wilson*," in *Presidents in the Movies*, ed. Iwan W. Morgan (New York: Palgrave Macmillan, 2011), 87.

34. Wheeler, "Darryl F. Zanuck's *Wilson*," 88.

35. Ross, *Power with Grace*, 296.

36. Ross, *Power with Grace*, 297.
37. Ross, *Power with Grace*, 298.
38. Levin, *Edith and Woodrow*, 510.
39. Cary Fuller, interview with the author, January 2022.
40. Woodrow Wilson Centennial Celebration Commission, *Woodrow Wilson Centennial: Final Report* (Washington, DC: U.S. Government Printing Office, 1958).
41. Washington National Cathedral, "Service of Dedication of Memorial Bay and Tomb of Woodrow Wilson President of the United States," November 11, 1956, WWP19663, Eleanor Wilson McAdoo Collection at the University of California–Santa Barbara.
42. Ross, *Power with Grace*, 340.
43. Richard Trenner, "Portrait of a Lady," *Princeton Alumni Weekly*, June 24, 2016.
44. Trenner, "Portrait of a Lady."
45. Fuller, interview with the author.
46. Fuller, interview with the author.
47. Kevin Ambrose and Jason Samenow, "How a Surprise Snowstorm Almost Spoiled Kennedy's Inauguration 60 Years Ago," *Washington Post*, January 19, 2021.
48. Thomas Sayre, interview with the author, January 2022.
49. Hatch, *Edith Bolling Wilson*, 275.
50. Elizabeth Karcher, interview with the author, January 2022.
51. Karcher, interview with the author.
52. "Wilson Memorial Closer," *News Leader* (Staunton, VA), October 8, 1961.
53. Joint Resolution Authorizing the Creation of a Commission to Consider and Formulate Plans for the Construction in the District of Columbia of an Appropriate Permanent Memorial to the Memory of Woodrow Wilson, Pub. L. No. 87-364, 75 Stat. 783 (1961).
54. "Wilson Memorial Commission Created," *Courier-News* (Bridgewater, NJ), October 5, 1961.
55. Ross, *Power with Grace*, 343.
56. "Mrs. Woodrow Wilson, 89, Dies on the Birthday of Her Husband; Center of Controversy During President's Illness, When She Was Intermediary," *New York Times*, December 29, 1961.
57. "Mrs. Woodrow Wilson," *Richmond Times-Dispatch*, December 30, 1961.
58. "The Regent Passes," editorial, *News & Observer* (Raleigh, NC), December 30, 1961.
59. Associated Press, "Wilson's Widow Dies," *Star Press* (Muncie, IN), December 29, 1961.
60. Associated Press, "Woodrow's Widow: Edith Wilson Dies; WWI First Lady," *Springfield (MO) News-Leader*, December 29, 1961.

BIBLIOGRAPHY

PAPERS AND CORRESPONDENCE

Cary T. Grayson Papers. Woodrow Wilson Presidential Library, Staunton, VA.

Jessie Wilson Sayre Collection. Seeley G. Mudd Manuscript Library, Princeton, NJ.

Edith Bolling Galt Wilson Papers. Library of Congress, Washington, DC.

Woodrow Wilson Papers. Library of Congress, Washington DC.

BOOKS

Adams, Henry. *The Education of Henry Adams*. Overland Park, KS: Neeland Media, 2004.

Allen, Frederick Lewis. *Only Yesterday: An Informal History of the 1920s*. New York: Open Road Media, 2015.

Anonymous. *Washington Merry-Go-Round*. New York: Liveright, 1931.

Bagby, Wesley M. *The Road to Normalcy*. Baltimore: Johns Hopkins Press, 1962.

Bennett, David J. *He Almost Changed the World: The Life and Times of Thomas Riley Marshall*. Bloomington, IN: AuthorHouse, 2007.

Berg, A. Scott. *Wilson*. New York: G.P. Putnam's Sons, 2013.

Berg, Scott W. *Grand Avenues: The Story of Pierre Charles L'Enfant, the French Visionary Who Designed Washington, D.C.* New York: Vintage, 2007.

Beschloss, Michael. *Presidents of War*. New York: Crown, 2018.

Blum, John Morton. *Joe Tumulty and the Wilson Era*. Cambridge, MA: Riverside Press, 1951.

Brands, H. W. *The Reckless Decade*. Chicago: University of Chicago Press, 1991.

Caroli, Betty Boyd. *First Ladies: From Martha Washington to Michelle Obama*. New York: Oxford University Press, 2010.

Cooper, John Milton. *Breaking the Heart of the World: Woodrow Wilson and the Fight for the League of Nations*. Cambridge: Cambridge University Press, 2001.

———. *Woodrow Wilson: A Biography*. New York: Knopf, 2009.

Cordery, Stacy A. *Alice: Alice Roosevelt Longworth, from White House Princess to Washington Power Broker*. New York: Penguin, 2008.

Covey, Joyce, and Farron Smith. *First Lady Mrs. Wilson and How the Sheep Helped Win the War*. Herndon, VA: Mascot Books, 2016.

Elliott, Margaret Axson. *My Aunt Louisa and Woodrow Wilson*. Chapel Hill: University of North Carolina Press, 1944.

Foner, Eric. *A Short History of Reconstruction*. New York: Harper, 2015.

Foster, Gaines M. *Ghosts of the Confederacy*. New York: Oxford University Press, 1987.

Furman, Bess. *White House Profile*. Indianapolis: Bobbs-Merrill, 1951.

Gann, Dolly. *Dolly Gann's Book*. New York: Doubleday, 1933.

Giblin, James Cross. *Edith Wilson: The Woman Who Ran the United States*. New York: Viking, 1992.

Grayson, Cary T. *Woodrow Wilson: An Intimate Memoir*. Washington, DC: Potomac Books, 1960.

Greenidge, Kerri K. *Black Radical: The Life and Times of William Monroe Trotter*. New York: Liveright, 2019.

Hager, Andrew. *Old Ike: The Fictionalized Story of Woodrow Wilson's Ram*. Middletown, DE: Presidential Pet Museum, 2017.

Harriman, Florence Jaffray Hurst. *From Pinafores to Politics*. New York: Henry Holt, 1923.

Hatch, Alden. *Edith Bolling Wilson: First Lady Extraordinary*. New York: Dodd, Mead, 1961.

Hazelgrove, William. *Madam President: The Secret Presidency of Edith Wilson*. Washington, DC: Regnery, 2016.

Helm, Edith Benham. *The Captains and the Kings*. New York: G.P. Putnam's Sons, 1954.

Hodgson, Godfrey. *Woodrow Wilson's Right Hand: The Life of Colonel Edward M. House*. New Haven, CT: Yale University Press, 2006.

Hoff, Joan. *Law, Gender & Injustice*. New York: New York University Press, 1991.

Hoover, Irwin (Ike) Hood. *Forty-Two Years in the White House.* Boston: Houghton Mifflin, 1934.

House, Edward Mandell. *The Intimate Papers of Colonel House.* Cambridge, MA: Riverside Press, 1926.

———. *What Really Happened at Paris.* New York: Scribner's, 1921.

Hulbert, Mary Allen. *The Story of Mrs. Peck.* New York: Minton, Balch, 1933.

Jacob, Kathryn Allamong. *Capital Elites.* Washington, DC: Smithsonian Institution Press, 1995.

Jones, Catherine A. *Intimate Reconstructions: Children in Postemancipation Virginia.* Charlottesville: University of Virginia Press, 2015.

Lane, Franklin K. *The Letters of Franklin K. Lane.* Boston: Houghton Mifflin, 1922.

Larson, Erik. *Dead Wake: The Last Crossing of the Lusitania.* New York: Penguin Random House, 2015.

Levin, Phyllis Lee. *Edith and Woodrow: The Wilson White House.* New York: Scribner, 2001.

Lewis, Tom. *Washington: A History of Our National City.* New York: Basic Books, 2015.

Link, Arthur S., ed. *The Papers of Woodrow Wilson.* Princeton, NJ: Princeton University Press, 1991.

Link, Arthur S. *Woodrow Wilson and a Revolutionary World, 1913–1921.* Chapel Hill: University of North Carolina Press, 1982.

Longworth, Alice Roosevelt. *Crowded Hours.* New York: Scribner's, 1933.

Marshall, Thomas R. *Recollections of Thomas R. Marshall: A Hoosier Salad.* Indianapolis: Bobbs-Merrill, 1925.

Marton, Kati. *Hidden Power: Presidential Marriages That Shaped Our History.* New York: Anchor Books, 2002.

McAdoo, Eleanor Wilson. *The Woodrow Wilsons.* New York: MacMillan, 1937.

McGerr, Michael. *A Fierce Discontent: The Rise and Fall of the Progressive Movement in America.* New York: Free Press, 2003.

Millard, Candice. *Destiny of the Republic.* New York: Anchor Books, 2011.

Miller, Kristie. *Ellen and Edith: Woodrow Wilson's First Ladies.* Lawrence: University Press of Kansas, 2010.

Ozer, Mark N. *Massachusetts Avenue in the Gilded Age: Palaces & Privilege.* Mount Pleasant, SC: Arcadia, 2010.

Painter, Nell Irvin. *Standing at Armageddon: A Grassroots History of the Progressive Era*. New York: W.W. Norton, 2008.

Parks, Lillian Rogers. *My Thirty Years Backstairs at the White House*. New York: Fleet, 1961.

Peck, Garrett. *The Great War in America: World War I and Its Aftermath*. New York: W.W. Norton, 2018.

Pietrusza, David. *1920: The Year of the Six Presidents*. New York: Basic, 2009.

Reed, Robert. *Old Washington, D.C. in Early Photographs 1846–1932*. Mineola, NY: Dover, 1980.

Reid, Edith Gittings. *Woodrow Wilson: The Caricature, the Myth and the Man*. New York: Oxford University Press, 1934.

Richardson, John P. *Alexander Robey Shepherd: The Man Who Built the Nation's Capital*. Athens: Ohio University Press, 2016.

Ridley, Jane. *George V: Never a Dull Moment*. New York: HarperCollins, 2022.

Roberts, John B. *Rating the First Ladies: The Women Who Influenced the Presidency*. New York: Citadel, 2003.

Roberts, Rebecca Boggs. *Suffragists in Washington, D.C: The 1913 Parade and the Fight for the Vote*. Mount Pleasant, SC: History Press, 2017.

Ross, Ishbel. *Power with Grace: The Life Story of Mrs. Woodrow Wilson*. New York: G.P. Putnam's Sons, 1975.

Shachtman, Tom. *Edith and Woodrow: A Presidential Romance*. New York: G.P. Putnam's Sons, 1981.

Shaw, Gwendolyn DuBois. *First Ladies of the United States*. Washington, DC: Smithsonian Books, 2020.

Slayden, Ellen Maury. *Washington Wife*. New York: Harper, 1962.

Smith, Gene. *When the Cheering Stopped: The Last Years of Woodrow Wilson*. New York: Open Road, 2016.

Smith, Marie, and Louise Durbin. *White House Brides*. Washington, DC: Acropolis Books, 1966.

Spinney, Laura. *Pale Rider: The Spanish Flu of 1918 and How It Changed the World*. New York: PublicAffairs, 2017.

Srodes, James. *On Dupont Circle: Franklin and Eleanor Roosevelt and the Progressives Who Shaped Our World*. Berkeley, CA: Counterpoint, 2012.

Starling, Edmund W. *Starling of the White House*. Chicago: Peoples Book Club, 1941.

Tribble, Edwin, ed. *President in Love: The Courtship Letters of Woodrow Wilson and Edith Bolling Galt*. Boston: Houghton Mifflin, 1981.

Tumulty, Joseph P. *Woodrow Wilson as I Know Him.* New York: Doubleday, 1921.

Twain, Mark. *Pudd'nhead Wilson.* 1894. Reprint, New York: W.W. Norton, 2004.

Weinstein, Edwin A. *Woodrow Wilson: A Medical and Psychological Biography.* Princeton, NJ: Princeton University Press, 1981.

Wertheimer, Molly Meijer, ed. *Inventing a Voice: The Rhetoric of American First Ladies of the Twentieth Century.* Lanham, MD: Rowman & Littlefield, 2004.

Wharton, Edith. *The Age of Innocence.* New York: W.W. Norton, 2002.

White, William Allen. *Woodrow Wilson.* Boston: Houghton Mifflin, 1929.

Wilson, Edith Bolling. *My Memoir.* Indianapolis: Bobbs-Merrill, 1939.

ARTICLES

Anthony, Carl. "A First Lady's Princess Complex: Royalty, Racism & Edith Wilson's Pocahontas Blood." Firstladies.org, September 18, 2012.

Egerton, George. "Diplomacy, Scandal and Military Intelligence: The Craufurd-Stuart Affair and Anglo-American Relations 1918–20." *Intelligence and National Security* 2, no. 4 (1987): 110–34. doi.org /10.1080/02684528708431918.

Fuller, Thomas. "'Go West, Young Man!'—an Elusive Slogan." *Indiana Magazine of History* 100, no. 3 (September 2004).

Gibson, Campbell. "Population of the 100 Largest Cities and Other Urban Places in the United States: 1790 to 1990." U.S. Census Bureau working paper no. POP-WP207, June 1998.

Jezierski, Bronislas A. "The Wilson Monument in Poland." *Polish American Studies* 12, no. 1/2 (1955): 19–34. jstor.org/stable/20147379.

King, Leslie. "The Devils in the Workhouses: Edith Bolling Wilson, Woman Suffrage, and Equity." *Wythe County Historical Review,* Summer 2011.

Knaplund, Kristine S. "The Evolution of Women's Rights in Inheritance." *Hastings Women's Law Journal* 19, no. 3 (2008): 3–51. repository.uchastings .edu/hwlj/vol19/iss1/2.

Maechling, Charles, Jr. "Scandal in Wartime Washington: The Craufurd-Stuart Affair of 1918." *International Journal of Intelligence and CounterIntelligence* 4, no. 3 (1990): 357–70.

Maillard, Kevin Noble. "The Pocahontas Exception: The Exemption of American Indian Ancestry from Racial Purity Law." *Michigan Journal of Race and Law* 12, no. 2 (2007): 351–86.

McRae, Elizabeth Gillespie. "Caretakers of Southern Civilization: Georgia Women and the Anti-suffrage Campaign, 1914–1920." *Georgia Historical Quarterly* 82, no. 4 (1998): 801–28. jstor.org/stable/40583906.

Ranney, Joseph A. "Anglicans, Merchants, and Feminists: A Comparative Study of the Evolution of Married Women's Rights in Virginia, New York, and Wisconsin." *William & Mary Journal of Women and the Law* 6, no. 3 (2000): 493–559.

Scharff, Virginia. "Femininity and the Electric Car." Automobile in American Life and Society, no date. autolife.umd.umich.edu/Gender/Scharff/G _casestudy.htm.

Trenner, Richard. "Portrait of a Lady." *Princeton Alumni Weekly*, June 24, 2016.

Welter, Barbara. "The Cult of True Womanhood: 1820–1860." *American Quarterly* 18, no. 2, part 1 (Summer 1966): 151–74

Wheeler, Mark. "Darryl F. Zanuck's *Wilson*." In *Presidents in the Movies*, edited by Iwan W. Morgan. New York: Palgrave Macmillan, 2011, 87–108.

NEWSPAPER ARTICLES

Ambrose, Kevin, and Jason Samenow. "How a Surprise Snowstorm Almost Spoiled Kennedy's Inauguration 60 Years Ago." *The Washington Post*, January 19, 2021.

Associated Press. "Wilson's Widow Dies." *Star Press* (Muncie, IN), December 29, 1961.

Associated Press. "Woodrow Wilson's Widow: Edith Wilson Dies; WWI First Lady." *Springfield (MO) News Leader*, December 29, 1961.

"The Book of the Week." *New York Daily News*, March 12, 1939.

"Chum of Wilson's Cousin." *Davey (NE) Mirror*, August 19, 1915.

"Deaths at Wytheville." *News* (Lynchburg VA), March 9, 1898.

"England Make Precedent by Welcoming Mrs. Wilson." *The Washington Post*, December 26, 1918.

"Galt Funeral Tomorrow." *The Washington Post*, January 29, 1908.

"Governor Smith." *The New York Times*, June 29, 1928.

Halloran, Liz. "A Glittering History." *Hartford Courant*, July 27, 2001.

"Ike, Famous Tobacco Chewing White House Sheep, Is Dead." *Spartanburg (SC) Herald*, August 14, 1927.

Jewish Telegraphic Agency. "Wilson Statue Dynamited by Nazis." February 7, 1940.

"Joy to Suffragists." *The New York Times*, October 1, 1918.

"Launch First Ship at Hog Island." *The New York Times*, August 6, 1918.

"More White House Sheep." *The Washington Post*, March 3, 1918.

"Mrs. Wilson Joins Lower Meat Drive." *The New York Times*, March 26, 1920.

"Mrs. Wilson and Society Leaders to Economize as Example to Country." *The Washington Post*, April 13, 1917.

"Mrs. Wilson's Birthday." *The New York Times*, October 16, 1916.

"Mrs. Wilson's Food Pledge." *The New York Times*, July 1, 1917.

"Mrs. Wilson's Posts Pledge." *The New York Times*, July 7, 1917.

"Mrs. Woodrow Wilson." *Richmond Times-Dispatch*, December 30, 1961.

"Mrs. Woodrow Wilson, 89, Dies on the Birthday of Her Husband; Center of Controversy During President's Illness, When She Was Intermediary." *The New York Times*, December 29, 1961.

"Norman Galt Dead." *Washington Herald*, January 28, 1908.

"Norman Galt's Death Shocks Business Friends; Prominent in Trade Bodies." *Washington Times*, January 28, 1908.

"Pershing's 'Jeff' Will Lead Parade." *The Washington Post*, April 12, 1920.

"President Suffers Collapse; Cancels Dates." *Belvidere (IL) Daily Republican*, September 26, 1919.

"President to Wed at Bride's Home, Not White House." *Brooklyn Daily Eagle*, October 7, 1915.

"President to Wed Mrs. Norman Galt." *Evening Star* (Washington, DC), October 7, 1915.

"President to Wed Once More? Ask Gossips." *Stockton (CA) Evening Mail*, July 29, 1915.

"Progress Made to Omaha After President Rests on Sunday at Des Moines." *Evening Star* (Washington, DC), September 8, 1919.

"The Regent Passes" (editorial). *News & Observer* (Raleigh, NC), December 30, 1961.

Roosevelt, Eleanor. My Day, December 9, 1941.

Seibold, Louis. "President Now in Foe's State." *Baltimore Sun*, September 17, 1919.

"Senators See President." *The New York Times*, December 6, 1919.

"Shows Fighting Temper." *Evening Star* (Washington, DC), September 5, 1919.

Small, Robert T. "Street Crowded Calm Greeting President." *The Washington Post*, September 9, 1919.

Town Topics, February 11, 1915; August 5, 1915; September 9, 1915; October 21, 1915; November 11, 1915; November 14, 1915; November 25, 1915; December 16, 1915; July 6, 1916; July 26, 1917; February 5, 1920; February 15, 1920; February 26, 1920. New York Public Library.

Watkins, Everett C. "Mrs. Woodrow Wilson's Story Sets Tongues Wagging." *Indianapolis Star*, March 12, 1939.

"White House Fiance Wears Happy Smile; to Buy Ring Today." *Atlanta Constitution*, October 8, 1915.

"Widow Forbids Publication of Wilson Letters." *The New York Times*, March 12, 1924.

"Wife of Late Pres. Wilson Favors Smith." *San Francisco Chronicle*, June 26, 1928.

"Wilson: Crescendo and Diminuendo." *Fort Worth Star-Telegram*, March 12, 1939.

"Wilson Ill: Cancels Tour." *Capital Times* (Madison, WI), September 26, 1919.

"Wilson on Long Trip." *The Washington Post*, September 4, 1919.

"Wilson Memorial Closer." *News Leader* (Staunton VA), October 8, 1961.

"Wilson Memorial Commission Created." *Courier News* (Bridgewater NJ), October 5, 1961.

"Wilson's Last Mad Act." *Los Angeles Times*, February 15, 1920.

"Wilson's Sheep Scared by Autos." *The Washington Post*, May 12, 1918.

ILLUSTRATION CREDITS

page 1 (top): Edith Bolling Wilson Birthplace Museum.

page 1 (bottom): University of Virginia Special Collections.

page 2 (top): Edith Bolling Wilson Birthplace Museum.

page 2 (bottom): Photograph by the author.

page 3 (top): Edith Bolling Galt Wilson, full-length portrait, seated on porch, facing slightly left, at age 15. 1887. Library of Congress, [LC-USZ62-127641].

page 3 (bottom): C.M. Bell, photographer. *Edith Bolling married Woodrow Wilson,* Between January 1891 and January 1894. Library of Congress, [LC-DIG-bellcm-03586].

page 4 (top): Edith Bolling Galt in the first electric automobile driven by a woman in Washington, D.C. Library of Congress, [LC-USZ62-139014].

page 4 (bottom): Harris & Ewing, photographer. *GALT, MRS. EDITH BOLLING. M. WOODROW WILSON, DEC. 18, . HER JEWELRY STORE, 'GALT & BRO.'* Library of Congress, [LC-DIG-hec-06261].

page 5 (top): Harris & Ewing, photographer. *Edith Bolling Galt Wilson, full-length portrait, standing, facing front, hands behind waist.* Library of Congress, [LC-USZ62-92811].

page 5 (bottom): Wilson family 1911 (Margaret, Ellen, Nell, Jesse, Woodrow). National Portrait Gallery, Smithsonian Institution.

page 6 (top): For President Woodrow Wilson, for Vice-President Thomas R. Marshall. By Manhattan Slide Company, Inc., New York City, 1912. Library of Congress, [LC-USZC2-6524].

page 6 (middle): Mrs. Cary Grayson in Mkt. Library of Congress, [LC-DIG-npcc-01306].

page 6 (bottom): Doctor Gary i.e. Cary Grayson, President Wilson's personal physician, photographed as he left the White House today. Library of Congress, [LC-USZ62-102803].

page 7 (top): Harris & Ewing, photographer. *HORSE SHOWS. MISS HELEN WOOD-ROW BONES; DR. CARY T. GRAYSON; MISS ELEANOR WILSON.* Library of Congress, [LC-DIG-hec-02565].

page 7 (bottom): Residence, Mrs. Norman Galt, 20th, Washington, D.C. Between 1910 and 1926. Library of Congress, [LC-DIG-npcc-32380].

pages 8, 9: Woodrow Wilson and Edith Bolling Galt, head-and-shoulders portraits cut in the shape of overlapping hearts with rose border; drawing of cupid in lower right and of the U.S. Capitol which is visible between the hearts. Library of Congress, [LC-USZ62-21328]

page 10 (top): Mrs. Woodrow Wilson Edith Bolling Galt, bust portrait, facing front. Between 1915 and 1921. Library of Congress, [LC-USZ62-25808].

page 10 (bottom): EBW WW Campaign trial 1916. Artist Harris & Ewing Studio. National Portrait Gallery, Smithsonian Institution; gift of Aileen Conkey. Object number S/NPG.84.277.

page 11 (top): Portrait by Adolfo Müller-Ury in 1916. Oil on canvas, 39 3/4 by 29 1/2 inches. White House Collection/White House Historical Association.

page 11 (bottom): Bain News Service, Publisher. *Wilson, Paris.* December 19, 1918. Library of Congress, [LC-DIG-ggbain-28213].

page 12 (top): Woodrow Wilson, half length, seated, facing right; and his wife Edith Bolling Galt holding flowers. Library of Congress, [LC-USZ62-65032].

page 12 (bottom): Woodrow Wilson, right, with personal secretary Joseph "Joe" Patrick Tumulty. Library of Congress, [LC-DIG-npcc-00356].

page 13(top): Bain News Service, Publisher. *R. Lansing, Paris.* December 17, 1918. Library of Congress, [LC-DIG-ggbain-28151].

page 13 (bottom): Pres. & Mrs. Wilson. March 20, 1920. Library of Congress, [LC-DIG-npcc-01264].

page 14 (top): Harris & Ewing, photographer. *President Woodrow Wilson, seated at desk with his wife, Edith Bolling Galt, standing at his side.* June, 1920. Library of Congress, [LC-DIG-ppmsca-13425].

page 14 (bottom): Portrait by Seymour Stone. Bruce White for the White House Historical Association/Collection of Woodrow Wilson House.

page 15 (top): Woodrow Wilson and Edith Wilson participating in Armistice Day festivities. November 11, 1922. Library of Congress, [LC-USZ62-137940].

page 15 (bottom): Portrait by Emile Alexay. Oil on canvas, 46 1/4 inches by 31 5/16 inches. National Portrait Gallery, Smithsonian Institution. Gift of Dr. Alan Urdang. Object no. NPG.69.43.

page 16: President John F. Kennedy Signs Bill to Establish the Woodrow Wilson Memorial Commission. Abbie Rowe. White House Photographs. John F. Kennedy Presidential Library and Museum, Boston. Accession number AR6818-B.

INDEX

papers of, 242
physical appearance of, 9, 24, 75
president's courtship of, 75–77, 78–88, 89–90. *See also* engagement of Edith to President Wilson
and president's desire for third term, 195, 197
president's first sighting of, 72
and president's legacy, 230
president's marriage proposal, 77–78
racial attitudes of, 82
social charms of, 75
and speeches, 230
and suffrage/suffragists, 58, 103, 117–19
travels. *See* travels of Edith Wilson
voice of, 24
See also First Lady role
Wilson, Eleanor. *See* McAdoo, Eleanor "Nell" Wilson
Wilson, Ellen Axson
awkward personality of, x, 52
burial site of, 220
death of, ix, 63–64
declining health of, 61, 63
and Eleanor's marriage, 60
move to Washington, 52
and presidential election of 1912, 50
and president's engagement to Edith, 97
and "proper"/"vulgar" family members, 60
role as husband's confidant, 52, 58
summer in New Hampshire, 62
Wilson, Jessie. *See* Sayre, Jessie Wilson
Wilson, Margaret
death of, 245
death of father, 219
death of mother, 64
and father's engagement to Edith, 94, 96
and First Lady responsibilities, 66
and funeral of president, 222
and presidential election of 1916, 114, 115
and "proper"/"vulgar" family members, 60
and retirement home of Edith and president, 205
singing career of, 66, 66n, 244
Slayden's memoirs on, 54
as suffragist, 118
and war effort, 126
and Washington society, 52–53
Wilson, Woodrow
and arming of merchant ships, 122–23
and armistice celebration at Italian Embassy, 140
automobile rides of, 71, 72, 191–92, 207
biographies and memoirs on, xiii, 209–10, 218–19, 225–27, 233
and Bryan, 82–83, 84, 87
burial site of, 220, 220n, 235, 235n, 246

calls for president to step down, 189, 191
congressional address on domestic agenda, 59–60
congressional address on U.S. joining war, 123–24
contingency plans in the event he lost 1916 election, 113–14
death and funeral of, 219–22
death of first wife, Ellen, ix, 63–64, 67–68
doctor of. *See* Grayson, Cary Travers
Edith as confidant of, 82–83, 87, 92–93, 110. *See also* political engagement of Edith
Edith courted by, xii–xiii, 75–77, 78–88, 89–90. *See also* engagement of Edith to President Wilson
Edith first sighted by, 72
Edith relied upon by, 83–84, 87, 96, 110, 130
and Edith's birthday celebration, 112–13
Edith's correspondence with, 75–76, 78–88, 91–92, 94–95, 96, 214, 241
Edith's first meeting with, 74
Edith's marriage to, ix, 104–6
education of, 79
and Eleanor's marriage, 60
favorite sweater of, 6, 8, 130, 178–79
female companionship needed by, 64, 96
flowers sent to Edith, 95
and foreign languages, 144
foreign policy experience, 64
Fourteen Points speech of, 134
golf game of, 61, 62, 71
gossip about love life of, 51, 72–73, 95–96
at Harlakenden House with Edith, 88–91
health issues of. *See* health of President Wilson
horseback riding of, 131
image cultivated by, 72
inaugurations of, 53, 54–56, 122
as lame duck president, 198
Lansing fired by, 189
law practice of, 207–8
legacy of, 230, 232, 234–36
life after the presidency. *See* retirement years
loneliness of, 67–68
and *Lusitania* attack, 83–84, 86
marriage proposal to Edith, 77–78
and Mary Peck, 51, 97–101
and *Mayflower* voyage in storm, 84–85
memorials/tributes to, 223–25, 232–33, 234–36, 238–39, 246
and midterm elections of 1918, 136–37
move to Washington, 52
and neutrality of U.S. in WWI, 68–69, 112, 121
New Freedom domestic agenda of, 58–59
Nobel Peace Prize given to, 200
papers/correspondence of, 225–27, 241–42

Wilson, Woodrow (*cont.*)
    and Paris Peace Conference, 140–45,
        147–51, 155
    political appointments made by, 58–59
    and presidential election of 1912, 48–52
    and presidential election of 1916, 90, 93–94,
        111–16
    and "proper"/"vulgar" family members, 60
    and public/social aspects of office, 54
    racial attitudes of, 69–71, 82
    review of Atlantic fleet, 84
    on roles of the president, 54
    sartorial choices of, 75
    schedule of, 109–10
    summer in New Hampshire, 62
    superstitious streak of, 151
    third term considered by, 194–98, 218
    and women' suffrage, 54–55, 103, 116–17, 136
    See also League of Nations; World War I
Wilson Centennial Commission, 238
Wilson Center (think tank), 239*n*
Wiseman, William, 168–69
women
    attitudes toward political ambitions in, 191
    and childhood lessons on roles of, 15
    and presidential election of 1916, 103, 116
    and president's engagement to Edith, 97
    profound changes in social roles of, x
    property rights of, 41–42
    and public/domestic spheres, x, 118–19
    and True Womanhood cult, 15, 19, 118–19
    voting in election of 1916, 97
    See also suffrage and suffragists
Women's National Democratic Club, 234
Wood, Waddy Butler, 201
Woodrow Wilson Birthplace Foundation, 232,
    234, 238, 241–42
Woodrow Wilson Foundation, 213
Woodrow Wilson House in Washington, 198*n*
Woodrow Wilson Memorial Commission, 239
Woodrow Wilson Presidential Library and
    Research Center, 234

Woodrow Wilson School of Public and
    International Affairs, 238
Woolley, Robert, 4–5, 196
World (New York), 195–96
World War I
    arming of U.S. merchant ships, 122–23
    armistice, 139–40
    and Armistice Day, 217
    assassination of Franz Ferdinand, 63
    attack of British steamship, 106
    and diplomatic reception at White House, 109
    Edith's wartime roles during, 125–30
    and high moral ground held by US, 134, 141
    and League of Nations, 120–21
    and *Lusitania* attack, 83–84, 86–87
    naming/renaming of ships, 129–30
    neutrality of U.S. in, 68–69, 83, 112, 121
    and Paris Peace Conference, 140–45, 147–51,
        155, 183
    and "peace without victory" proposal, 120–21
    and plan to annex U.S. railroads, 133–34
    and presidential election of 1916, 112, 113–14
    president's congressional address on U.S.
        joining war, 123–24
    and president's Fourteen Points speech, 134
    and president's lack of foreign policy
        experience, 64
    and president's "peace note," 119–20
    submarine warfare, 83–84, 106, 121
    and war effort in the U.S., 125–30
    war resolution passed by Congress, 124–25
    and women's roles, x
    See also Treaty of Versailles
Wright brothers, 44
Wytheville home of Bolling family
    and childhood/youth of Edith, 11–12, 18, 27
    and death of William Bolling, 29
    and Edith Bolling Wilson Birthplace Museum,
        xiv, 227*n*, 237*n*, 246–47

Zanuck, Darryl, 233
Zimmerman, Arthur, 121